Communications in Computer and Information Science 2536

Series Editors

Rationale
The CCIS series is devoted to the publication of proceedings of computer science conferences. Its aim is to efficiently disseminate original research results in informatics in printed and electronic form. While the focus is on publication of peer-reviewed full papers presenting mature work, inclusion of reviewed short papers reporting on work in progress is welcome, too. Besides globally relevant meetings with internationally representative program committees guaranteeing a strict peer-reviewing and paper selection process, conferences run by societies or of high regional or national relevance are also considered for publication.

Topics
The topical scope of CCIS spans the entire spectrum of informatics ranging from foundational topics in the theory of computing to information and communications science and technology and a broad variety of interdisciplinary application fields.

Information for Volume Editors and Authors
Publication in CCIS is free of charge. No royalties are paid, however, we offer registered conference participants temporary free access to the online version of the conference proceedings on SpringerLink (http://link.springer.com) by means of an http referrer from the conference website and/or a number of complimentary printed copies, as specified in the official acceptance email of the event.

CCIS proceedings can be published in time for distribution at conferences or as post-proceedings, and delivered in the form of printed books and/or electronically as USBs and/or e-content licenses for accessing proceedings at SpringerLink. Furthermore, CCIS proceedings are included in the CCIS electronic book series hosted in the SpringerLink digital library at http://link.springer.com/bookseries/7899. Conferences publishing in CCIS are allowed to use Online Conference Service (OCS) for managing the whole proceedings lifecycle (from submission and reviewing to preparing for publication) free of charge.

Publication process
The language of publication is exclusively English. Authors publishing in CCIS have to sign the Springer CCIS copyright transfer form, however, they are free to use their material published in CCIS for substantially changed, more elaborate subsequent publications elsewhere. For the preparation of the camera-ready papers/files, authors have to strictly adhere to the Springer CCIS Authors' Instructions and are strongly encouraged to use the CCIS LaTeX style files or templates.

Abstracting/Indexing
CCIS is abstracted/indexed in DBLP, Google Scholar, EI-Compendex, Mathematical Reviews, SCImago, Scopus. CCIS volumes are also submitted for the inclusion in ISI Proceedings.

How to start
To start the evaluation of your proposal for inclusion in the CCIS series, please send an e-mail to ccis@springer.com.

Abdoulaye Sere ·
Borlli Michel Jonas Some ·
Moustapha Bikienga ·
Tounwendyam Frédéric Ouedraogo
Editors

Africa Data, Artificial Intelligence and Innovations

First International Conference, AFRI2 2025
Koudougou, Burkina Faso, February 27–28, 2025
Proceedings

Editors
Abdoulaye Sere
Université Nazi BONI
Bobo-Dioulasso, Burkina Faso

Borlli Michel Jonas Some
Université Nazi BONI
Bobo-Dioulasso, Burkina Faso

Moustapha Bikienga
Université Norbert ZONGO
Koudougou, Burkina Faso

Tounwendyam Frédéric Ouedraogo
Université Norbert ZONGO
Koudougou, Burkina Faso

ISSN 1865-0929 ISSN 1865-0937 (electronic)
Communications in Computer and Information Science
ISBN 978-3-031-98326-9 ISBN 978-3-031-98327-6 (eBook)
https://doi.org/10.1007/978-3-031-98327-6

This Springer imprint is published by the registered company Springer Nature Switzerland AG
The registered company address is: Gewerbestrasse 11, 6330 Cham, Switzerland

Preface

It was with pleasure and happiness, immense gratitude and excitement that we extend a warm thanks to all participants, researchers, professionals, and enthusiasts who joined us at the first International Conference on Africa Data, Artificial Intelligence, and Innovations (AFRI2). This distinguished conference, organized by "Réseau des Enseignant chercheurs et Chercheurs en Informatique du Faso" RECIF, took place from February 27–28, 2025, at the Université Norbert Zongo in Burkina Faso. The conference was held as a hybrid event and brought an opportunity for local and international academics, scientists, and experts to discuss the latest research results in topics related to data science, artificial intelligence, and innovations.

The success of AFRI2 in Burkina Faso was made possible through the collaborative effort of numerous individuals, and we would like to extend our heartfelt thanks to all involved. Success would also not have been possible without the dedication and hard work of the local committee, the technical program committee, the steering committee, authors, and reviewers.

Fifty (50) papers were submitted to the conference. Each paper was reviewed by at least three reviewers. Reviews were double-blind and the reviewers were scientists from different countries in Africa and Europe. Fourteen (14) papers were accepted. During the conference, twelve (12) papers were presented by the authors.

Special thanks go to Oluwatope O. Ayodeji from Obafemi Awolowo University for his visionary talk regarding artificial intelligence applications in the African context, in the inaugural conference. His insights into the role of artificial intelligence in the African context sparked meaningful discussions and added significant value to the conference.

This conference plays a crucial role in bridging the gap between technological advancements and the unique challenges faced by the continent. It serves as a platform for collaboration, knowledge exchange, and the exploration of solutions tailored to the specific needs of African nations. As we reflect on the first conference's success, we extend our gratitude to the organizing committee, sponsors such as "Autorité de Régulation des Communications Électroniques et des Postes" (ARCEP), and all those who played a pivotal role in making this conference a reality.

We eagerly anticipate your continued engagement and participation in future editions of AFRI2 that will occur in different countries in Africa, as we collectively strive to explore ideas, innovations, and partnerships for the advancement of artificial intelligence in Africa.

Abdoulaye Sere
Borlli Michel Jonas Some

Organization

Steering Committee

Rashid Abdulhaleem Saeed	Taif University, Saudi Arabia
Alain Mille	Claude Bernard University Lyon 1, France
Eugène C. Ezin	University of Abomey-Calavi, Benin
Elmustafa Sayed Ali Ahmed	Red Sea University, Sudan

Organizing Committee

General Chair

André Conseibo	Université Norbert Zongo, Burkina Faso

General Co-chairs

Tounwendyam Frédéric Ouedraogo	Université Norbert Zongo, Burkina Faso
Rashid Abdulhaleem Saeed	Taif University, Saudi Arabia

TPC Chair and Co-chairs

Abdoulaye Sere	Université Nazi Boni, Burkina Faso
Borlli Michel Jonas Some	Université Nazi Boni, Burkina Faso
Elmustafa Sayed Ali Ahmed	Red Sea University, Sudan

Sponsorship and Exhibit Chair

Mamadou Diarra	École Polytechnique de Ouagadougou, Burkina Faso

Local Chair

Moustapha Bikienga	Université Norbert Zongo, Burkina Faso

Local Co-chair

Mamadi Boulou | Université Norbert Zongo, Burkina Faso

Publicity and Social Media Chair

Stéphane Aimé Metchebon | Takougang, Université Aube Nouvelle, Burkina Faso

Publications Chair

Abdoulaye Sere | Université Nazi Boni, Burkina Faso

Web Chair

Abdoulaye Sere | Université Nazi Boni, Burkina Faso

Technical Program Committee

Oumarou Sie	Université Joseph Ki-Zerbo, Burkina Faso
Abdoulaye Sere	Université Nazi Boni, Burkina Faso
Borlli Michel Jonas Some	Université Nazi Boni, Burkina Faso
Tounwendyam Frédéric Ouedraogo	Université Norbert Zongo, Burkina Faso
Rashid Abdulhaleem Saeed	Taif University, Saudi Arabia
Alain Mille	Université Claude Bernard Lyon 1, France
Eugène C. Ezin	Université Abomey-Calavi, Benin
Elmustafa Sayed Ali Ahmed	Red Sea University, Sudan
Idowu Diyaolu Obafemi	Obafemi Awolowo University, Nigeria
Ayodeji O. Oluwatope	Obafemi Awolowo University, Nigeria
Arsène Sabas	Canadian Nuclear Safety Commission, Canada; Institut de Mathématiques et de Sciences Physiques, Benin
Didier Bassole	Université Joseph Ki-Zerbo, Burkina Faso
Idy Diop	Université Cheikh Anta Diop, Senegal
Kouamé Koffi Fernand	Université Virtuelle de Côte d'Ivoire, Côte d'Ivoire
Babri Michel	Institut National Polytechnique Félix Houphouët Boigny, Côte d'Ivoire
Loum Georges	Institut National Polytechnique Félix Houphouët Boigny, Côte d'Ivoire

Horia F. Pop	Université Babèş-Bolyai, Romania
Mohamed Salim Bouhlel	Sfax University, Tunisia
Amedeo Napoli	CNRS, LORIA, France
Michel Paindavoine	Université de Bourgogne, France
Pierre Lescanne	École Normale Supérieure, Lyon, France
Moussa Lo	Université Virtuelle du Sénégal, Sénégal
Karim Konate	Université Cheikh Anta Diop, Senegal
Cherif Diallo	Université Gaston Berger, Senegal
Tiguiane Yelemou	Université Nazi Boni, Burkina Faso
Harouna Naroua	Université Abdou-Moumouni de Niamey, Niger
Koné Tiémoman	Université Virtuelle de Côte d'Ivoire, Côte d'Ivoire
Bi Tra Goore	Institut National Polytechnique Félix Houphouët Boigny, Côte d'Ivoire
Konan Marcellin Brou	Institut National Polytechnique Félix Houphouët Boigny, Côte d'Ivoire
Ntakpé Tchimou Guépié Euloge	Université Nangui Abrogoua, Côte d'Ivoire
Moustapha Diaby	École Supérieure Africaine des TIC, Côte d'Ivoire
Issa Traore	Université Félix Houphouët Boigny, Côte d'Ivoire
Edi Kouassi Hilaire	Université Nangui Abrogoua, Côte d'Ivoire
Pasteur Poda	Université Nazi Boni, Burkina Faso
Telesphore Tiendrebeogo	Université Nazi Boni, Burkina Faso
Toundé Mesmin Dandjinou	Université Nazi Boni, Burkina Faso
Mahamadou Belem	Université Nazi Boni, Burkina Faso
Seydou Golo Barro	Université Nazi Boni, Burkina Faso
Joelle Ouattara/Compaore	Université Nazi Boni, Burkina Faso
Hamadoun Tall	Université Nazi Boni, Burkina Faso
Didier Bassole	Université Joseph Ki-Zerbo, Burkina Faso
Tégawende Bissyande	Université Joseph Ki-Zerbo, Burkina Faso
Aminata Sabane	Université Joseph Ki-Zerbo, Burkina Faso
Yaya Traore	Université Joseph Ki-Zerbo, Burkina Faso
Kisito K. Kabore	Université Joseph Ki-Zerbo, Burkina Faso
Justin Kouraogo	Université Joseph Ki-Zerbo, Burkina Faso
Ferdinand Guinko	Université Joseph Ki-Zerbo, Burkina Faso
Désiré Guel	Université Joseph Ki-Zerbo, Burkina Faso
Jean Serge Dimitri Ouattara	Université Joseph Ki-Zerbo, Burkina Faso
Boureima Zerbo	Université Thomas Sankara, Burkina Faso
Moustapha Bikienga	Université Norbert Zongo, Burkina Faso
Stéphane Aimé Metchebon Takougang	Université Aube Nouvelle, Burkina Faso
Boris Ouedraogo	École Polytechnique de Ouagadougou, Burkina Faso

Sibiri Tiemounou	École Polytechnique de Ouagadougou, Burkina Faso
Souleymane Zio	École Polytechnique de Ouagadougou, Burkina Faso
Bernard Lamien	École Polytechnique de Ouagadougou, Burkina Faso
Mamadou Diarra	École Polytechnique de Ouagadougou, Burkina Faso
Mohamed Beidari	École Polytechnique de Ouagadougou, Burkina Faso
Marc Assogba	Université d'Abomey-Calavi, Benin
Yahaya Coulibaly	Université des Sciences, des techniques et des Technologies de Bamako, Mali
Franklin Tchakounte	Université de Ngaoundere, Cameroon
Aïda Ouangraoua	Université de Sherbrooke, Canada
Rodrigue Kafando	Université Virtuelle du Burkina Faso, Burkina Faso
Mahamadi Boulou	Université Norbert Zongo, Burkina Faso
Melatagia Yonta Paulin	Université Yaoundé 1, Cameroon
Lossan Bonde	Adventist University of Africa, Kenya
Benkrid Soumia	École Nationale Supérieure d'Informatique, Algeria
Zakaria Sawadogo	École Polytechnique de Ouagadougou, Burkina Faso
Ismaila Ouedraogo	Université de Bordeaux, France
Gono Denon Arthur Richmond	Institut National Polytechnique Félix Houphouët-Boigny, Côte d'Ivoire
Jean Marie Dembele	Université Gaston Berger de Saint Louis, Senegal
Abdoul-Hadi Konfé	École Polytechnique de Ouagadougou, Burkina Faso
Doda Afoussatou Rollande Sanou	Université Virtuelle du Burkina Faso, Burkina Faso
Sanda Mahama Amadou Tidjani	Université d'Abomey-Calavi, Benin
Boureima Sangare	Université Nazi Boni, Burkina Faso
Wendpuiré Ousmane Compaore	Université Nazi Boni, Burkina Faso
Deussom Djomadji Eric Michel	École Nationale Supérieure Polytechnique de Yaoundé, Cameroon
Traoré Cheick Amed Diloma Gabriel	École Polytechnique de Ouagadougou, Burkina Faso
Mbaiossoum Bery Leouro	Université de N'Djamena, Chad
Julie Thiombiano	École Polytechnique de Ouagadougou, Burkina Faso

Pegdwendé Nicolas Sawadogo	Université Virtuelle du Burkina Faso, Burkina Faso
Gayo Diallo	Université de Bordeaux, France
Bawindsom Marcel Kebre	Université Joseph Ki-Zerbo, Burkina Faso
Gouayon Koala	Université Joseph Ki-Zerbo, Burkina Faso
Kouaho N'Guessan Narcisse Tehia	Université Nazi Boni, Burkina Faso
Flavien Hervé Somda	Université Joseph Ki-Zerbo, Burkina Faso
Satafa Sanogo	École Polytechnique de Ouagadougou, Burkina Faso
Franklin Oladiipo Asahiah	Obafemi Awolowo University, Nigeria
Yamba Dabone	Université Joseph Ki-Zerbo, Burkina Faso
Ahouandjinou Sèmèvo Arnaud Roland Martial	Université d'Abomey-Calavi, Benin
Sekou-Harouna Kangoye	Université Joseph Ki-Zerbo, Burkina Faso
Batoure Bamana Apollinaire	Université de Ngaoundéré, Cameroon
Pengwendé Zongo	Université Norbert Zongo, Burkina Faso
Abdoul Azize Kindo	Université Nazi Boni, Burkina Faso
Dagba Théophile Komlan	Université d'Abomey-Calavi, Benin
Houngue Pelagie	Université d'Abomey-Calavi, Benin
Téeg-Wendé Zougmore	Université Nazi Boni, Burkina Faso

Contents

Artificial Intelligence Application: Large language Models (LLMs)

Beyond Syntax: Testing LLM Semantic Understanding of Code

Aminata Sabané[1,2(✉)] and Tegawendé F. Bissyandé[1,2]

[1] Université Joseph Ki-Zerbo, Ouagadougou, Burkina Faso
aminata.sabane@ujkz.bf

[2] CITADEL, Université Virtuelle du Burkina Faso, Ouagadougou, Burkina Faso
tegawende.bissyande@citadel.bf
https://www.citadel.bf

Abstract. While Large Language Models (LLMs) have shown promise in various software engineering tasks, their deep understanding of code semantics remains a challenging area. This paper introduces a novel methodology to probe the semantic understanding of LLMs by subjecting them to a rigorous test: identifying trivial equivalent mutations in C code generated by csmith. By leveraging the diversity and complexity of csmith-generated programs, we can challenge the LLM on its comprehension of code semantics. Our evaluation focuses on the LLM's ability to recognize semantic equivalence, provide sound justifications, and generate counterexamples when necessary. Through our experiments, we aim to shed light on the limitations and potential of current LLMs in understanding code semantics, paving the way for future advancements in AI-assisted software development.

Keywords: LLM · Code understanding · Mutation equivalence

1 Introduction

Large Language Models (LLMs) have rapidly advanced in recent years, demonstrating state-of-the-art capabilities in various natural language processing (NLP) tasks [6]. These models are already starting to revolutionize numerous fields, including software engineering. By leveraging their ability to understand and generate natural language, LLMs can assist developers in various ways, such as code generation, code summarization, and bug detection. However, a fundamental question remains: **To what extent do LLMs truly understand the semantics of code?**

While LLMs can increasingly generate syntactically correct code, given enough training data, their ability to reason about program execution, identify equivalent transformations, and comprehend the underlying logic remains a subject of ongoing research. A deep understanding of code semantics is essential for tasks such as code refactoring, debugging, and security analysis, which are challenging for developers and where automation is particularly sought.

A. Sere et al. (Eds.): AFRI2 2025, CCIS 2536, pp. 3–16, 2026.
https://doi.org/10.1007/978-3-031-98327-6_1

To address this fundamental question, we propose a novel methodology to assess the semantic understanding of LLMs in the context of code. Specifically, we aim to answer the following research questions:

❶ Can LLMs accurately identify semantically equivalent code transformations?

❷ To what extent can LLMs provide meaningful explanations for their judgments about code equivalence?

To investigate these questions, we leverage the power of csmith [10], a state-of-the-art tool for generating diverse C programs, originally intended for differential testing of compilers. By applying trivial equivalent mutations to csmith-generated code, we create a controlled environment to test the LLM's ability to recognize semantic equivalence.

This Paper. Our study makes the following contributions:

- *Novel Methodology*: We introduce a new methodology to evaluate LLM code understanding, combining csmith-generated code with trivial equivalent mutations.
- *Comprehensive Evaluation*: We conduct a comprehensive evaluation, considering both quantitative and qualitative metrics.
- *In-depth Analysis*: We delve into the limitations and strengths of LLMs in understanding code semantics, providing insights for future research.

The remainder of this paper is organized as follows: Sect. 2 reviews related work on LLMs in software engineering and code understanding techniques. Section 3 details our methodology, including the LLM model, csmith code generation, and the mutation process. Section 4 presents our experimental setup and results. Section 5 discusses the implications of our findings and future research directions. Finally, Sect. 6 concludes the paper.

2 Related Work

The intersection of LLMs and software engineering has seen significant growth in recent years. LLMs have been applied to various software engineering tasks, including code generation, code summarization, bug detection, and security analysis. However, assessing the depth of LLM understanding of code semantics remains a challenging and under-explored area.

2.1 LLMs in Software Engineering

Several studies have explored the potential of LLMs in software engineering. For instance, Chen et al. [2] introduced Codex, an LLM capable of generating code from natural language descriptions. While impressive, these models often rely on statistical patterns and may not fully understand the underlying semantics. Le Scao et al. [3] investigated the ability of LLMs to translate between different programming languages. While these models can often produce syntactically correct code, their ability to preserve semantic equivalence has been scarcely assessed.

2.2 Code Understanding and Reasoning

Traditional approaches to code understanding and reasoning have relied on static analysis and symbolic execution techniques. However, these methods can be computationally expensive and may struggle with complex code. Recent advancements in neural network architectures, such as Graph Neural Networks (GNNs) [9], have shown promise in capturing the structural and semantic information within code. CodeGPT [5] was then proposed as an LLM-based approach for code generation and understanding. While it can generate code and answer questions about code, its ability to perform deep semantic reasoning remains to be validated.

2.3 Code Generation Tools

Code generation tools like csmith have been widely used to generate code samples. By introducing subtle variations, csmith can create test cases that challenge the robustness of software systems. In our work, we leverage csmith to generate a diverse set of C programs and apply trivial equivalent mutations to test the semantic understanding of LLMs.

In contrast to previous work, our approach focuses on systematically evaluating the LLM's ability to recognize semantic equivalence, provide explanations for its judgments, and handle complex code scenarios.

3 Methodology

3.1 LLM Model

LLMs are a class of artificial intelligence models that are trained on massive amounts of text data. These models are have been demonstrated capable of generating human-quality text, translating languages, writing different kinds of creative content, and answering questions in an informative way. Because code can be considered as text written in programming language, LLMs have been applied in software engineering tasks.

For our experiments, we leverage the LLAMA [8] model. LLAMA is a powerful language model that has been trained on a massive dataset of text and code. Its extensive training, and its open source nature, has made it extremely appealing for software engineering researchers and practitioners, making it an ideal candidate for our study.

The LLAMA model was trained using a masked language modeling objective. This involves masking certain tokens in a text sequence and training the model to predict the missing tokens based on the context of the surrounding words. This training process helps the model to develop a deep understanding of language and code, enabling it to generate and understand complex code structures.

3.2 Code Generation with csmith

csmith is a state-of-the-art software testing tool designed to generate diverse and complex C programs. By systematically exploring the C language's grammar and semantics, csmith can produce a wide range of programs, from simple to complex, with varying levels of control flow, data structures, and arithmetic operations.

To generate a diverse set of C programs for our experiments, we parameterize csmith with different seed values and configuration options. For example, we can use specific parameter settings to generate a set of simple and complex programs as described in Table 1 for two different experiments.

Table 1. csmith Configuration Parameters

Parameter	Exp. 1: Simple Programs	Exp. 2: Complex Programs
Seed value	12345	98765
Maximum number of statements	10	50
Maximum depth of nested blocks	2	5
Maximum complexity of expressions	3	10
Probability of pointers	0.2	0.8
Probability of arrays	0.2	0.8
Probability of function calls	0.1	0.5

By varying these parameters, we can generate a wide range of C programs with varying levels of complexity and diversity, providing a challenging and realistic environment to evaluate the LLM's code understanding capabilities (Table 2).

Table 2. Example C Programs Generated by csmith

Simple Program

```
#include <stdio.h>

int main(void) {
    int i = 0;
    int j = 2;

    while (i < 10) {
        i++;
        j += i;
    }

    printf("%d\n", j);
    return 0;
}
```

Complex Program

```
#include <stdio.h>

int main(void) {
    int i, j, k, l;
    int a[10];

    for (i = 0; i < 10; i++) {
        a[i] = i * 2;
    }

    for (j = 0; j < 10; j++) {
        for (k = 0; k < 5; k++) {
            l = a[j] + k;
            if (l % 2 == 0) {
                printf("%d\n", l);
            }
        }
    }

    return 0;
}
```

3.3 Trivial Equivalent Mutations

To rigorously evaluate the LLM's understanding of code semantics, we apply a set of carefully designed trivial equivalent mutations to the csmith-generated programs. These mutations involve minor changes to the code that do not alter its overall behavior. By identifying and applying these mutations, we can test the LLM's ability to recognize semantic equivalence. Table 3 enumerates the mutation trivial equivalent mutations that we applied.

Table 3. Mutation Operators

Mutation Operator	Description	Example
Variable Renaming	Replace variable names with semantically equivalent names.	‘int x = 10;’ becomes ‘int y = 10;’
Expression Reordering	Rearrange the order of operands in commutative expressions.	‘a + b‘ becomes ‘b + a’
Constant Folding	Replace constant expressions with their evaluated values.	‘2 * 3’ becomes ‘6’
Dead Code Elimination	Remove unused code.	Removing a ‘printf‘ statement that is never executed.
Loop Invariant Code Motion	Move code that does not change within a loop to outside the loop.	Moving ‘int x = 10;‘ outside a loop where ‘x‘ is not modified inside the loop.
Strength Reduction	Replace expensive operations with less expensive ones.	Replacing ‘x * 2’ with ‘x ¡¡ 1’
Conditional Simplification	Simplify conditional expressions.	Replacing ‘if (x ¿ 0 && x ¡ 10)’ with ‘if (0 ¡ x && x ¡ 10)’
Type Casting	Cast variables to compatible types.	Casting an ‘int‘ to a ‘float’ or vice versa.
Array Index Manipulation	Modify array indices.	Changing ‘a[i]’ to ‘a[i-1]’
Function Inlining	Replace function calls with their corresponding code.	Inlining a simple function with a few lines of code.

To apply the trivial equivalent mutations, we use a combination of static analysis techniques and heuristic rules. We identify potential mutation sites by analyzing the abstract syntax tree (AST) of the code. Once potential sites are identified, we apply the appropriate mutation operator, ensuring that the resulting code is still syntactically correct and semantically equivalent to the original code.

By systematically applying these mutation operators, we can generate a diverse set of semantically equivalent code variants. These variants can then be used to test the LLM's ability to recognize equivalence, explain the reasons for equivalence, and identify potential errors in the LLM's reasoning.

4 Experimental Setup and Results

4.1 Dataset

For our experiments, we generated a dataset of 2,000 C programs using csmith, covering a wide range of syntactic and semantic complexities. For each program, we applied a set of 10 different trivial equivalent mutations, resulting in a total of 20,000 program pairs.

4.2 Computational Resources and Time

The experiments were conducted on a cluster of 2 A100 GPUs. Assuming an average processing time of 1 min per program pair, the total estimated time for processing all 20,000 pairs is approximately 167 h, or roughly 7 days.

4.3 LLM Model and Prompting

We focus on the LLAMA model to evaluate its ability to understand and reason about code. For each pair of original and mutated code snippets, we presented the LLM with the following prompt:

```
Prompt >> Given the following two code snippets,
determine if they are semantically equivalent.
If so, explain why. If not, provide a counter-example.
```

4.4 Evaluation Metrics

We evaluated the LLM's performance using the following metrics:

- Accuracy: The proportion of correct judgments made by the LLM.
- Precision: The proportion of correct positive judgments out of all positive judgments.
- Recall: The proportion of correct positive judgments out of all actual positive instances.
- F1-Score: The harmonic mean of precision and recall.
- Qualitative Evaluation: Human experts assessed the quality of the LLM's explanations and counter-examples.

4.5 Results and Analysis

Semantic Equivalence Identification. The LLM demonstrated a high level of accuracy in identifying semantically equivalent code transformations, particularly for simple mutations like variable renaming and constant folding. For instance, the LLM correctly identified that the following two code snippets are semantically equivalent (Table 4):

However, for more complex mutations, such as loop unrolling, common subexpression elimination, and strength reduction, the LLM's performance was more varied (Table 5).

To quantify the LLM's performance on different types of mutations, we categorized the mutations into three levels of complexity:

Table 4. Example of Identified semantic equivalence: Expression reordering

Original	Mutated
`int x = 10;`	`int x = 10;`
`int y = 20;`	`int y = 20;`
`int z = x + y;`	`int z = y + x;`

Table 5. Example of Non-Identified semantic equivalence: Loop unfolding

Original	Mutated

`for (int i = 0; i < 10; i++) {`
`  sum += i;`
`}`
	`int sum = 0;`
	`sum += 0;`
	`sum += 1;`
	`// ...`
	`sum += 9;`

1. *Simple Mutations*: These mutations involve straightforward transformations like variable renaming, constant folding, and simple expression reordering.
2. *Moderate Mutations*: These mutations involve more complex transformations, such as loop unrolling, common subexpression elimination, and strength reduction.
3. *Complex Mutations*: These mutations involve significant changes to the program's structure, such as function inlining, loop transformations, and code restructuring.

We found that LLAMA achieved high accuracy on simple mutations, with an accuracy rate of about 97%. However, the accuracy decreased for moderate and complex mutations, with rates of around 85% and 72%, respectively. This means that the accuracy can drop by 25% depending on the type of mutations that are applied (Table 6).

Table 6. Performance on Different Mutation Categories

Mutation Category	Accuracy	Precision	Recall	F1-Score
Simple	0.97	0.98	0.96	0.97
Moderate	0.85	0.82	0.88	0.85
Complex	0.72	0.68	0.78	0.73

These results suggest that the LLM's understanding of code semantics is still limited, especially when dealing with complex transformations that require deeper reasoning and analysis. Future research should focus on improving the LLM's ability to handle these more challenging scenarios.

Explanation Quality. Assessing the quality of explanations generated by LLMs is crucial for several reasons:

1. *Trust*: High-quality explanations enhance the trustworthiness of the LLM's decisions.
2. *Debugging*: Detailed and accurate explanations can help identify potential errors or biases in the LLM's reasoning.
3. *Human-AI Collaboration*: Clear and concise explanations facilitate effective human-AI collaboration.
4. *Education*: Well-structured explanations can serve as a valuable educational tool.
5. *Benchmarking*: By analyzing the quality of explanations, researchers can identify areas for improvement in LLM training and fine-tuning.

To quantitatively evaluate the quality of explanations, we employed a combination of automatic metrics and human evaluation. We used metrics such as BLEU, METEOR, and ROUGE to assess the semantic similarity between the generated explanation and a set of reference explanations. To create a dataset of such reference explanations, we sampled a subset of 100 pairs (original and mutated csmith-generated code) and asked Computer science undergraduates to write justifications about why and how these pairs are semantically equivalent.

Table 7 illustrates an example where the LLM judgment is good.

Table 7. Example of Correct Judgment: Dead Code Elimination

Original	Mutated

`int x = 10;`
`int y = 20;`
`int z = x + y;`
`// Unnecessary code:`
`int unused = 5;`
	`int x = 10;`
	`int y = 20;`
	`int z = x + y;`

LLM Judgment: *Semantically equivalent.*
LLM Explanation: *The second code snippet is a simplified version of the first. The declaration and initialization of the unused variable do not affect the final output of the program.*

Table 8, however, illustrates an example where the LLM judgment is bad.

Table 8. Example of Incorrect Judgment: Incorrect Loop Unrolling

Original	Mutated

`int x = 10;`
`int y = x++;`
	`int x = 10;`
	`int y = x;`
	`x = x + 1;`

LLM Judgment: *Semantically equivalent.*
LLM Explanation: *Both code snippets assign the value of x to y.*

This explanation is incorrect. While both snippets assign the value of x to y, the first snippet increments x before the assignment, leading to a different final value for x.

By analyzing these case studies, we can see that the LLM's performance is influenced by the complexity of the code transformations and its ability to reason about the underlying semantics. While the LLM can handle simple transformations accurately, more complex scenarios, especially those involving subtle side effects and intricate control flow, can pose challenges.

Table 9 presents the overall evaluation results. The BLEU [7] score is the highest at 0.82: it measures the precision of the LLM judgment compared to the set of reference explanations. The METEOR [1] score however is slightly lower: it measures the similarity between the LLM judgment and the reference explanation, considering synonyms and paraphrasing. Actually, we observe that METEOR seems to be penalizing the LLM for not capturing the exact semantic nuances of the student-generated explanations, even if the generated text is grammatically correct and lexically similar. We also consider the ROUGE-L [4] score, which represents the overlap between the generated judgment and the reference explanations.

It is further noteworthy that the aforementioned metrics may not fully capture the nuances of human language and reasoning. Therefore, human evaluation is essential to assess the clarity, coherence, and correctness of the explanations. Human experts rated the explanations on a scale of 1 to 5, considering factors such as correctness, relevance, clarity, and comprehensiveness.

Table 9. Explanation Quality Metrics

Metric	Value
BLEU score	0.82
METEOR	0.75
ROUGE-L	0.80
Human Evaluation Score (average)	3.8/5

These results indicate that the LLM is capable of generating reasonably good explanations, but there is still room for improvement, especially for more complex mutations. Future work should focus on improving the LLM's ability to generate more informative and insightful explanations.

Counter-Example Generation. To further assess the LLM's understanding of code semantics, we tested its ability to generate counter-examples for non-equivalent code snippets. A good counter-example should highlight the semantic difference between the two code snippets and provide a clear explanation of why they are not equivalent.

Experimentally, we must generate pairs of cases where the mutation does not preserve equivalence. To that end we randomly mutate again the mutated programs using *first-order mutation operators.* These are simple transformations applied to a single syntactic element. While they can introduce subtle changes, they may not always preserve the original program's semantic behavior. We enumerate the first-order mutation operators that were applied to the mutated Csmith-generated code:

Arithmetic Operator Mutation

- Replace arithmetic operators (+, −, ∗, /, %) with other operators:

$$x + y \rightarrow x - y$$

- Modify operands by adding or subtracting a constant value:

$$x + y \rightarrow x + y + 1$$

Logical Operator Mutation

- Replace logical operators (&&, $\|\|$, ¬) with other operators.

$$x \&\& y \rightarrow x \|\| y$$

- Negate the condition of an 'if' or 'while' statement:

$$\text{if } x > y \text{ then ...} \rightarrow \text{if } \ \text{x} \leq y \text{ then ...}$$

Bitwise Operator Mutation

- Replace bitwise operators (&, |, ∧, ∼, ≪, ≫) with other operators:

$$x \& y \rightarrow x | y$$

- Modify operands by performing bitwise operations with a constant value:

$$x \& y \rightarrow x \& (y \oplus 0xFF)$$

Control Flow Mutation

- Remove the condition of an 'if' or 'while' statement: if $x > y$ then ... → ...
- Add unnecessary conditions to 'if' or 'while' statements:

$$\text{if } x > y \text{ then ...} \rightarrow \text{if } x > y \text{ and } x \neq y \text{ then ...}$$

- Swap the 'then' and 'else' branches of an 'if' statement:

$$\text{if } x > y \text{ then } A \text{ else } B \rightarrow \text{if } x > y \text{ then } B \text{ else } A$$

Variable Mutation

- Modify the initial values of variables: $int\ x = 10; \rightarrow int\ x = 20;$
- Replace variable names with other valid identifiers: int $x = 10; \rightarrow$ int $y = 10;$

Function Mutation

- Remove function calls: $f(x, y); \rightarrow$ (empty statement)
- Modify the number or types of function arguments: $f(\text{int } x, \text{int } y) \rightarrow f(\text{int } x)$

By applying these mutations to Csmith-generated code, you can create a diverse set of mutant programs that can be used to evaluate the effectiveness of testing techniques and tools. However, it's important to note that not all mutations will result in semantically different programs. Some mutations may be equivalent to the original code, may lead to compilation errors or may simply exhibit different execution behavior.

Table 10 illustrates an example of code pairs where the LLM succeeds in generating an appropriate counter-example to demonstrate that the code is not semantically equivalent.

Table 10. Example of Semantic inequivalence

Original	Double-Mutated inequivalent code

`int arr[5] = {5, 4, 3, 2, 1};`
`int *ptr = arr;`
`int x = 1 + *ptr;`
	`int arr[5] = {5, 4, 3, 2, 1};`
	`int *ptr = arr;`
	`int x = *ptr++;`

LLM-Generated Counter-Example: The first code snippet adds 1 to the value pointed to by ptr, while the second code snippet first dereferences ptr to get the value, then increments the pointer. This leads to different values for x in the two cases.

```
LLM COUNTER-EXAMPLE <<< In the first code snippet, *ptr is 5, so x
becomes 6. In the second code snippet, *ptr is also 5 initially, but
the ++ operator increments ptr to point to the next element, which
is 4.  Therefore, x becomes 4 in the second case. >>>
```

To evaluate the quality of the generated counter-examples, we again asked students to manually rate 100 generated counter-examples on a scale of 1 to 5, considering factors such as correctness, relevance, simplicity, and completeness.

- *Correctness* measures whether the counter-example correctly highlights the semantic difference between the two code snippets.

- *Relevance* measures how relevant the counter-example is to the specific semantic difference.
- *Simplicity* measures the simplicity and clarity of the counter-example.
- *Completeness* measures whether the counter-example covers all relevant aspects of the semantic difference.

Figure 1 provides the boxplot distributions of the scores on the different metrics.

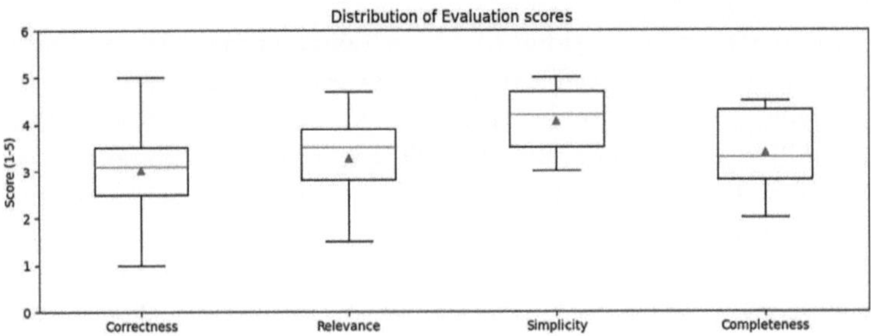

Fig. 1. Distribution of Scores in the Evaluation of Counter-Examples Generated by the LLM

The analysis of the evaluation scores clearly shows that the counter-examples are generally simple, sometimes relevant, but often incomplete and incorrect.

4.6 Threats to Validity

While this study makes a notable contribution to understanding LLM capabilities in code comprehension, several threats to validity should be considered:

Internal Validity: First, the dataset, while diverse, may not fully capture the complexity and variability of real-world code. Second, the specific LLM used may have inherent biases or limitations that could affect the results. Finally, the design of prompts could influence the LLM's responses, potentially leading to biased results.

External Validity: The results may not generalize to other LLMs or programming languages. Furthermore, the controlled experimental setting may not fully reflect the complexities of real-world software development.

Construct Validity: The definition of semantic equivalence can be subjective and may vary depending on the context. The choice of mutation operators may also influence the difficulty of the tasks and the LLM's performance.

Conclusion Validity: The sample size of the experiments may not be sufficient to detect statistically significant differences. However, 10 000 programs have been evaluated, making it among the largest studies related to LLM prompting.

To mitigate these threats, future research should focus on expanding the dataset, exploring different LLM architectures, and refining the evaluation methodology. Additionally, incorporating expert developers (instead of students) in the evaluation process can help to address the subjective nature of semantic equivalence and explanation quality.

5 Discussion

The experimental results demonstrate that LLMs have the potential to accurately identify semantically equivalent code transformations, particularly for simple mutations. However, the performance degrades as the complexity of the transformations increases. This suggests that while LLMs can recognize basic syntactic and semantic patterns, they may struggle with more intricate reasoning and analysis.

One of the key challenges in assessing LLM code understanding is the lack of large-scale, high-quality datasets of code pairs with explicit semantic equivalence labels. While csmith is a powerful tool for generating diverse code, it may not always capture the full range of semantic nuances and edge cases.

Furthermore, the evaluation metrics used in this study, such as accuracy, precision, recall, and F1-score, primarily focus on the correctness of the LLM's judgments. While these metrics are useful for assessing the overall performance, they do not provide insights into the LLM's reasoning process or the quality of its explanations.

To improve the evaluation of LLM code understanding, future research could explore the following directions:

- Expanding the Dataset: Develop larger and more diverse datasets of code pairs with explicit semantic equivalence labels, including a wider range of programming languages and code styles.
- Enhancing LLM Training: Train LLMs on a more diverse and comprehensive dataset of code, including examples of complex transformations and edge cases.
- Improving Explanation Generation: Develop techniques to improve the quality and coherence of LLM-generated explanations, such as incorporating knowledge graphs or symbolic reasoning.
- Leveraging Formal Verification: Integrate formal verification techniques to provide rigorous proofs of code equivalence, which can be used to assess the accuracy of the LLM's judgments.
- Human-in-the-Loop Evaluation: Involve human experts in the evaluation process to provide more nuanced and detailed assessments of the LLM's performance.

By addressing these challenges and exploring these research directions, we can further advance the state-of-the-art in LLM-based code understanding and analysis.

6 Conclusion

In this paper, we presented a methodology to assess the semantic understanding of code by LLMs via leveraging csmith-generated code and trivial equivalent mutations. Our experiments demonstrated that LLMs can accurately identify simple semantic equivalences but struggle with more complex transformations.

We also explored the quality of the LLM's explanations and its ability to generate counter-examples for non-equivalent code. While the LLM was able to generate reasonable explanations for simple cases, it again struggled with slightly-evolved scenarios.

Our findings highlight the limitations of current LLMs in understanding code semantics, suggesting that there are threats to experimental validity on leveraging LLMs withough adequate test suites to validate code execution behavior. By addressing these limitations and improving the LLM's reasoning capabilities, specifically on code, we can unlock the full potential of AI-powered software development tools.

References

1. Banerjee, S., Meteor, A.L.: An automatic metric for MT evaluation with improved correlation with human judgments. In: Proceedings of the ACL Workshop on Intrinsic and Extrinsic Evaluation Measures for Machine Translation and/or Summarization, pp. 65–72 (2005)
2. Chen, M., et al.: Evaluating large language models trained on code. arXiv preprint arXiv:2107.03374 (2021)
3. Le Scao, T., et al.: Bloom: a 176b-parameter open-access multilingual language model (2023)
4. Lin, C.-Y.: Rouge: a package for automatic evaluation of summaries. In: Text Summarization Branches Out, pp. 74–81 (2004)
5. Lu, S., et al.: Codexglue: a machine learning benchmark dataset for code understanding and generation. arXiv preprint arXiv:2102.04664 (2021)
6. Mann, B., et al. Language models are few-shot learners. arXiv preprint arXiv:2005.14165 (2020)
7. Papineni, K., Roukos, S., Ward, T., Zhu, W.-J.: Bleu: a method for automatic evaluation of machine translation. In: Proceedings of the 40th Annual Meeting of the Association for Computational Linguistics, pp. 311–318 (2002)
8. Touvron, H., et al.: Llama: open and efficient foundation language models. arXiv preprint arXiv:2302.13971 (2023)
9. Wu, Z., Pan, S., Chen, F., Long, G., Zhang, C., Philip, S.Y.: A comprehensive survey on graph neural networks. IEEE Trans. Neural Networks Learn. Syst. **32**(1), 4–24 (2020)
10. Yang, X., Chen, Y., Eide, E., Regehr, J.: Finding and understanding bugs in c compilers. In: Proceedings of the 32nd ACM SIGPLAN Conference on Programming Language Design and Implementation, pp. 283–294 (2011)

Greeting Voice Translation Using Deep Learning for Low Resource Language: Case of Mooré into English and English into Mooré

Go Issa Traoré[1(✉)], Borlli Michel Jonas Some[1], Hamado Kongo[2], Ozias Bombiri[1], and Rachid Gaetan Nabolle[2]

[1] Université Nazi BONI, Laboratoire d'algébre, de Mathématiques discrétes et d'Informatique, Bobo-Dioulasso, Burkina Faso
goissatraore@yahoo.fr

[2] Burkina Institute of Technology, Koudougou, Burkina Faso

Abstract. This study addresses communication challenges between non-English-speaking traders and their business partners by proposing a Mooré-to-English and English-to-Mooré voice translation mobile app using Artificial Intelligence. One of the main goals of this project is to overcome the language barrier between non-English-speaking traders and their business partners. After data collection, several algorithms were tested on the initial dataset for voice translation from Mooré to English and English to Mooré. The best accuracy, 79.92%, was achieved by combining the architecture of CNN+BiLSTM on our initial dataset. By using data augmentation techniques, CNN+BiLSTM achieved an accuracy of 96.25%. Our contribution in this paper is twofold: first, we provide a dataset for the scientific community. This dataset contains recordings of basic greetings in the Mooré language. This is an important step for studies on low-resource languages like Mooré and contributes to reducing the data scarcity challenge for local languages. The second contribution concerns the Mooré speech recognition model using deep learning techniques, which can help develop further studies related to our local languages.

Keywords: Translation · Low Resource Language · Deep Learning · Natural Language Processing · Voice Recognition · Mooré · English

1 Introduction

Burkina Faso is a country located in West Africa. Like the other countries in this location, a lot of Burkina Faso people don't have the chance to go to school. Based on the 5th Population and Housing Census (PHC) of 2019 in Burkina Faso [1], only 29.7% of people older than 15 years old went to school. Among them, as they can't work in public institutions, many become traders by deciding

A. Sere et al. (Eds.): AFRI2 2025, CCIS 2536, pp. 17–31, 2026.
https://doi.org/10.1007/978-3-031-98327-6_2

to sell traditional clothes, smartphones, crops (rice, corn, millet), traditional craft products etc. They work with international partners in China, Germany, England, USA etc. which usually speak English. Language barriers often pose communication difficulties between them.

To overcome these difficulties, and taking inspiration from solutions like Siri, Google Translate, and Alexa that can translate speech from one language to another, we propose using deep learning techniques to provide similar solutions for our local languages in order to help business partners communicate effectively with traders. The problematic we aim to solve through this work is: How can deep learning techniques been used to unleash language barrier between non-English speaking traders and their business partners through a mobile app? Considering that most of their international partners understand and are able to speak English, and also that Mooré is the most spoken language in Burkina Faso according to the 5th PHC with a rate of 52.9%, we are making through this study a system for translating voice from Mooré into English and from English into Mooré".

This study, which only takes into account greeting expressions in Mooré language, is the first step in a major project that we aim to built which will permit to translate all expressions, words and phrases from Mooré into English and vice versa, like deepl [7] and google translate [10].

To carry out this project, firstly, we collected the basic Mooré greeting using JotForm[1] and cleaned it. Secondly, we experimented several deep learning algorithms in order to select the best one for the model. Thirdly we built an Application Programming Interface (API) using FastApi[2] to serve our model and then we developed a mobile app using Flutter to consume the model through the API. We named this application No-Reesa. The rest of this paper is organised as follows: in Sect. 2 we present the state of knowledge in voice recognition, in Sect. 3 we show the methodology used to conduct the project. The Sect. 4 presents the results of experiments. In the Sect. 5, we conclude and present future studies.

2 Related Work

Research on voice recognition and voice translation using AI has been conducted for many years. Notable studies include:

C. A. Montgomery et al. [14] implemented Machine-Aided Voice Translation to help Air Force interrogation personnel interact with potential prisoners in unfamiliar foreign languages. The study focused on English-to-Spanish translation, with the authors describing the challenges of handling each language's unique features during implementation. I. Lezhenin et al. [9] studied urban sound classification using Long Short Term Memory (LSTM) networks. They used the UrbanSound8K audio dataset and evaluated their proposed network using 5-fold cross-validation, comparing it with Convolutional Neural Networks (CNNs). Their results showed that the LSTM model outperformed existing solutions, achieving 84.25% accuracy compared to 80.48% for the CNN.

[1] https://www.jotform.com/myforms/.

[2] https://fastapi.tiangolo.com/.

Regarding low-resource languages in Africa, several AI-based works on local languages have been conducted. C. C. Emezue et al. [3] worked on Fon-French Neural Machine Translation (FFR v1.0), proposing a model for Fon-to-French machine translation based on the GRU architecture. The results were evaluated using two metrics: BLEU and GLEU. Two types of model structures were used: with diacritics and without diacritics. They showed that the model with diacritic coding achieved better performance, reaching 30.55% (BLEU) and 18.18% (GLEU) compared to 24.53% (BLEU) and 13.0% (GLEU) for the model without diacritical coding. L. Martinus et al. [11] studied neural machine translation for South Africa's official languages and proposed MT models to translate the official languages of South Africa into English. Their objective was to create a BLEU reference score for neural translation between English and the ten official languages of South Africa. Their model was based on the Transformer architecture, which has shown strong performance in MT. Their data source was the JW300 corpus. The results showed a BLEU score of 40 G. Hacheme [4] developed English2Gbe, a multilingual machine translation model for Fon and Ewe (languages of the Gbe family). The study proposed a multilingual machine translation model from English into Fon and Ewe. The main objective was to demonstrate the effectiveness of a multilingual machine translation approach. Three translation models were developed: a bilingual model for English-to-Ewe translation, a bilingual model for English-to-Fon translation, and a multilingual model for English-to-Ewe/Fon translation. The models were compared using the BLEU metric and were based on the Transformer architecture. The training data was sourced from the JW300 corpus.

As far as Burkina Faso's languages are concerned, some similar AI-based studies have already been conducted. Ouedraogo et al. [16] worked on deploying a speech recognition model for low-resourced languages, with a case study on Dioula wake words (1, 2, 3, and 4). They used a combination of CNN and Bidirectional Long Short-Term Memory (BiLSTM) to build a voice recognition model for Dioula numbers 1, 2, 3, and 4. The model was designed to help the Dioula linguistic community access malaria awareness messages through a voice interface that allowed them to select messages by number from a predefined list.

3 Methodology

3.1 Data Collection

This part consists of collecting Mooré voices to train our algorithm for Mooré speech recognition. Since no speech dataset exists in Mooré for translation purposes, we created an online form (JotForm) to collect greetings from Mooré speakers. We shared this form with our contacts and visited schools, universities, and shops for data collection. After 4 months, we collected 310 different submissions, including approximately 123 women and 187 men, with ages ranging from 15 to 35 years. The form was designed to collect ten basic greetings in the Mooré language. We used greeting transcriptions from the Dictionary [19]. For data collection, each participant clicked the record button next to each

Mooré expression, read the expression, and submitted the completed form. The expressions and their meanings are recorded in Table 1.

Table 1. Greeting expressions in Mooré and their meaning in English

Mooré greeting expressions	Meaning in English
Ney yibeoogo	Good morning
Ney zaabre	Good evening
Ney windga	Good afternoon
Laafi	I am fine
Byaa laafi	There are fine
Windga kibare	How your afternoon is going?
Yibeogo kibare	How your morning is going?
Yam yika laafi	Did you wake up well?
Zaabre kibare	How your evening is going?
Zak ramba	And your family?

3.2 Data Pre-processing

In this part, we reviewed each submission to identify and remove any poor quality voice recordings that could negatively affect our algorithm's performance, as user submitted data requires validation. During this process, we removed numerous audio recordings due to incorrect pronunciation, empty recordings, or unrelated French conversations. After this validation process, our final dataset composition is shown in Fig. 1.

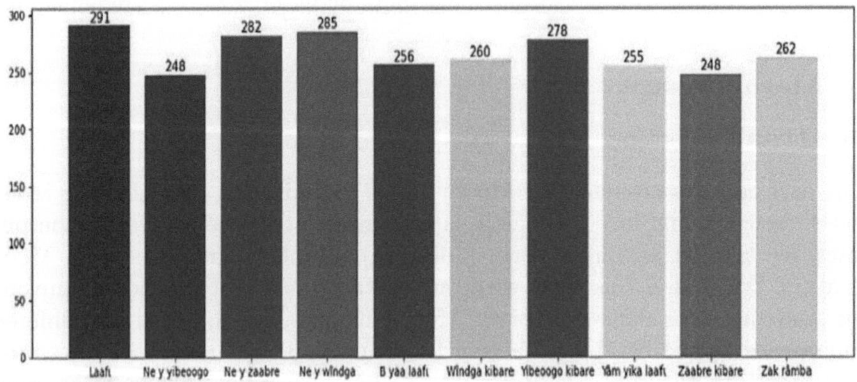

Fig. 1. Initial Cleaned Dataset

The performance of a deep learning model depends on the quality and quantity of data. Our dataset showed limitations in volume, as it was insufficient for building a robust deep learning model. Therefore, we applied audio data augmentation techniques to expand our dataset.

3.3 Data Augmentation Techniques

To increase the diversity of the Mooré dataset, several augmentation techniques [15] were applied:

- Time Stretching: Adjusts the speed of the audio without changing pitch, simulating faster or slower speech patterns to help the model recognize different speaking rates.
- Pitch Shifting: Alters the pitch to mimic variations in vocal range, which enables the model to adapt to different speaker characteristics.
- Noise Addition: Adds background noise, such as white noise or ambient sounds, to prepare the model for real-world environments with background sounds.
- Volume Variation: Changes audio volume to simulate different speaking volumes, helping the model handle both loud and soft speech.

Together, these techniques expanded the dataset's variability, making the model more resilient to diverse conditions and speaker differences. The composition of the dataset after augmentation is shown in Fig. 2.

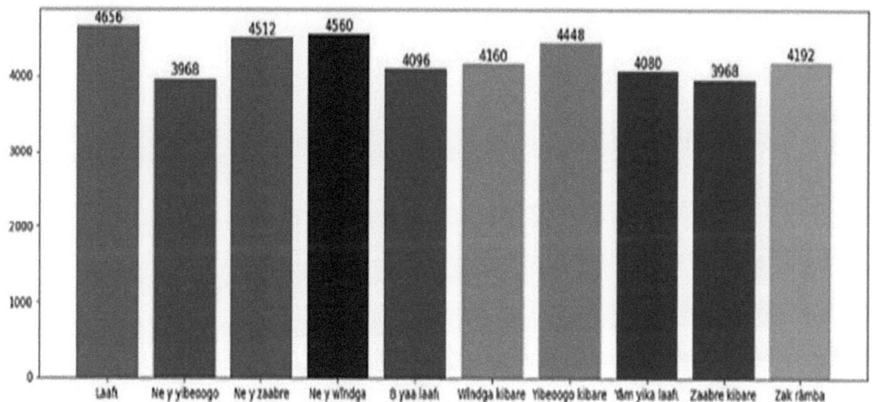

Fig. 2. Augmented dataset

3.4 Features Extraction

Features extraction permits to create the voiceprint from the speech signal [18]. This voiceprint will allow us to have the characteristics of the speech signal.

There are other methods for extracting speech features [2,5,12] but the cepstral parameters obtained from the Mel Frequency Cepstral Coefficients(MFCC) method continue to be used since many years. The MFCC has the advantage of being closer to the original audio signal [3]. The MFCC extraction consist in six (06) steps including cutting of speech signal into several overlapping windows; Hamming window is application In order to reduce the spectral distortion, the application of Fast Fourier Transform (FFT), the modulation of the spectrum, the calculation of the logarithm to obtain spectral envelope in decibels, the application of an inverse Fourier transform to the Filter Bank. These steps are detail in [12]. To carry out our study, we used MFCC to extract speech features.

3.5 Model Development

The core of the project's AI component was a voice recognition model designed to handle Mooré to English translation and English to Mooré. The model architecture combined CNN and BiLSTM networks to capture both spatial and temporal features in the audio data. 05 models were tested for this project: CNN, LSTM, BiLSTM, CNN-LSTM, and CNN-BiLSTM. The CNN-BiLSTM approach performed best with an accuracy of approximately 79.92% with initial dataset.

- CNN [8] are a type of deep learning algorithm that perform well at learning images. That's because they can learn patterns that are translation invariant and have spatial hierarchies. The Fig. 3 resumes how CNNs work to classify and input data.

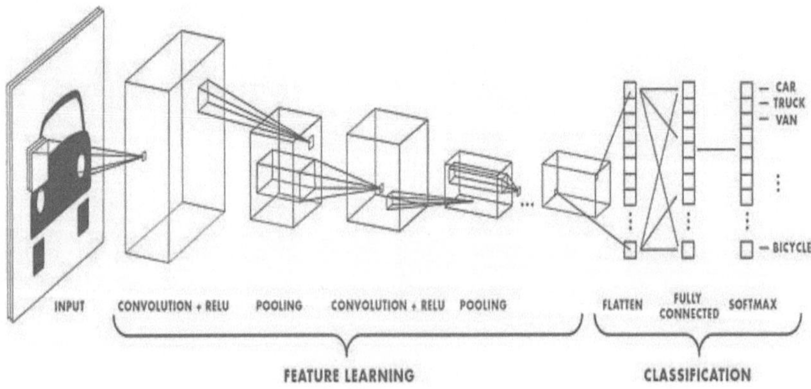

Fig. 3. CNN architecture with many convolutional layers [17]

- BiLSTM [13] is a recurrent neural network used primarily on natural language processing. Unlike standard LSTM, the input flows in both directions, and it's capable of utilizing information from both sides. It's also a powerful tool for modeling the sequential dependencies between words and phrases in both directions of the sequence. BiLSTM adds one more LSTM layer, which reverses the direction of information flow. Briefly, it means that the input sequence flows backward in the additional LSTM layer. The Fig. 4 shows the architecture of BiLSTM

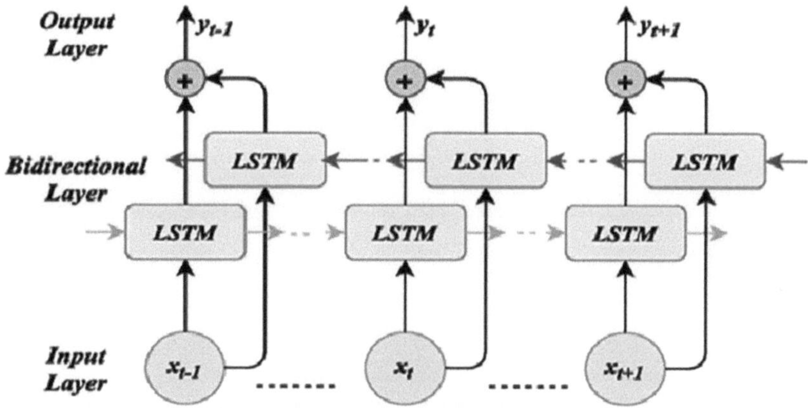

Fig. 4. Bi-LSTMs' architecture [6]

3.6 Mobile App Development

The mobile app was developed using Flutter (with Dart) to allow cross-platform compatibility on both Android and iOS devices. Flutter was chosen due to its simplicity in creating smooth and interactive user interfaces and its ability to handle real-time audio input efficiently. The app's user interface included:

- Speech Input Module: Users can record Mooré or English audio input.
- Translation Output Module: Translated speech is displayed and played back to users.

3.7 API Development

The backend API was developed using FastAPI, chosen for its speed, lightweight nature, and easy integration with Python based machine learning models. The API handled data pre-processing, model inference, and returned audio translations. FastAPI's asynchronous request handling supported real-time translation and minimized delays. The API use a Python library for google text-to-speech and speech-to-text[3] for handling English part. The Fig. 5 shows the Mooré into English translation architecture while the Fig. 6 shows the English into Mooré translation architecture.

[3] https://cloud.google.com/speech-to-text/docs.

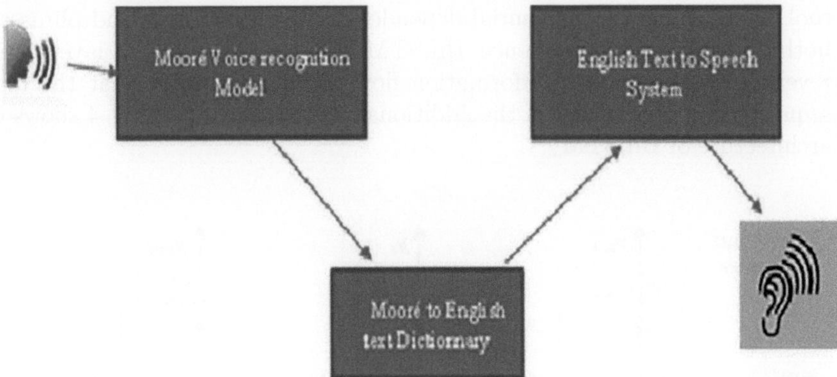

Fig. 5. Mooré to English translation architecture

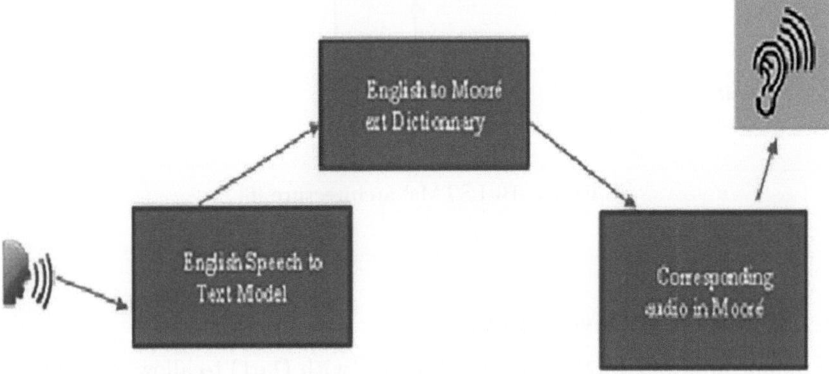

Fig. 6. English to Mooré translation system architecture

4 Experiments and Results

We used the opensource machine learning tool TensorFlow and the Python programming language to create the models. We used 5 algorithms for the experiments. For each algorithm, we split the dataset into 80% for model training and 20% for testing, both on the initial data and on the augmented data. These algorithms include a simple architecture algorithms and hybrid architecture algorithms. Some hyperparameters of the algorithms used is presented by the Table 2. Performances (in accuracy) are shown in Table 3.

The hybrid CNN-BiLSTM architecture gave better results in terms of accuracy. This means that this architecture adapts better to our data and can better determine its structure. The loss curves and learning curves, which give a better understanding of how the model learns from the data, are shown in Fig. 7a and Fig. 7b respectively, using the CNN-BiLSTM architecture.

Table 2. Some hyperparameters of the algorithms used

Hyperparameters types	Hyperparameters name	Values
Layer hyperparameters	Number of neurons in the first layer	150
	The number of filters for convolutional layers	64
	Number of neurons in the output layer	10
	Number of units for the dense layer	128
	Droupout	0.3
	Hidden layers activation method	relu
	Finale layers activation method	sofmax
Model compilation parameters	Optimizer	Adam
	Loss function	Categorical_crossentropy
Model execution hyperparameters	Batch size	64
	Number of epochs	20

Table 3. Results with different algorithms used to train the model with the initial dataset

Algorithm	CNN	LSTM	BiLSTM	CNN-LSTM	CNN-BILSTM
Accuracy (%)	21.76	76.73	73.73	75.98	79.92

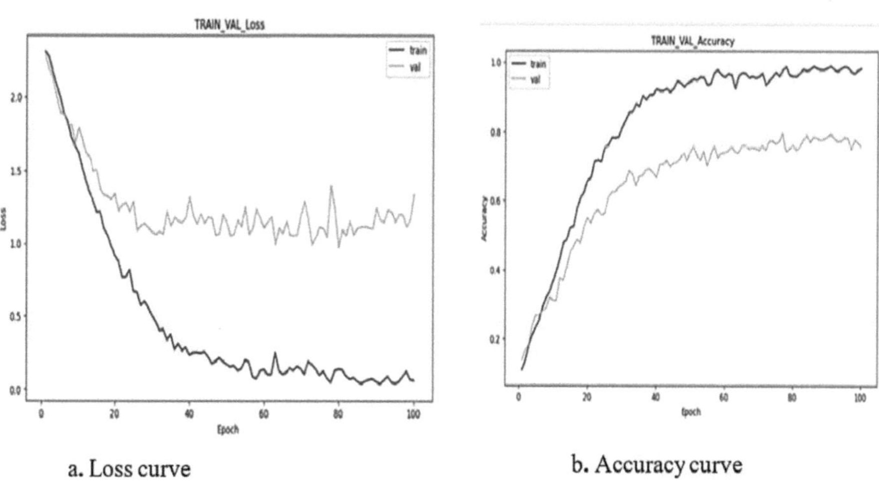

Fig. 7. Loss and Accuracy curves of the model trained using the initial dataset

Figure 8 shows the confusion matrix of the model using the CNN-BiLSTM algorithm on the initial data. This matrix shows the predictions made by each expression class as well as the classification errors made for each class. It shows that the model made a lot of confusion in the recognition of the "windga kibare" and "yibeoogo kibare" classes. We also note that these two classes have the common suffix "kibare". This confusion had a negative impact on the overall accuracy of the model.

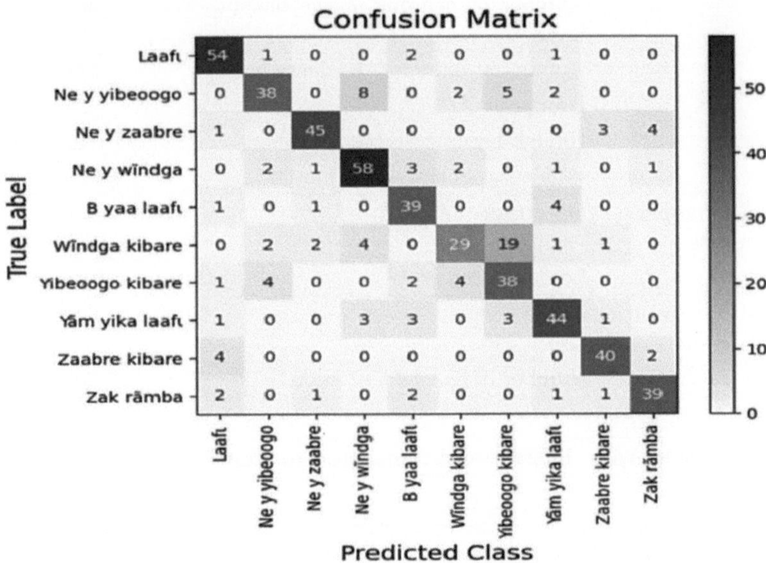

Fig. 8. Confusion Matrix of the model trained with initial dataset

Figure 9 shows the recognition rate by expression class. We can see a fairly good recognition rate for all expressions, with the exception of the "windga kibare" and "yibeoogo Kibare" classes, which have relatively low recognition rates (61% and 67% respectively).

Based on loss curve, we can remark that the training loss is decreasing, the validation loss plot suggests that the model is overfitting. In addition, while the model shows strong learning capability through the accuracy curve on the training set, its performance on the validation set indicates also an overfitting. Through the confusion matrix, we can observe that the model seems to struggle differentiating "W?ndga kibare" and "Yibeoogo kibare". Overfitting is due to the fact that the training data is not sufficient to allow the model to learn to correctly identify all classes. This phenomenon led us to apply the data augmentation technique, which enabled us to achieve better performance (96.25%. of accuracy) with CNN-BiLSTM. Figure 10a and Fig. 10b show the loss curve and accuracy curve, respectively, of the CNN-BiLSTM algorithm after data augmentation.

```
F1 Score for class Laafɩ: 0.89
F1 Score for class Ne y yibeoogo: 0.75
F1 Score for class Ne y zaabre: 0.87
F1 Score for class Ne y wĩndga: 0.82
F1 Score for class B yaa laafɩ: 0.81
F1 Score for class Wĩndga kibare: 0.61
F1 Score for class Yibeoogo kibare: 0.67
F1 Score for class Yãm yika laafɩ: 0.81
F1 Score for class Zaabre kibare: 0.87
F1 Score for class Zak rãmba: 0.85
```

Fig. 9. Scores per classes of the model trained with initial dataset

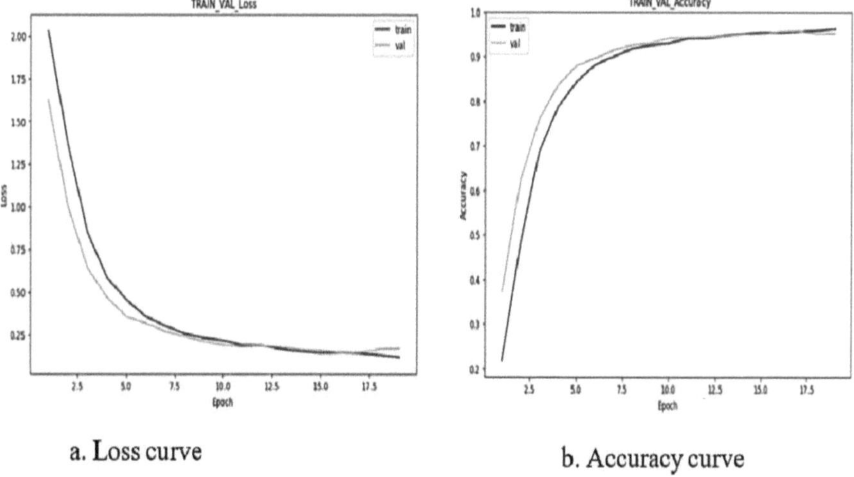

Fig. 10. Loss and Accuracy Curves of the model trained with augmented dataset

The loss and accuracy curves suggest that the model training is progressing well. The rapid initial decrease of loss curve and increase of accuracy curve followed by a stabilisation indicates effective learning. Since the validation loss follows the training loss closely and the validation accuracy follows the training accuracy closely, all eventually stabilize, the model generalizes well to the validation set without overfitting. The confusion matrix (see Fig. 11) shows that, the classifier performs well across most classes, with high true positive rates and relatively low misclassifications.

Some classes (see Fig. 12) show particularly strong performance while the others have slightly higher misclassifications, these classes have oral similarity.

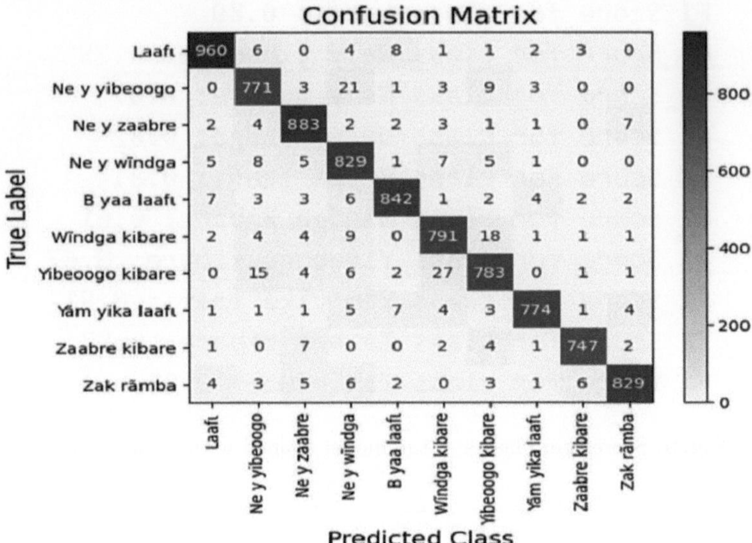

Fig. 11. Confusion Matrix of the model trained with augmented dataset

```
F1 Score for class Laafɩ: 0.98
F1 Score for class Ne y yibeoogo: 0.95
F1 Score for class Ne y zaabre: 0.97
F1 Score for class Ne y wĩndga: 0.95
F1 Score for class B yaa laafɩ: 0.97
F1 Score for class Wĩndga kibare: 0.95
F1 Score for class Yibeoogo kibare: 0.94
F1 Score for class Yãm yika laafɩ: 0.97
F1 Score for class Zaabre kibare: 0.98
F1 Score for class Zak rãmba: 0.97
```

Fig. 12. Scores per classes of the model trained with augmented dataset

After analyzing these results, we can say that the augmentation of the dataset helped to improve the model accuracy but more data will help to level up the model for better results. In addition, the strong performance of some classes compared to others may be caused by the unbalanced size of the data per classes. It would also be important to balance the data by class for future works.

To make an AI model accessible and easy to use for everyone, including non-IT specialists, it's important to create an application with user-friendly interfaces which embarks the model. The interfaces in Fig. 13a, 13b, 14a and 14b represent the screens of the mobile application that embeds the translation system.

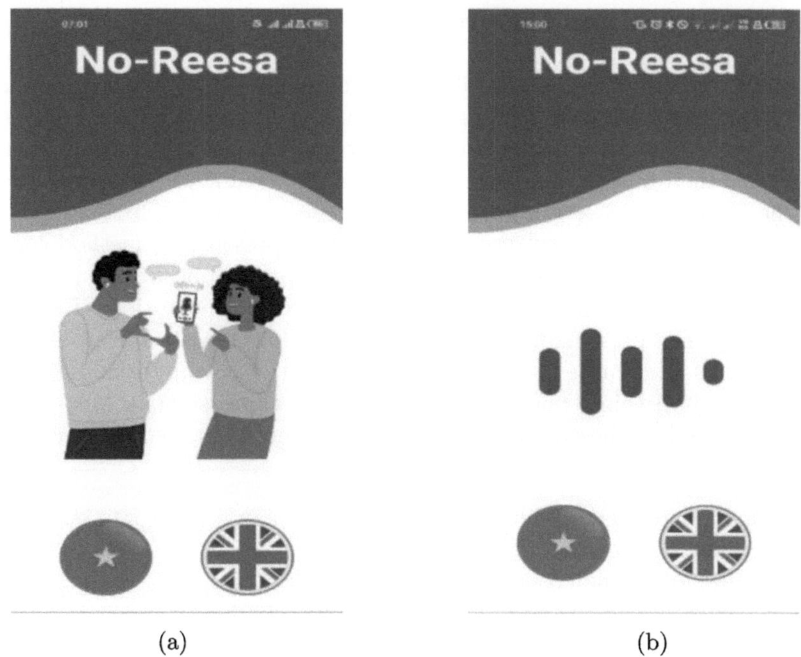

(a) (b)

Fig. 13. (a) Home Page of the mobile App. (b) App playing an audio

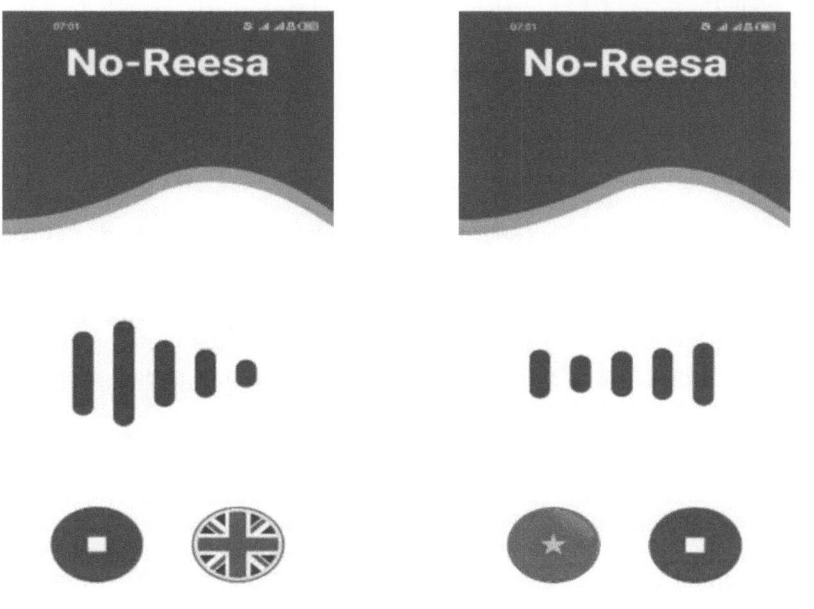

(a) Mooré to English translation interface

(b) English to Mooré translation interface

Fig. 14. Main interfaces of the mobile application.

5 Conclusion and Future Work

This paper describes our study about the development of a voice translation mobile app using artificial intelligence including Mooré language. This study aims to contribute to unleash language barrier between non-English speaking traders and their business partners. This was a challenging project due to the fact that the Mooré language is a low resource language. To do so, firstly, we present the similar studies on voice recognition, then we present the methodology followed to achieved the results which consisted in data collection, data processing, data augmentation, features extraction and experimentations. Finally, the results have been presented; model performances and mobile app screens.

Despite the difficulties met during data collection, competitive results have been achieved on voice translation using greeting expressions in Mooré, a local language. Based on these preliminary results, we intend in the next stages of the project to:

- Add more expressions including phrases other than greetings to our datasets to increase the scope of translation;
- Add other local languages like Dioula, Fulfulde etc.;
- Make the difference between men, women and children voices;
- Do a speech to text instead of predicting the classes;
- Implement a text-to-text model from our local languages to English;
- Implement a text to speech for our local languages;
- Merge all these models together to do a real automatic speech to speech system;
- Integrate the model in earphones for automatic translation.

References

1. Résultats du 5E Recensement Général de la Population et de l'Habitation — INSD (2019). https://www.insd.bf/fr/file-download/download/public/2071
2. Dehak, N., Kenny, P.J., Dehak, R., Dumouchel, P., Ouellet, P.: Front-end factor analysis for speaker verification. IEEE Trans. Audio Speech Lang. Process. **19**(4), 788–798 (2011). https://doi.org/10.1109/TASL.2010.2064307
3. Emezue, C.C., Dossou, F.P.B.: Ffr v1.1: Fon-French neural machine translation. In: Proceedings of the Fourth Widening Natural Language Processing Workshop, pp. 83–87 (2020). https://doi.org/10.18653/v1/2020.winlp-1.21
4. Hacheme, G.: English2gbe: a multilingual machine translation model for Fon/Ewegbe (2021). http://arxiv.org/abs/2112.11482. Accessed 12 Aug 2024
5. Hermansky, H., Sharma, S.: Temporal patterns (traps) in ASR of noisy speech. In: 1999 IEEE International Conference on Acoustics, Speech, and Signal Processing, ICASSP99, vol. 1, pp. 289–292 (1999). https://doi.org/10.1109/ICASSP.1999.758119
6. Ihianle, I., Nwajana, A., Ebenuwa, S., Otuka, R., Owa, K., Orisatoki, M.: A deep learning approach for human activities recognition from multimodal sensing devices. IEEE Access **8**, 179028–179038 (2020). https://doi.org/10.1109/ACCESS.2020.3027979

7. Kamaluddin, M.I., Rasyid, M.W.K., Abqoriyyah, F.H., Saehu, A.: Accuracy analysis of deepl: breakthroughs in machine translation technology. J. Engl. Educ. Forum JEEF **4**(2), 122–126 (2024). https://doi.org/10.29303/jeef.v4i2.681
8. Kozek, T., Roska, T., Chua, L.O.: Genetic algorithm for CNN template learning. IEEE Trans. Circuits Syst. Fundam. Theory Appl. **40**(6), 392–402 (1993). https://doi.org/10.1109/81.238343
9. Lezhenin, I., Bogach, N., Pyshkin, E.: Urban sound classification using long short-term memory neural network. In: 2019 Federated Conference on Computer Science and Information Systems, pp. 57–60 (2019). https://doi.org/10.15439/2019F185
10. Li, H., Graesser, A.C., Cai, Z.: Comparison of google translation with human translation, unpublished
11. Martinus, L., Webster, J., Moonsamy, J., Jnr, M.S., Moosa, R., Fairon, R.: Neural machine translation for south Africa's official languages (2020). http://arxiv.org/abs/2005.06609. Accessed 12 Aug 2024
12. Miró, X.A., Bonastre, J.F.: Fast speaker diarization based on binary keys. In: 2011 IEEE International Conference on Acoustics, Speech and Signal Processing (ICASSP), pp. 4428–4431 (2011). https://api.semanticscholar.org/CorpusID:14321864
13. Mohine, S., Bansod, B.S., Bhalla, R., Basra, A.: Acoustic modality based hybrid deep 1D CNN-bilstm algorithm for moving vehicle classification. IEEE Trans. Intell. Transp. Syst. **23**(9), 16206–16216 (2022). https://doi.org/10.1109/TITS.2022.3148783
14. Montgomery, C., Stalls, B., Stumberger, R., Li, N., Beivin, R.: Machine-aided voice translation (MAVT) (1996)
15. Muthumari, M., Bhuvaneswari, C.A., Babu, J.E.N.S.K., Raju, S.P.: Data augmentation model for audio signal extraction. In: 2022 3rd International Conference on Electronics and Sustainable Communication Systems (ICESC), pp. 334–340 (2022). https://doi.org/10.1109/ICESC54411.2022.9885539
16. Ouedraogo, I., et al.: Deploying a speech recognition model for under-resourced languages: a case study on dioula wake words 1, 2, 3, and 4. In: Proceedings of the 2023 7th International Conference on Natural Language Processing and Information Retrieval. NLPIR '23, New York, NY, USA, pp. 111–118. Association for Computing Machinery (2024). https://doi.org/10.1145/3639233.3639345, https://doi.org/10.1145/3639233.3639345
17. Raghav, P.: Understanding of convolutional neural network (CNN) — deep learning. https://medium.com/@RaghavPrabhu/understanding-of-convolutional-neural-network-cnn-deep-learning-99760835f148. Accessed 15 Oct 2024
18. Traore, G.I., Some, B.M.J.: Speech processing: a literature review (2024). https://eudl.eu/doi/10.4108/eai.18-12-2023.2348132. presented at the Proceedings of the 6th Computer Science Research Days, JRI 2023, 18-20 December 2023, Ouagadougou, Burkina Faso
19. Yibéogo, N.: Salutations suivant le moment de la journée, unpublished

Data Protection, Cybersecurity and System

Datasets Analysis for Effective Cyberattacks Mitigation in Software-Defined Networking

B. O. S. Biaou[1(✉)], A. O. Oluwatope[1], and B. S. Ogundare[2]

[1] Department of Computer Science and Engineering, OAU, Ile-Ife, Nigeria
bsbiaou@pg-student.oauife.edu.ng

[2] Department of Mathematics, OAU, Ile-Ife, Nigeria

Abstract. The The rapid propagation of many Cyberattacks presents a serious danger to the flexibility of Software-Defined Networking (SDN). The Cyberattacks such as Botnet, Distributed Denial of Service (DDoS), Probe, Brute-Force-Attack (BFA), User-to-Root attack (U2R), Web attack and many more are disrupting the emerging technologies. The selection of a dataset for the Intrusion Detection System (IDS) is therefore crucial in achieving a comprehensive awareness of the threat environment, which is necessary to mitigate these sophisticated attacks. In this study, technical details of the properties of the data set that are essential to create efficient cyber attack mitigation techniques in SDN are covered. In the light of the critical role that datasets play in comprehending, modeling, and reducing cyberattacks, this study carefully examines selected existing datasets to determine and evaluate their applicability for cyberattacks in SDN. The insights into the characteristics of ten common datasets are covered. Datasets analysis for SDN-based cyberattacks is accessed. The statistical analysis of the InSDN dataset is evaluated to provide a solid foundation for developing better cyberattack mitigation techniques in SDN. Dataset preparation is done using Python libraries like Scikit-learn and Pandas, ensuring standardized and efficient data processing. The implementation uses Support Vector Machine (SVM), K-Nearest Neighbors (KNN), and Naïve Bayes (NB) algorithms, with preprocessing steps including feature scaling and class balancing to improve model performance. Finally, accuracy, precision, recall, and F1-score are measured to evaluate classification effectiveness.

Keywords: Cyberattacks · SDN · Datasets

1 Introduction

The Internet is a vast, interconnected system linking billions of devices worldwide, serving as a global network of networks that enables seamless access to information, services, and resources across the globe. It makes it easier to communicate, share information, do online business, have fun, and more. The provision of digital services like e-commerce, online learning, telemedicine, and remote

A. Sere et al. (Eds.): AFRI2 2025, CCIS 2536, pp. 35–49, 2026.
https://doi.org/10.1007/978-3-031-98327-6_3

work is made possible through global interconnections of computer devices. Emerging technologies like SDN, 5G, Internet of Things (IoT), and edge computing, which enable new capabilities and applications, continue to advance networking [1]. Though conventional networking has long been the basis of networking, its flaws make it less suited to the dynamic, resource-efficient, and programmable demands of contemporary networks [2]. Traditional networking makes extensive use of specialized equipment, including load balancers, switches, routers, and firewalls [3]. Since many restrictions limited the traditional network, networks and businesses such as Google, Facebook, Microsoft Azure, Verizon, and China Telecom to increase network flexibility, effectiveness, and management capabilities have effectively deployed SDN [4]. Fundamentally, SDN divides the control plane of the network from the data plane, enabling centralized network management and dynamic network setup using software [5]. The interaction between the application layer and the control layer entails the management of the traffic flow via the northbound (NB) interface, whereas the southbound (SB) interface serves as the conduit linking the control layer to the infrastructure layer [6].

Nevertheless, in the area of network design and management, a revolutionary paradigm (SDN) has emerged as a result of the quick development of communication technology. However, Cyberattacks are a big security risk for these networks. The most frequent and important network attacks, including those on IoT, cloud computing, and 5G/6G communication networks, are Botnet, DDoS, Probe and web attacks [7]. Such attacks, among others, represent a significant threat to the performance, reliability, and availability of SDN infrastructures [8]. The main goal of many cyberattacks is to prevent network services or applications from being available. Cyberattacks frequently target certain network resources in an effort to deplete them, reduce service quality, or make the service unavailable [9]. Attackers seek to overwhelm network resources such as firewalls, load balancers, or routers with an excessive amount of traffic or to take advantage of weaknesses in how they handle network packets [3].

However, a dataset is defined as a collection of related sets of information that composed of separate elements but can be manipulated as a unit by a computer. Meanwhile, it is impossible to neglect the value of datasets in dealing with cyber attacks. When it comes to addressing cyber-dangers, datasets are essential to offer a basis for comprehending, evaluating, and reducing a variety of security risks [10]. Realistic datasets aid in the creation of useful and efficient defense systems.

According to the authors of the paper [11], the general properties that scholarly data should fulfill were defined as FAIR. Where FAIR stands for Findability, Accessibility, Interoperability and Reusability. Those four principles of FAIR are truly needed to be considered at the level of general concept but limited to a specific environment like SDN. Therefore, additional properties for a suitable dataset for analysing cyberattacks in SDN environment are listed below:

- Sufficient benign and attack traffic for balanced analysis.
- Labeling of all attack types recorded in the dataset.
- Enough SDN-based features to capture key network behaviors.

- Captured within an SDN environment for real-world relevance.

The goal of this manuscript is to generate useful information that can be used by cybersecurity researchers and practitioners to make decision in the choice of datasets in the study of cyberattacks in SDN environment. In this paper, we defined the relations between the datasets, the peculiarities of each dataset and evaluated the quality of intrusion detection in the datasets. Further, we pointed out the analysis of datasets for cyberattacks in the SDN environment. Also, we evaluated the statistical analysis of the InSDN dataset that provides a foundation for developing cyberattack mitigation techniques in SDN.

This section of the paper has presented the introduction. The Sect. 2 illustrates the state of the art on Datasets for IDS. Section 3 presents the analysis of the datasets for cyberattacks in SDN. In the Sect. 4, the statistical analysis of the InSDN dataset are presented. Section 5 presents the classification metrics of DDoS in InSDN dataset while Sect. 6 is specifically for discussion and conclusion remarks.

2 State of the Art on Datasets for IDS

2.1 Background on Common and Available Datasets for IDS

Numerous datasets have been considered by researchers to address different types of attacks in the area of cybersecurity. Ten common and widely used datasets for intrusion detection system are presented below.

- **KDD'99 dataset**: This dataset was developed under the sponsorship of Defense Advanced Research Projects Agency (DARPA) and Air Force Research Laboratory (AFRL) in 1998. The MIT Lincoln Labs has gathered and disseminated the dataset [12]. The dataset contains 4,898,431 instances where the instances of attacks are too high in relation with those of normal traffic with the complexity of the calculations [13].
- **NSL-KDD dataset**: To settle the issues of KDD Cup informational index, National Institute of Standards and Technology (NIST) proposed the NSL-KDD dataset. The dataset comprised of chosen records of the total KDD Cup'99 informational index [10]. The NSL-KDD dataset is made up of a respectable number of well chosen features by eliminating duplicate and redundant instances from the KDD CUP 99 dataset [14] and [15].
- **Kyoto dataset**: The dataset was constructed over a three-year period through honeypot servers of Kyoto University [16]. During the observation period, there were 43,043,255 attack sessions, 425,719 unknown attacks sessions, and 50,033,015 normal sessions [17]. The imbalanced class appropriation of the dataset is viewed as the fundamental limit of Kyoto 2006+ since most of the deals information are noxious [18].
- **ISOT Dataset**: The Fake News Dataset, ISOT was developed in 2010 at Lawrence Berkeley National Laboratory and Ericsson Research in Hungary (LBNL) [19]. P2P botnet detection was accomplished with ISOT [20].

- **ISCX2012 dataset**: The Canadian Institute for Cybersecurity created the ISCX 2012 dataset, which was produced by the Information Security Center of Excellence within 7 days (ISCX) [21]. A substantial portion of network traffic were left unlabeled, and attack scenarios were not thoroughly explained [22]. Besides, the dataset incorporates just HTTP traffic, which did not reflect present day deals, where most of current Internet follows depend on HTTPS traffic [23].
- **UNSW-NB15 Dataset**: The UNSW-NB15 dataset was generated over a 31-hour period in a tiny simulated environment using the IXIA Perfect Storm tool. The dataset offers 45 unique IP addresses in addition to predefined splits for training and testing [24].
- **CIDDS-001 Dataset**: The Coburg Intrusion Detection DataSet is a labelled flow-based dataset built within 28 days. This dataset developed for the evaluation purpose of Anomaly-based Network Intrusion Detection System (NIDS). There are 16 million flows in the CIDDS001 dataset and was built over the course of two weeks [25].
- **CICIDS2017 dataset**: The dataset was published by "Information Security Center of Excellence (ISCX) of the University of New Brunswick, Canada". [26]. The dataset was built in 2017 within a period of 5 days with about 203 missing data [27].
- **CSE-CIC-IDS2018 dataset**: This dataset is the aftereffect of a cooperative task between the Communications Security Establishment (CSE) and the Canadian Institute for Cybersecurity (CIC). The dataset covers similar attack situations as in CICIDS 2017 dataset. Notwithstanding, the dataset experiences similar intrinsic issues of CICIDS 2017, and furthermore the utilization of manufactured traffic [28].
- **InSDN dataset**: InSDN is an attack-specific SDN dataset and was developed in 2020. It is publicly available to the researchers since 2020 at Research Repository UCD ASEADOS Lab (University College Dublin), Ireland. The dataset was implemented using only ONOS SDN controller [29].

2.2 Datasets Properties

The evaluation basis of every dataset in the area of IDS must be defined within some common properties. The purpose of carrying out the closest relationship among datasets based properties is to facilitate the choice of appropriate datasets for the researchers in regard of the goal and the environment of the research. In general, a survey should not be used to determine the relevance of any given property because it relies on the particular evaluation circumstance. Instead, the goal should be to enable readers to come across the reasons embedded on the choice of the right datasets for their purposes. Therefore, the major dataset properties are categorized in five such as general information, nature of the data, data volume, recording environment and evaluation [17,27] and [15]. Figure 1 presents and explain briefly the components of each category.

Table 1 is therefore derived from the understanding of the information given by Fig. 1 to establish the comparative analysis of the ten datasets. Henceforth,

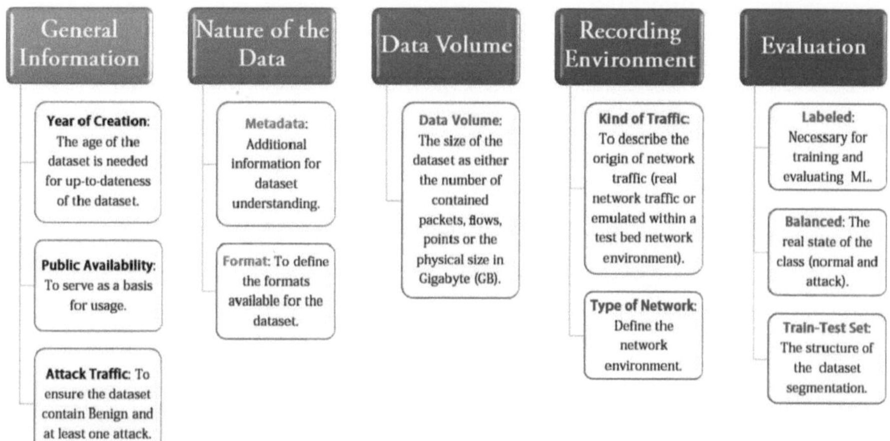

Fig. 1. Datasets Properties.

all the ten datasets have many useful properties in common such as the availability for usage, the presence of normal and abnormal class of labels and the unbalanced data to engage the feature engineering. However, some other properties are specific to every dataset in term of the year of creation, the data volume, the recording environment and the structure of the dataset. Therefore, it is imperative to consider each of those properties in relation with the type of threats and the environment targeted of the research. Those characteristics are needed not to judge the dataset but rather to facilitate the choice of the best datasets accordingly.

However, some useful key guidance points can be summarized based on the outcome results presented in Table 1.

- The KDD'99, NSL-KDD and Kyoto datasets were without any additional information to ease the clear understanding of the meaning of the features' names (metadat). Though, those datasets were the most oldest but the KDD'99 and NSL-KDD datasets were gathered in a small network and segmented into training and testing set [15] while the Kyoto dataset was obtained in a real network traffic for a single host (honeypot) [25].
- The ISOT, ISCX2012 and UNSW-NB15 datasets were all built in a small test bed network environment within 2010 and 2015 with the availability of the metadata. The datasets were segmented into training and testing set except the ISCX2012 dataset [22].
- The CIDDS-001, CICIDS2017, CSE-CIC-IDS2018 and InSDN datasets are the most recent available datasets (2017-2020) with detail additional metadata. The datasets were built in a small test bed network environment [25] except the InSDN, which is specially obtained from a real SDN environment [29].

Table 1. Comparative Analysis of Ten Common Datasets

Dataset		General Information			Nature of Data		Data Volume	Recording Environment		Evaluation		
No	Dataset	Year of Creation	Availability	Attack Traffic	Metadata	Format	Volume	Kind of Traffic	Type of Network	Labeled	Balanced	Training-Test. Set
1	KDD'99	1998	Yes	Yes	No	cvs, Others	71.4 MB	Emulated	Small Network	Yes	No	Yes
2	NSL-KDD	1998	Yes	Yes	No	cvs, Others	15 MB	Emulated	Small Network	Yes	No	Yes
3	Kyoto 2006+	2006 to 2009	Yes	Yes	No	cvs, Others	60.1 MB	Real	Honeypots	Yes	No	No
4	ISOT	2010	Yes	Yes	Yes	Packet, PCAP	11 GB	Emulated	Small Network	Yes	No	Yes
5	ISCX2012	2012	Yes	Yes	Yes	Packet, bi. flow	1,012 MB	Emulated	Small Network	Yes	No	No
6	UNSW-NB15	2015	Yes	Yes	Yes	Packets, csv	2M Data points	Emulated	Small Network	Yes	No	Yes
7	CIDDS-001	2017	Yes	Yes	Yes	uni. flow	32M Data flows	Emulated and Real	Small Network	Yes	No	No
8	CICIDS 2017	2017	Yes	Yes	Yes	Packet bi. flow	494 MB	Emulated	Small Network	Yes	No	No
9	CSE-CIC-IDS2018	2018	Yes	Yes	Yes	cvs, PCAP	5M Data flows	Emulated	Small Network	Yes	No	No
10	InSDN	2020	Yes	Yes	Yes	Packet, flow, cvs	5.46 GB	Emulated and Real	SDN Network	Yes	No	No

3 Datasets Analysis for Cyber Attacks in SDN

Every dataset has a total number of features that majorly composed of nominal, integer, binary, float and timestamp [17]. In a SDN environment, only flow statistics information can be read from the SDN controller through API queries. Those features must be found in every dataset that is suitable for IDS in SDN and are thirteen in number [29] and [26] include: (F1) Protocol type, (F2) Length of the connection, (F3) Maximum expire time of flow, (F4) Data bytes in bidirectional flow. (F5) Packets in bidirectional flow, (F6) Data bytes from source to destination, (F7) Data bytes from destination to source, (F8) Flow permanence time, (F9) Inter arrival time, (F10) Inter arrival time from source to destination, (F11) Inter arrival time from destination to source, (F12) Packet per second from source to destination and (F13) Packet per second from destination to source. Figure 2 therefore summarizes the number of features, the number of statistical features and the number of statistical features based SDN in each of the ten popular and available datasets [15,17,20,24] and [29].

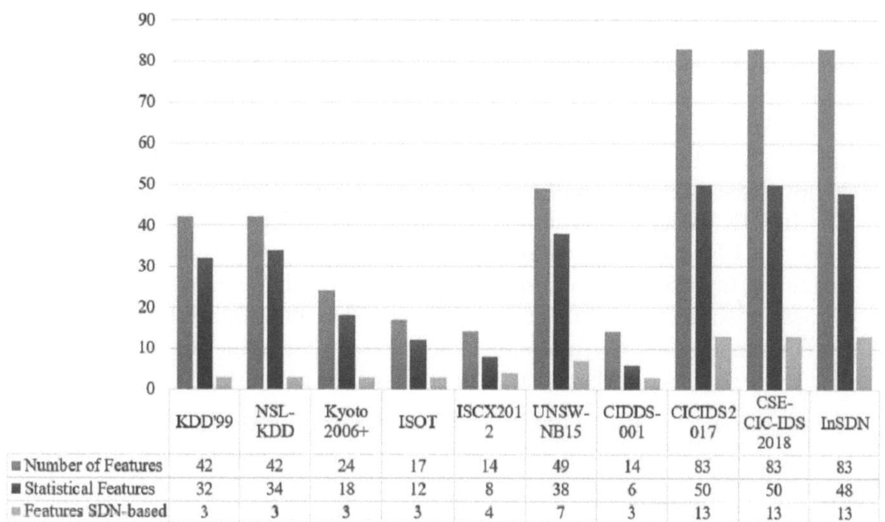

	KDD'99	NSL-KDD	Kyoto 2006+	ISOT	ISCX2012	UNSW-NB15	CIDDS-001	CICIDS2017	CSE-CIC-IDS 2018	InSDN
Number of Features	42	42	24	17	14	49	14	83	83	83
Statistical Features	32	34	18	12	8	38	6	50	50	48
Features SDN-based	3	3	3	3	4	7	3	13	13	13

Fig. 2. Datasets Analysis in SDN Environment.

However, the suitable SDN dataset must include diverse traffic patterns, realistic attack scenarios, and sufficient volume to reflect dynamic network conditions. Key criteria include accurate labeling, balanced class distribution, and the 13 SDN-based features as confirmed by [29] and [26]. Hence, the comparative analysis of the listed datasets in the area of SDN as shown in Fig. 2 can be summarized as follow:

- The KDD'99 and NSL-KDD datasets contain the same number of features (42) while 32 and 34 statistical features were obtained respectively from

KDD'99 and NSL-KDD [15]. Both datasets contain only 3 over 13 major SDN-based features. Moreover, the number of SDN-based features in those datasets is far away from the required condition to fit for IDS in SDN. Consequently, KDD'99 and NSL-KDD datasets are not suitable to carry out an effective analysis of the attacks in the area of SDN.
- The CIDDS-001, ISOT, Kyoto and ISCX2012 datasets contain 14, 17, 24 and 14 features respectively with different number (6, 12, 18 and 8) of statistical features [17,20] and [15]. Except the ISCX2012 dataset that contains 4 SDN-based features, the remaining three contain only 3 SDN-based features. Hence, the CIDDS-001, ISOT, Kyoto and ISCX2012 datasets did not reach the required condition for IDS in SDN and then failed to be suitable for effective cyberattacks analysis in SDN environment.
- The UNSW-NB15 dataset contains a total number of 49 features with 38 and 7 respectively of statistical features and SDN-based features [24]. Even though, the dataset has more than half of the required condition to fit for IDS in SDN, UNSW-NB15 is not worthy to be considered for cyberattacks in the area of SDN.
- The CICIDS2017 and CSE-CIC-IDS2018 datasets contain the same number of features (83), the same number of statistical features and the same number of SDN-based features [17]. CICIDS2017 and CSE-CIC-IDS2018 have truly reached the required condition for IDS in SDN. Consequently, the CICIDS2017 and CSE-CIC-IDS2018 datasets are suitable to carry out an analysis of cyber attacks in SDN even though both were not built in a SDN environment but in a small conventional network as shown in Table 1.
- The InSDN dataset contain a total number of 83 features, 48 statistical features and 13 featured-based SDN [29]. The dataset meets the essential requirements for Intrusion Detection Systems (IDS) in SDN and stands as the only dataset specifically constructed within an SDN environment. Consequently, InSDN emerges as the most suitable choice for conducting a rigorous and effective analysis of cyberattacks in SDN-based networks.

Nevertheless, Table 2 is obtained from the graphical representation of the evolution of the datasets in term of the number of features as presented in Fig. 2.

However, from the analysis of the results displayed in Fig. 2, there is an attend to affirm that as time goes on, the datasets become more dynamic and suitable to carryout effective attacks mitigation. It is remarkable that most recent datasets upgrade in term of number of features (CICIDS2017, CSE-CIC-IDS2018 and InSDN datasets). This can be probably explained by the rapid advancement of the technologies and tools used for data collection as the major step in dataset building.

4 Statistical Analysis of InSDN Dataset

The InSDN dataset stands as a well-structured benchmark for evaluating intrusion detection systems (IDS) in SDN environments. Capturing 100 days of network traffic, it offers a rich and diverse collection of data encompassing both

Table 2. Comparative Analysis of the Datasets in SDN

No	Dataset	[F1]	[F2]	[F3]	[F4]	[F5]	[F6]	[F7]	[F8]	[F9]	F10	F11	F12	[F13]
1	KDD'99	●	●	●	○	○	○	○	○	○	○	○	○	○
2	NSL-KDD	●	●	●	○	○	○	○	○	○	○	○	○	○
3	Kyoto 2006+	●	●	●	○	○	○	○	○	○	○	○	○	○
4	ISOT	●	●	●	○	○	○	○	○	○	○	○	○	○
5	ISCX2012	●	●	●	○	○	●	○	○	○	○	○	○	○
6	UNSW-NB15	●	●	●	○	○	●	●	●	●	○	○	○	○
7	CIDDS-001	●	●	●	○	○	○	○	○	○	○	○	○	○
8	CICIDS 2017	●	●	●	●	●	●	●	●	●	●	●	●	●
9	CSECICIDS2018	●	●	●	●	●	●	●	●	●	●	●	●	●
10	InSDN	●	●	●	●	●	●	●	●	●	●	●	●	●

normal and attack scenarios [29]. Traffic was meticulously gathered at the switch level, yielding 83 attributes and 41 traffic features, including key packet header details such as source and destination IPs, ports, and protocol types. This dataset is particularly well-suited for supervised machine learning applications, as it contains both benign and malicious traffic patterns [10].

However, the InSDN dataset is systematically structured into three distinct subgroups, offering a granular approach to traffic analysis. The Normal group consists exclusively of legitimate network activities, including Skype calls, Facebook interactions, file transfers, YouTube streaming, email exchanges, DNS queries, online chats, and web browsing, and accounts for 19.90% of the total instances in the dataset. In contrast, the Metasploitable-2 group captures a diverse set of five cyberattacks–DDoS, Probe, DoS, Brute-Force Attacks (BFA), and User-to-Root exploits and representing 39.76% of the total instances. Expanding the attack diversity further, the OVS group introduces Web attacks and Botnet activities, alongside DoS, DDoS, Probe, and BFA intrusions, making up 40.34% of the total instances. This well-defined segmentation enables researchers to strategically select datasets aligned with their specific study objectives, ensuring a targeted and effective evaluation framework for intrusion detection and cybersecurity advancements.

A detailed breakdown of the dataset composition is illustrated in Fig. 3, emphasizing the distribution of instances across the three subgroups. Moreover, Fig. 4 highlights the overall traffic distribution, revealing that among the seven recorded attack types, DDoS, Probe, and DoS attacks exhibit a significantly high number of instances. This abundance makes them particularly valuable for availability analysis and the development of resilient IDS models. By offering a well-defined structure, diverse attack representation, and realistic traffic patterns,

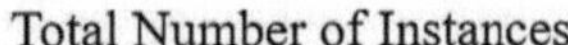

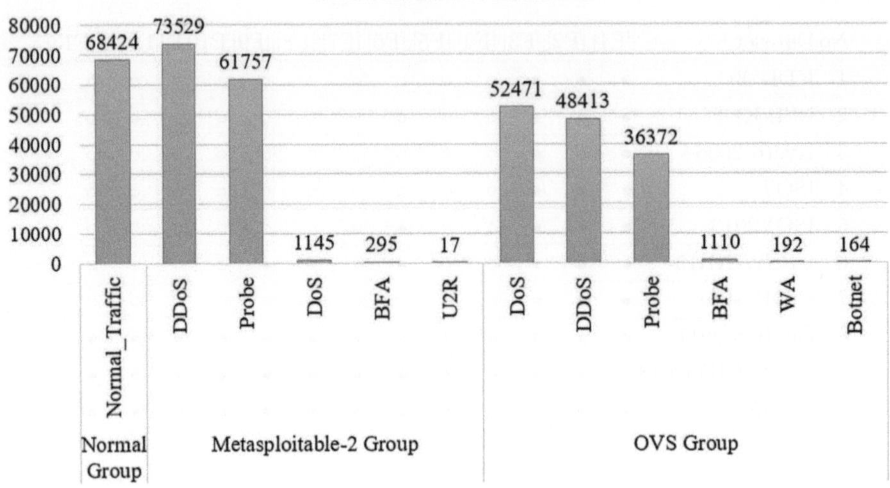

Fig. 3. Group of Instances in InSDN Dataset.

the InSDN dataset presents an essential foundation for advancing cybersecurity research and SDN-based threat mitigation strategies.

5 Classification Metrics of DDoS in InSDN Dataset

The selection of DDoS attacks from the InSDN dataset is driven by their dominant presence and high frequency compared to other attack types (Fig. 3), making them statistically significant for analysis. Given their ability to exploit SDN vulnerabilities, DDoS attacks pose a severe threat to network stability, warranting focused mitigation strategies. Their prevalence in the dataset ensures a comprehensive evaluation of detection models, enhancing the reliability of classification performance and real-world applicability. Moreover, their complex attack patterns and traffic amplification effects provide a challenging yet critical benchmark for assessing the adaptability and effectiveness of security mechanisms.

The InSDN dataset, collected from a real-world SDN environment at University College Dublin (UCD) in 2020, is sourced from the Research Repository. Prior to model training, preprocessing is conducted to enhance dataset suitability and mitigate overfitting, which involves filtering out excessive information. The final dataset retains 48 essential features, ensuring relevance within the SDN context. The modeling process employs three supervised learning algorithms: Naïve Bayes, K-Nearest Neighbors, and Support Vector Machines. The dataset is split into 80% training data and 20% testing data, facilitating optimal model selection for unseen inputs. Implementation is carried out in Python, utilizing core machine learning libraries such as scikit-learn, Seaborn, Pandas, NumPy, and Matplotlib, integrated within the Anaconda environment. Each

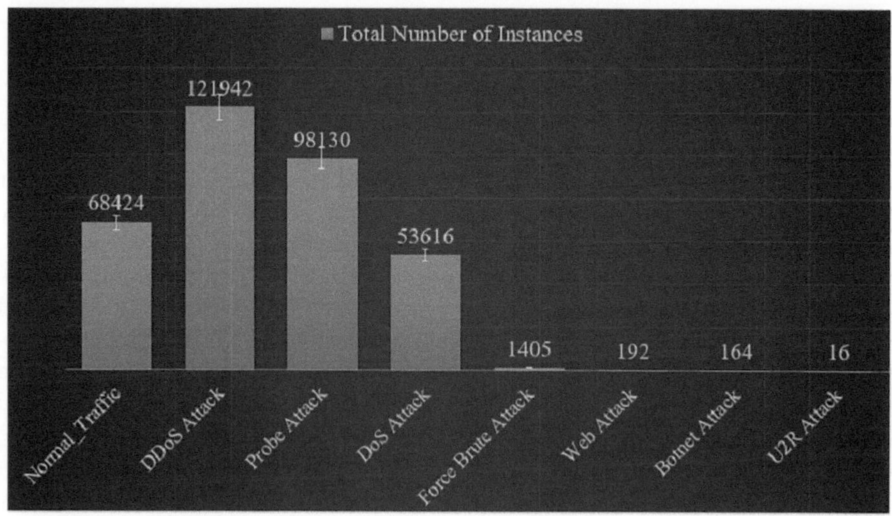

Fig. 4. Traffics in InSDN Dataset.

algorithm is instantiated, trained, and validated against the test set, with performance assessed through accuracy, precision, sensitivity, and F1-score.

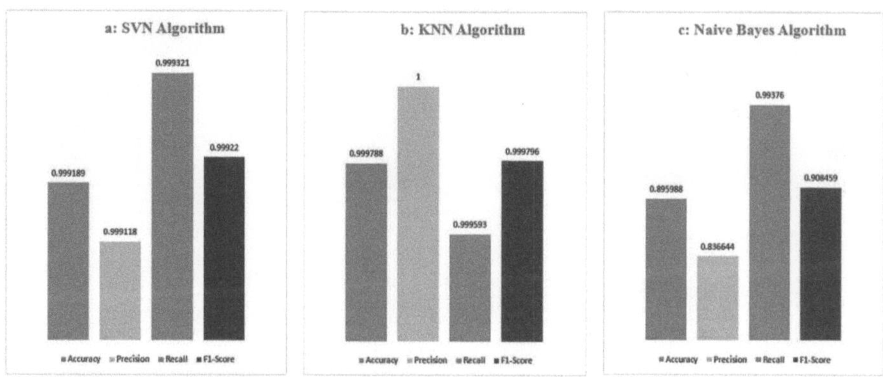

Fig. 5. Metrics Performance of Each Algorithm.

The implementation results reveal significant performance variations, highlighting the effectiveness of the chosen models in achieving high classification accuracy with minimal errors. The SVM and KNN algorithms demonstrate exceptional classification performance across all evaluation metrics. SVM achieves an accuracy of 99.92% and KNN slightly surpasses it at 99.98%, with precision values of 99.91% and 100%, respectively. Their specificity scores

(99.93% for SVM and 99.96% for KNN) indicate an extremely low false positive rate, while their F1-Scores (99.92% and 99.98%) confirm a strong balance between precision and recall, as illustrated in Figs. 5a and 5b. The KNN model marginally outperforms SVM in accuracy, precision, and specificity, yet both exhibit near-perfect classification capabilities. In contrast, the Naïve Bayes (NB) algorithm, while still achieving a high accuracy of 89.6%, lags behind with lower precision (83.66%) and F1-Score (90.85%), as depicted in Fig. 5c. Its specificity (99.38%), though relatively strong, is notably lower than that of SVM and KNN, indicating a higher tendency toward misclassification. The evaluation of the implemented models reveals significant performance differences, with SVM and KNN achieving near-perfect classification accuracy, while NB exhibits comparatively higher misclassification rates, as further illustrated through the confusion matrices. The confusion matrices, depicted in Fig. 6, provide a detailed visual comparison of classification performance for the NB (Fig. 6a), SVM (Fig. 6b), and KNN (Fig. 6c) algorithms. These matrices highlight the distribution of correctly and incorrectly classified instances, offering insights into each of the ability of the model to distinguish between classes.

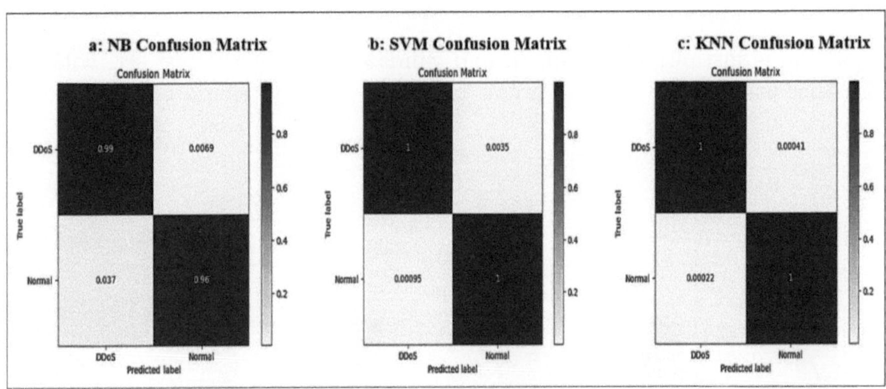

Fig. 6. Confusion Matrix of Each Algorithm.

6 Discussion and Conclusion

6.1 Discussion

The InSDN dataset enables network operators and cybersecurity teams to enhance anomaly detection by providing a comprehensive collection of SDN-specific traffic patterns, which is critical for identifying sophisticated attacks like control plane attacks or flow table manipulation, common in modern SDN environments. For instance, its detailed labeling of network events allows for the development of machine learning models that can accurately detect and mitigate attacks such as DDoS, helping to improve real-time intrusion response and reduce the risk of network disruptions.

The obtained results (Fig. 2 and Table 2) so far demonstrate that the quality and realism of any attack mitigation approaches are highly dependent on the suitability of the dataset. The relevance of the chosen dataset is paramount in ensuring that cybersecurity mitigation strategies are tailored to the specific system or environment under study. A contextually appropriate dataset captures the intricacies of network configurations, system architectures, and user behaviors, providing a realistic foundation for analyzing cyber threats. By selecting a dataset that aligns with the target environment, researchers can enhance the accuracy and effectiveness of data-driven threat mitigation techniques. From the comprehensive analysis of ten cybersecurity datasets for SDN, Table 2 and Fig. 2 clearly highlight CICIDS2017, CSE-CIC-IDS2018, and InSDN as the three most suitable choices. Additionally, the results in Fig. 5 and Fig. 6 indicate that SVM and KNN algorithms perform exceptionally well in classification tasks, particularly in scenarios requiring high precision and recall. Specifically, KNN and SVM demonstrate good effectiveness in detecting DDoS attacks within the SDN framework using the InSDN dataset, making them optimal choices for attack classification and mitigation strategies.

However, a critical factor in cyberattack analysis is the environment in which the dataset was collected. Since cyber threats can emerge in virtually any network setting, the presence of diverse attack types across datasets underscores the importance of dataset suitability for the intended study. The InSDN dataset, for instance, offers a broad spectrum of attack types, including DDoS, Probe, DoS, Brute-Force Attacks (BFA), User-to-Root attacks, Web attacks, and Botnets. The key challenge remains: how well does the dataset represent the target environment? Ensuring dataset suitability is crucial for accurate attack detection, reliable model training, and the development of practical mitigation frameworks in real-world SDN deployments.

6.2 Conclusion

This work has conducted a thorough investigation of the selected datasets necessary to advance techniques for mitigating cyberattacks in network environment. The obtained results highlight the significant properties to be considered in choosing the right datasets in the study of cyberattack mitigation in SDN. The comparative evaluation will help cybersecurity researchers and practitioners to arrive at informed decisions in their studies. Therefore, among the ten datasets considered, CICIDS2017, CSE-CIC-IDS2018 and InSDN datasets are the most appropriates in the development of data-driven technique in the mitigation of cyberattacks in SDN.

While InSDN effectively mitigates cyberattacks in SDN environments, its adaptability and potential data biases require further analysis. Future research will focus on optimizing resource efficiency, integrating adaptive threat intelligence, and enhancing data diversity to strengthen its resilience and applicability.

References

1. Gaurav, A., Gupta, B.B., Alhalabi, W., Visvizi, A., Asiri, Y.: A comprehensive survey on DDoS attacks on various intelligent systems and it is defense techniques. Int. J. Intell. Syst. **37**(12), 11407–11431 (2022)
2. Mishra, K., Saini, D.K.: SEIRS epidemic model with delay for transmission of malicious objects in computer network. Appl. Math. Comput. **188**(2), 1476–1482 (2007)
3. Belgaum, M.R., Musa, S., Alam, M.M., Su'ud, M.M.: A systematic review of load balancing techniques in software-defined networking. IEEE Access **8**, 98612–98636 (2020)
4. Shakil, M., Mohammed, F.Y.A., Arul, R., Bashir, A.K., Choi, J.K.: A novel dynamic framework to detect DDoS in SDN using metaheuristic clustering. Trans. Emerg. Telecommun. Technol. **33**(3), e3622 (2022)
5. Biaou, B.O.S., Oluwatope, A.O.: Development of machine learning-based blockchain architecture to mitigate DDoS attacks in SDN. In: Proceedings of the Obafemi Awolowo University, Faculty of Technology Conference (2022)
6. Biaou, B.O.S., Oluwatope, A.O., Ogundare, B.S.: Mathematical analysis of DDoS attacks in SDN-based 5G. In: Saeed, R.A., Bakari, A.D., Sheikh, Y.H. (eds.) Towards new e-Infrastructure and e-Services for Developing Countries, vol. 499, pp. 87–100. Springer, Cham (2023). https://doi.org/10.1007/978-3-031-34896-9_7
7. Cui, Y., et al.: Towards DDoS detection mechanisms in software-defined networking. J. Netw. Comput. Appl. **190**, 103156 (2021)
8. Gadze, J.D., Bamfo-Asante, A.A., Agyemang, J.O., Nunoo-Mensah, H., Opare, K.A.-B.: An investigation into the application of deep learning in the detection and mitigation of DDOS attack on SDN controllers. Technologies **9**(1), 14 (2021)
9. Mahjabin, T., Xiao, Y., Sun, G., Jiang, W.: A survey of distributed denial-of-service attack, prevention, and mitigation techniques. Int. J. Distrib. Sens. Netw. **13**(12), 155014771774146 (2017)
10. Chuang, H.-M., Liu, F., Tsai, C.-H.: Early detection of abnormal attacks in software-defined networking using machine learning approaches. Symmetry **14**(6), 1178 (2022)
11. Wilkinson, M.D., et al.: The FAIR Guiding Principles for scientific data management and stewardship. Sci. Data **18**(3), 160018 (2016)
12. Choudhary, S., Kesswani, N.: Analysis of KDD-Cup'99, NSL-KDD and UNSW-NB15 datasets using deep learning in IoT. Procedia Comput. Sci. **167**, 1561–1573 (2020)
13. Gifty Jeya, P., Ravichandran, M., Ravichandran, C.S.: Efficient classifier for R2L and U2R Attacks. Int. J. Comput. Appl. **45**(21), 28–32 (2012)
14. Kavitha, P., Usha, M.: Anomaly based intrusion detection in WLAN using discrimination algorithm combined with Naïve Bayesian classifier Naïve Bayesian classifier. J. Theor. Appl. Inf. Technol. **62**(1) (2014)
15. Protić, D.D.: Review of KDD Cup '99, NSL-KDD and Kyoto 2006+ datasets. Vojnotehnički glasnik/Military Techn. Courier **66**(3), 580–596 (2018)
16. Sato, M., Yamaki, H., Takakura, H.: Unknown attacks detection using feature extraction from anomaly-based ids alerts. In: 2012 IEEE/IPSJ 12th International Symposium on Applications and the Internet. IEEE(2012)
17. Ghurab, M., Gaphari, G., Alshami, F., Alshamy, R., Othman, S.: A detailed analysis of benchmark datasets for network intrusion detection system. Asian J. Res. Comput. Sci. **7**(4), 14–33 (2021)

18. Song, J., Takakura, H., Okabe, Y.: Description of Kyoto University Benchmark Data (2006). http://www.takakura.com/Kyoto_data/BenchmarkData-Description-v5.pdf. Accessed 26 Jan 2023
19. Szabó, G., Orincsay, D., Malomsoky, S., Szabó, I.: On the validation of traffic classification algorithms. In: Claypool, M., Uhlig, S. (eds.) PAM 2008. LNCS, vol. 4979, pp. 72–81. Springer, Heidelberg (2008). https://doi.org/10.1007/978-3-540-79232-1_8
20. Saad, S., et al.: Detecting P2P botnets through network behavior analysis and machine learning. In: 2011 Ninth Annual International Conference on Privacy, Security and Trust, pp. 174–180. IEEE (2011)
21. Shiravi, A.: Toward developing a systematic approach to generate benchmark datasets for intrusion detection. Comput. Secur. **31**(3), 357–374 (2012)
22. Pektaş, A., Acarman, T.: A deep learning method to detect network intrusion through flow-based features. Int. J. Netw. Manag. **29**(3), e2050 (2019)
23. Haider, S., et al.: A deep CNN ensemble framework for efficient DDoS attack detection in software defined networks. IEEE Access **8**, 53972–53983 (2020)
24. Moustafa, N., Slay, J.: UNSW-NB15: a comprehensive data set for network intrusion detection systems (UNSW-NB15 network data set). In: 2015 Military Communications and Information Systems Conference (MilCIS) (2015). https://doi.org/10.1109/milcis.2015.7348942.
25. Ring, M., Wunderlich, S., Grüdl, D., Landes, D., Hotho, A.: Flow-based benchmark data sets for intrusion detection. In: Proceedings of the 16th European Conference on Cyber Warfare and Security. ACPI, pp. 361–369 (2017)
26. Krishnan, P., Duttagupta, S., Achuthan, K.: VARMAN: multi-plane security framework for software defined networks. Comput. Commun. **148**, 215–239 (2019)
27. Ring, M., Wunderlich, S., Scheuring, D., Landes, D., Hotho, A.: A survey of network-based intrusion detection data sets. Comput. Secur. **86**, 147–167 (2019)
28. Leevy, J.L., Khoshgoftaar, T.M.: A survey and analysis of intrusion detection models based on CSE-CIC-IDS2018 big data. J. Big Data **7**(1), 104 (2020)
29. Elsayed, M.S., Le-Khac, N.-A., Jurcut, A.D.: InSDN: a novel SDN intrusion dataset. IEEE Access **8**, 165263–165284 (2020)

A New Stegano-Watermarking Scheme for the Creation of Medical Image Datasets

Boureima Koussoube[1(✉)], Moustapha Bikienga[2], Telesphore Tiendrebeogo[1], and Cheick Yacouba Rachid Coulibaly[1]

[1] Nazi Boni University, Bobo-dioulasso, Burkina Faso
koussoubebrm@gmail.com

[2] Nobert Zongo University, Koudougou, Burkina Faso

Abstract. Digitisation of medical images is improving diagnosis and clinical research, but poses major challenges in terms of security and traceability. This paper proposes a hybrid solution combining digital watermarking and steganography to securely trace these images, while enabling automatic watermarking detection via adapted neural networks. We evaluated several watermarking techniques, including Discrete Cosine Transform (DCT), Discrete Wavelet Transform (DWT) and Singular Value Decomposition (SVD), in terms of their robustness to alteration, imperceptibility and impact on file size. Our results show that the DWT method applied to the LL sub-band offers a good compromise between visual quality and robustness, with almost total imperceptibility and a low impact on image size. This work provides an integrated methodology to strengthen the protection of medical data and support the development of high-performance watermarking detection algorithms in digital medical environments.

Keywords: Digital Watermarking · Steganography · Image traceability · Medical data security · Neural networks

1 Introduction

The digitisation of medical images has revolutionised the field of healthcare, facilitating diagnosis and clinical research. However, this progress comes with major challenges in terms of data security and traceability. Medical images contain sensitive and confidential information, making them vulnerable to unauthorised modification, illicit access and fraud. These concerns raise important issues relating to patient confidentiality and data integrity.

To meet these challenges, this study proposes a hybrid approach combining digital watermarking [17] and steganography [16,20]. Digital watermarking involves inserting information into an image in such a way that it is invisible to a human observer, while still being recoverable by specific algorithms. Steganography, on the other hand, aims to conceal a message in a medium, ensuring that

A. Sere et al. (Eds.): AFRI2 2025, CCIS 2536, pp. 50–64, 2026.
https://doi.org/10.1007/978-3-031-98327-6_4

the original medium and the steganographic medium remain indistinguishable. By merging these two techniques, we aim to insert an invisible watermark into medical images, guaranteeing their security and traceability while minimising the impact on their visual quality and size.

As well as improving the security and traceability of medical images, our approach has significant potential to facilitate the secure sharing of medical data between different healthcare professionals. By enabling the insertion of invisible digital watermarks that do not degrade image quality, our method ensures that images can be shared without compromising their integrity. This is particularly crucial in contexts where frequent exchanges of images are necessary, for example between different hospitals or during international collaboration for clinical research.

What's more, our solution could help improve medical diagnosis. The neural networks we propose to train on watermarked images could not only automatically detect inserted watermarks, but also verify the integrity of the images over time. This would prevent any unauthorized alteration or corruption of medical data, ensuring that healthcare professionals always have access to reliable information for their diagnoses. In the long term, this approach could be integrated into clinical imaging systems to provide automated tracking of data throughout the patient's care pathway.

The contributions of this article include the development of a new digital watermarking method incorporating steganography, as well as the evaluation of several watermarking techniques in terms of robustness, imperceptibility and impact on file size. The ultimate goal of this work is to provide a robust methodology to strengthen the protection of medical data and support the development of high-performance watermarking detection algorithms in digital medical environments.

2 Image Steganography and Watermarking

2.1 Image Steganography

Steganography is a form of secret communication [16,20] that seeks to conceal a secret message in an (unimportant) medium in such a way that the original medium and the steganographic medium are indistinguishable. It should be noted that the hidden message has no connection with the medium.

For a medicum digital image, this involves inserting information into the image while minimizing distortion. Plusieurs techniques de steganographie ont été proposé. Ces techniques sont basées sur les méthodes traditionnelles [16] et les plus récents sont les reseaux de neurone [20]. Despite their robustness, these techniques are not suitable for medical images where the hidden information is linked to the image.

2.2 Digital Image Watermarking

Digital watermarking is a technique for concealing information (called a mark, watermark, etc.) in a document (text, image, sound, video, etc.). Unlike steganography, in digital watermarking the message is linked to the document. It is generally used to protect intellectual property and copyright, trace content and check data integrity.

2.3 General Scheme of Watermarking

Typically, a watermarking scheme consists of a watermark generation phase, watermark insertion and watermark detection and/or extraction.

Watermark Generation. The watermark is generated according to the objectives of the watermarking application. This process can be modeled by the following function:

$$G(DO) = W \tag{1}$$

where G: watermark generation function; DO: Original data and W: watermark.

A watermark can be a text or an image. Watermark generators are generally based on cryptographic keys, chaotic functions or neural networks [6,22] [19].

Watermark Insertion. In general the watermark insertion function must define where and how to insert the watermark. This insertion function is based on a secret key and can be defined by:

$$Ins(IO, W, K) = IW \tag{2}$$

where In : insert function; IO: original image; W: watermark; K: secret key and IW: watermarked image

The different insertion techniques are presented in Sect. 3.

Watermark Detection or Extraction. The detection or extraction of the watermark is the opposite process of the insertion. The extraction function Ext takes as input the watermarked image IW and the secret keys K, and returns as output an extracted watermark WE:

$$Ext(IW, K) = WE \tag{3}$$

2.4 Evaluation Metrics

The Peak Signal to Noise Ratio(PSNR). The PSNR indicates a similarity between the original image and the watermarked image by measuring imperceptibility. In general, the visual quality is considered acceptable for PSNR values above 30 (dB). Let's consider an original image I of dimension N*M and Iw the watermarked image

$$PSNR(I, Iw) = 10\log(\frac{3 \times N \times M \times 255^2}{\sum_{i=1}^{3}\sum_{x=1}^{N}\sum_{y=1}^{M}[I_i(x,y) - Iw_i(x,y)]^2}) \tag{4}$$

The SSIM (Structural SIMilarity). It is a measure of similarity between two images, the value 1 indicates the total similarity of the two images.

$$SSIM(I, Iw) = \frac{(2\mu_I \times \mu_{Iw} + c_1) \times (2 \times cov_{Iw} + c_2)}{(2{\mu_I}^2 \times \mu_{Iw}^2 + c_1) \times (\sigma_I^2 \times \sigma_{Iw}^2 + c_2)} \tag{5}$$

μ_I and μ_{Iw} are the means of I and Iw, respectively; σ_I^2 and σ_{Iw}^2 are the variances of I and Iw, respectively; cov_{Iw} is the covariance of Iw

Normalized Correlation. Robustness can be measured by a metric called Normalized Correlation (NC). It measures the similarity between the original watermark and the extracted watermark. The NC is between 0 and 1, if the value of NC is closer to 1, it means that the two images are more similar.

$$NC(I, Iw) = \frac{\sum_{i=1}^{3}\sum_{x=1}^{N}\sum_{y=1}^{M}[I_i(x,y) - Iw_i(x,y)]}{\sqrt{\sum_{i=1}^{3}\sum_{x=1}^{N}\sum_{y=1}^{M}[I_i(x,y)]^2} \times \sqrt{\sum_{i=1}^{3}\sum_{x=1}^{N}\sum_{y=1}^{M}[Iw_i(x,y)]^2}} \tag{6}$$

3 Image Representation and Watermarking

3.1 Matrix Representation

A digital image is defined on a two-dimensional grid. The elements of this grid are called pixels. If we consider the fact that it is imperceptible to the human eye a change a variation of one unit of gray, then we can consider the last bit (LBS: Least Significant Bit) that is not important and change it as we wish. This is the technique used to hide a binary image in a grayscale image.

The LBS technique is in [13,18] to insert the watermark. It produces good quality watermarked images. In most works using this technique, there is confusion between watermarking and steganography.

3.2 Discrete Cosine Decomposition

The discrete cosine transform (DCT) is a technique for representing signals or images in cosine components of different frequencies. DCT is particularly useful for representing data with a high concentration of energy in the low coefficients. For an image (Fig. 1), DCT of the image produces a frequency spectrum that contains information about the frequency distribution in the image.

- The low frequencies (upper left corner of the matrix) correspond to the uniform parts of the image.
- The high frequencies (upper left corner of the matrix) correspond to the fine details and edges of the image.
- The high frequencies (in the bottom corner of the matrix) represent the fine details and noise in the image.

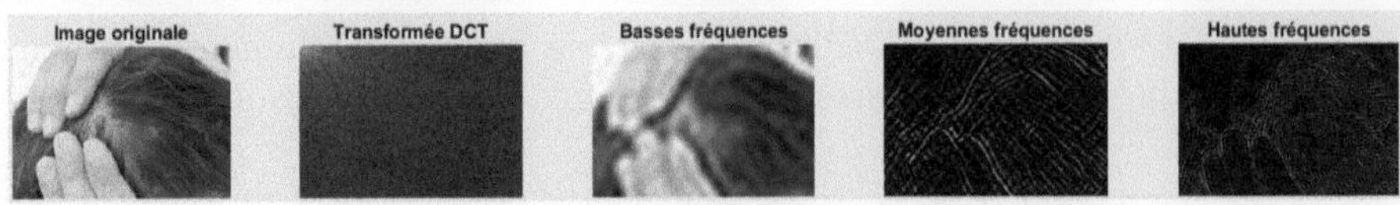

Fig. 1. The different zones of the DCT spectrum

Several DCT-based watermarking solutions have been proposed. In [3] the authors have proposed a new approach which modifies the DCT coefficients of the image according to the watermark. With this new approach, the watermarked images are of very good quality. However, it does not allow traceability because the mark incorporates information about its owner. On the other hand, in [1] the authors have proposed an approach which generates a watermark according to the selected coefficient. The watermark is also based on a pseudo-random sequence. The approach proposed in [11] is resistant to JPEG compression.

3.3 Discrete Fourier Decomposition

The Discrete Fourier Transform (DFT) is a mathematical method for breaking down an image into its frequency components. Unlike DCT, which uses only cosines, DFT uses complex exponential functions. For an image (Fig. 2) the DFT produces a frequency spectrum that contains information about the frequency distribution in the image.

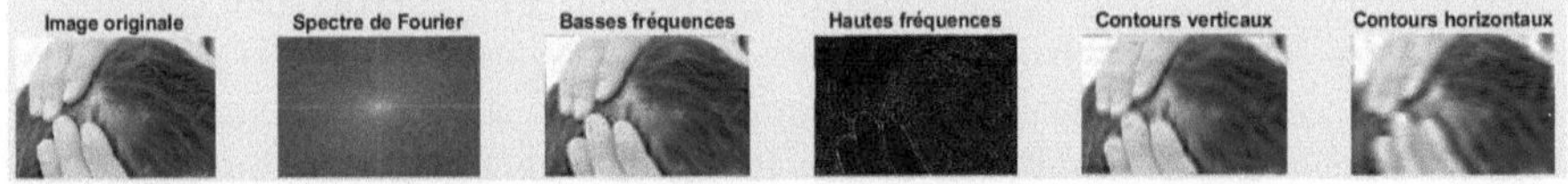

Fig. 2. The different zones of the DFT spectrum

1. The low frequencies (near the origin of the spectrum) correspond to unified, degraded zones;
2. The high frequencies (at the edge of the spectrum) correspond to contours and details;
3. The coefficients on the horizontal axis correspond to the vertical contours;
4. The coefficients on the vertical axis correspond to the horizontal contours.

In [4] the authors inserted a watermark formed from a random sequence in the high frequencies of the image. In [8], it was shown that inserting the watermark in the high frequencies makes it possible to resist geometry attacks (rotation, translation and scaling).

3.4 Discrete Wavelet Decomposition

Discrete Wavelet Decomposition (DWT) uses functions called wavelets to represent signals more locally. For an image (Fig. 3), DWT decomposes the image into four sub-bands as follows:

1. **LL**: low-low frequency band (Approximation)
2. **LH**: low-high frequency band (Horizontal details)
3. **HL**: high-low frequency band (Vertical details)
4. **HH**: high-high frequency band (Diagonal details)

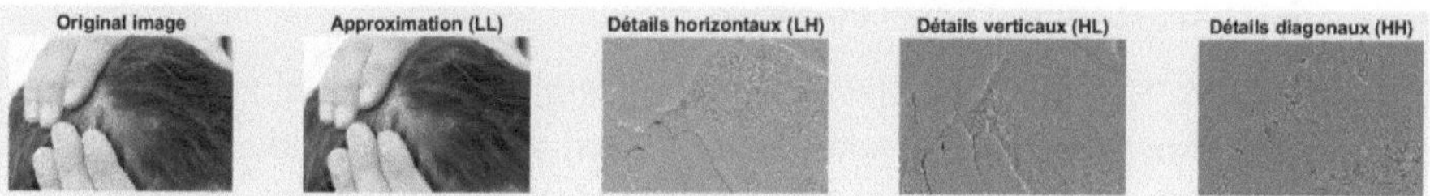

Fig. 3. The four sub-bands of an image

In [10] the authors used the LL level 3 coefficient to sum the watermarks. This technique is compared to the one using level 2 and 1. This study reveals that the higher the level of decomposition, the better the visual quality of the watermarked image. Other authors [7] have proposed a hybrid solution using DWT and DCT. They applied the DCT transformation to the LL sub-band before adding an encrypted watermark.

3.5 Singular Value Decomposition

Singular Value Decomposition (SVD) decomposes a matrix (such as an image) into three distinct matrices. For a matrix A or image (Fig. 4) of dimensions M×N, the SVD decomposition is defined by the following equation:

$$A = U.S.V^T \tag{7}$$

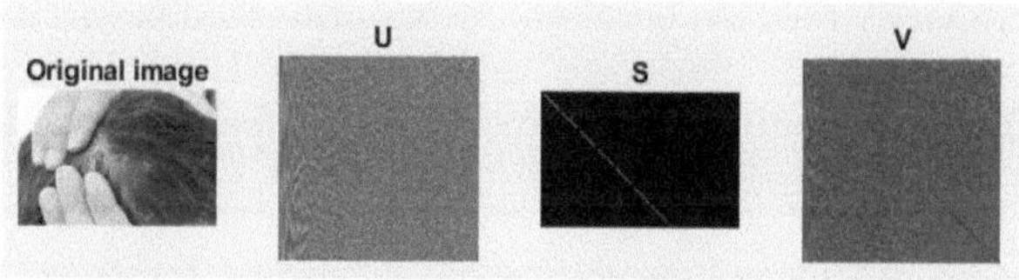

Fig. 4. Image singular value decomposition

- U represents the orthogonal matrix (containing the eigenvectors of $A.A^T$) capturing the vertical patterns in the image.
- S represents the diagonal matrix containing the singular values. These values represent the importance or energy of the different components in the image.
- V^T represents the transpose of an orthogonal matrix and contains the eigenvectors of $A^T.A$. It captures the horizontal patterns in the image.

Watermarking schemes using SVD are presented in [21]. In [15] the authors propose a scheme based on DWT and SVD that offers a good compromise between robustness and invisibility.

3.6 Medical Image Watermarking

William PUECH and al [17] proposed a combination of digital watermarking and cryptography techniques to secure medical images. The images used were in DICOM format. The authors first generated a key to encrypt the image and then inserted the key and the patient's data (name, first name, age and place of acquisition of the image) in the encrypted image. Regarding the watermarking technique, they considered the Least Significant Bit (LSB) technique.

Chokri CHEMAK and al [5] applied a digital watermarking during medical image transfers. They inserted the medical information of the patient in the medical image and tried to find this information as accurately as possible. This information included the identity of the patient, the different examinations, the diseases, and the different treatments. This information was coded with the algorithm of tubo code and the decoding was done with the alorithm of viterbi with flexible output. As for the digital watermarking technique, the authors used a multi-resolution approach based on the decomposition of the image into multi-level discrete odelettes before inserting the coded information. The use of discrete odelettes makes the watermarking solution robust to image compression.

In [12], the authors implemented four watermarking techniques which are DWT, DCT, DFT and LSB. They used a medical image as the host image and a logo as the watermark. The DFT technique had the best PSNR value and the others had PSNR values that were about the same. On the other hand, DFT has the lowest SR value. This study was done without considering ROI and RONI.

In [2] the authors propose a new approach of watermarking which uses a reference watermark contained in the image. Indeed the signature of the image is based on a similarity relation between the watermarked blocks and the selected blocks. The selection of the blocks was done with the Harris detector in order to make the method robust to geometrical features. The watermarking technique used is the spread spectrum.

4 Stegano-Watermarking Sheme Description

Our proposed scheme is described in figure (Fig. 5). In our approach, we will generate an identifier through patient information. Based on this identifier, we will generate a mark. The mark is then inserted into the contours of a host image. The host image has no connection with the mark, which is referred to as steganography. The marked host image must be of good quality. Finally, the marked host image is regarded as the new watermark, which must be inserted in a frequency domain of the medical image. These three phases are described in the following sub-sections.

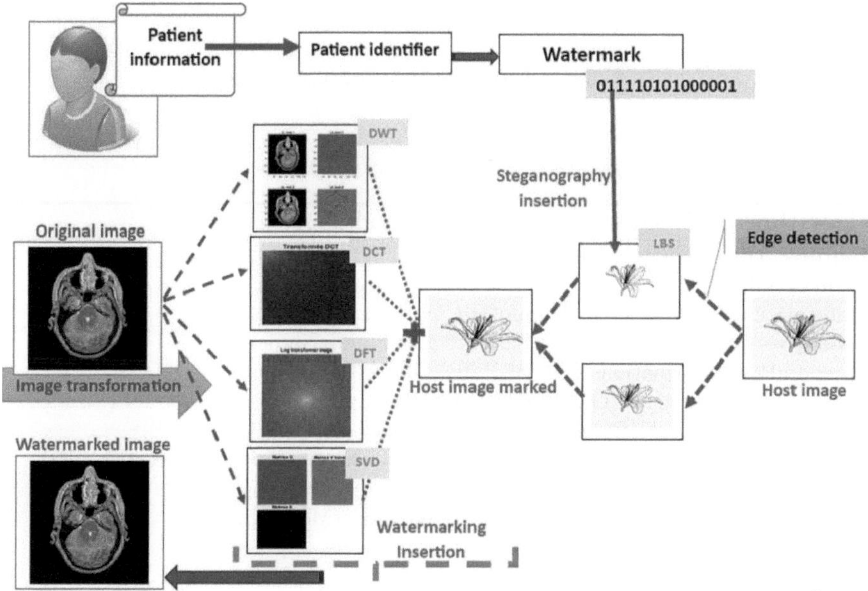

Fig. 5. Watermarking scheme

4.1 Generate Patient Identifier and Mark

Before watermarking an image, it is crucial to anonymize the metadata to guarantee the confidentiality of patient information. Our proposed Algorithm 1 generates a DICOM image identifier and mark, but could be adapted to other formats.

- Step 1: This step is not necessary for those who already have a identifier. Generate a unique identifier from the patient's details (surname, first name, registration number, birth and city of birth).

$$IDp = fonctionIDp(Lname, Fname, NumR, dateB, cityB) \tag{8}$$

  Our $functionIDp$ is described by the following steps
  - Sub-step 1.1: Data normalisation (minuscule without accent and without space), concatenation of first and last name and concatenation of different dates

- Sub-step 1.2: Hashage of name and surname
- Sub-step 1.3: For the city of birth, give the country code before the name of the city.
- Sub-step 1.4: Link data with an underscore. Example: fonctionIDp (BARA, Dimi, 0343, 02/03/1980, Bouakéé) = 48143511f896cd7a07b588369424a338_0343_02031980_225bouake

– Step 2: Generate a mark

$$Mark = fonctionMerk(IdP, dateA, materialA) \tag{9}$$

- Link IdP, $dateA$ and $materialA$ with an underscore
- Hashing data

Algorithm 1. Generate patient identifier and mark

Require: DICOMimage, NumR, i0, longueurID
Ensure: IdP, Mark

```
informationsDICOM ← dicominfo(DICOMimage);
nomP ← informationsDICOM.PatientName.FamilyName;
prenomP ← informationsDICOM.PatientName.GivenName;
bD ← informationsDICOM.PatientBirthDate;
bP ← informationsDICOM.PatientBirthPlace;
IdP ← strcat(normalization((Hash(nomP), Hash(prenomP), NumR, bD, bP));
dateAcq ← informationsDICOM.StudyDate;
materielUti ← informationsDICOM.ManufacturerModelName;
Mark0 ← strcat(IdP, dateAcq, materielUti);
Mark0 ← DataHash(Mark0);
Mark ← Mark0(i0:i0+longueurID);
```

4.2 Edge Detection and Mark Insertion

The host image should be chosen according to its contours. Images with more contours are preferred. This phase is described by the Algorithm 2 and the following steps

– Detection and selection of image edges (high-frequency zone): this can be done using one of the following filters [14] [9] (Canny, Sobel, Prewitt, Roberts)
– Watermark binarization,
– Insert binary watermark in least significant bit

The marked host image will be used as a watermark in the next phase.

Algorithm 2. Mark insertion

```
Require: hote, mark
Ensure: hoteMarked
  hoteMarked ← hote;
  edgeDetection ← edge(hote);
  edgePixel ← find(edgeDetection);
  binaryMark ← binary(mark, 8)
  markLength ← length(binaryMark);
  edgeLength ← length(edgePixel);
  if edgeLength < markLength then
    binaryMark ← imresize(binaryMark, edgeLength)
  end if
  for i : 1, edgeLength do
    pixelvalue = hoteMarked(edgePixel(i));
    hoteMarked(edgePixel(i)) = bitset(pixelvalue, 1, binaryMark(i));
  end for
```

4.3 Frequency-Domain Watermarking Insertion

The watermarking phase is described by the Algorithm 3 and the following steps.

- Image decomposition in the frequency domain (DCT or DFT or DWT or SVD). The choice of domain depends on the quality of the watermarked image, but also on the impact of the mark insertion on the size of the watermarked image.
- Select the sub-band that will carry the watermak. Choose the sub-band that offers a watermarked image with the least distortion.
- Multiply the watermark by a factor of α: the choice of α is very decisive for the quality of the watermarked image and the detection of the watermark by neural networks.
- Add the multiplied watermark and the selected sub-band.

Algorithm 3. Watermark insertion

```
Require: image, watermark
Ensure: imageWatermarked
  imageFrequentiel ← tranformation(image);
  WatermarkFrequentiel ← tranformation(Watermark);
  bandSelection ← selection(imageFrequentiel);
  bandWatermarked ← bandSelection + α × WatermarkFrequentiel;
  imageWatermarked ← remplace(imageFrequentiel, bandWatermarked)
  imageWatermarked ← transformeInverse( imageWatermarked)
```

The aim of such an approach is to have images watermarked with the same watermark. Such images can be used to test future detection algorithms based on neural networks.

4.4 Neural Networks and Watermark Detection

Our approach favours the use of modern neural networks to detect the watermark. To our knowledge, there are no watermark detectors based on neural networks [6] [19,22]. Indeed, modern neural networks can play a crucial role in improving the robustness and detection capabilities of digital watermarks in medical imaging. Thanks to their ability to analyse large amounts of data and identify complex patterns, these models can be trained to recognise and extract digital watermarks even after potential image modifications, such as compression or geometric transformations. By integrating deep neural network architectures, it is possible to increase the accuracy of watermarking detection while preserving the visual quality of images. This guarantees not only the security and traceability of medical data, but also the integrity of information throughout its lifecycle in clinical systems.

5 Simulations

5.1 Steganography: Mark Insertion

For this section, we have selected image types (Table 1) that can be used as host images. For each host image we have the Canny, Sobel, De Prewits and

Table 1. Steganography: edge detection and mark insertion

Hotes	Canny	Sobel	Prewitt	Roberts	Evaluation metrics
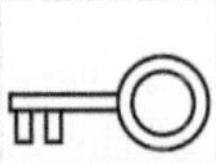	1778	1539	1542	1822	PNSR = 69.846739 SSIM = 0.999999 NC = 1.000000
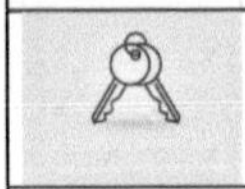	3358	1193	1193	1703	PNSR = 71.482295 SSIM = 0.999935 NC = 1.000000
	8370	5118	4438	1988	PNSR = 70.936743 SSIM = 0.999996 NC = 1.000000
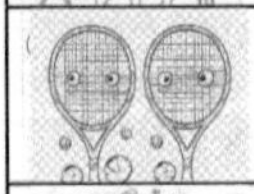	122623	51674	51989	43579	PNSR = 82.333709 SSIM = 0.999998 NC = 1.000000
	6668	4256	4065	1845	PNSR = 71.001755 SSIM = 0.999997 NC = 1.000000
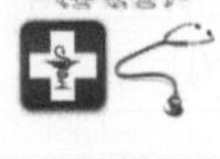	5165	3989	3975	4279	PNSR = 76.087527 SSIM = 0.999994 NC = 1.000000
	5165	3989	3975	4279	PNSR = 89.697497 SSIM = 1.000000 NC = 1.000000

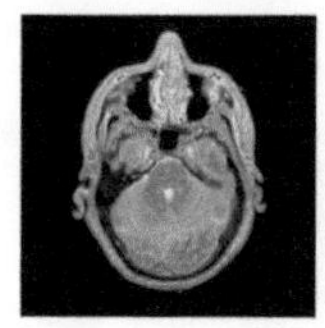 

Fig. 6. Image and watermark

Roberts filters [9,14] for edge detection. We then determined the number of edge pixels for each filter (columns 2, 3, 4 and 5 of Table 1). With the Canny filter, we have more pixels detected for most of the host images considered. After selecting the pixels we inserted a watermark. The values of the various metries are very satisfactory, demonstrating the good quality of the watermarked host images.

5.2 Watermarking: Watermark Insertion

Table 2 shows the impact of the α insertion factor on the quality of watermarked images and the robustness of digital watermarks in medical images (Fig. 6).

Table 2. α variation and watermark insertion

α	Metrics	DCT	DFT	DWT-LL	DWT-LH	DWT-HL	DWT-HH	SVD-S	SVD-U	SVD-V
1	PNSR	–47.54	–47.54	-41.51	–41.51	–41.51	–41.51	–39.82	–37.11	–37.87
	SSIM	0.19	0.19	0.28	0.06	0.06	0.06	0.24	0.33	-0.23
	NC	0.74	0.74	0.84	0.60	0.60	0.59	0.88	0.90	0.87
	Size(bytes)	21823	21823	584	2634	3225	3592	21947	38682	41972
0.1	PNSR	–27.54	–27.54	–21.51	–21.51	–21.51	–21.51	–27.35	–18.85	-18.86
	SSIM	0.44	0.44	0.52	0.36	0.36	0.36	0.83	0.79	0.63
	NC	0.98	0.98	0.99	0.99	0.99	0.99	1	1	1
	Size(bytes)	36296	36293	584	1826	2113	2247	36714	37084	37154
0.01	PNSR	–7.54	–7.54	1.51	–1.51	–1.51	–1.51	–7.56	1.05	0.62
	SSIM	0.77	0.77	0.88	0.73	0.73	0.73	0.98	0.96	0.94
	NC	1	1	1	1	1	1	1	1	1
	Size(bytes)	36101	36101	806	7118	8721	8090	36131	36140	36153
0.001	PNSR	12.46	12.46	18.49	18.49	18.49	18.49	15.68	Inf	Inf
	SSIM	0.98	0.98	0.99	0.99	0.99	0.99	1	1	1
	NC	1	1	1	1	1	1	1	1	1
	Size(bytes)	36085	36085	8029	10970	11584	10185	36091	36085	36085
0.0001	PNSR	32.46	32.46	38.49	38.49	38.49	38.49	Inf	Inf	Inf
	SSIM	1	1	1	1	1	1	1	1	1
	NC	1	1	1	1	1	1	1	1	1
	Size(bytes)	36085	36085	8743	10751	13704	12306	36085	36085	36085

Table 3. Insertion du watermark dans des images avec α=0.0001

Technics	Metrics						
	Size	38634	30881	35309	27323	25845	22666
DCT	PNSR	32.46	32.46	32.46	32.46	32.46	32.46
	SSIM	1.00	1.00	1.00	1.00	1.00	1.00
	NC	1.00	1.00	1.00	1.00	1.00	1.00
	SIZE	38634	30881	35309	27323	25845	22666
DFT	PNSR	32.46	32.46	32.46	32.46	32.46	32.46
	SSIM	1.00	1.00	1.00	1.00	1.00	1.00
	NC	1.00	1.00	1.00	1.00	1.00	1.00
	SIZE	38634	30881	35309	27323	25845	22666
DWT-LL1	PNSR	38.49	38.49	38.49	38.49	38.49	38.49
	SSIM	1.00	1.00	1.00	1.00	1.00	1.00
	NC	1.00	1.00	1.00	1.00	1.00	1.00
	SIZE	610	662	1181	2114	632	584
DWT-LH1	PNSR	38.49	38.49	38.49	38.49	38.49	38.49
	SSIM	1.00	1.00	1.00	0.99	1.00	0.98
	NC	1.00	1.00	1.00	1.00	1.00	1.00
	SIZE	627	681	1776	3078	634	584
DWT-HL1	PNSR	38.49	38.49	38.49	38.49	38.49	38.49
	SSIM	1.00	1.00	1.00	0.99	1.00	0.98
	NC	1.00	1.00	1.00	1.00	1.00	1.00
	SIZE	620	692	1542	3155	634	584
DWT-HH1	PNSR	38.49	38.49	38.49	38.49	38.49	38.49
	SSIM	1.00	1.00	1.00	0.99	1.00	0.98
	NC	1.00	1.00	1.00	1.00	1.00	1.00
	SIZE	617	688	1947	3448	635	584
SVD-S	PNSR	Inf	Inf	Inf	Inf	Inf	Inf
	SSIM	1.00	1.00	1.00	1.00	1.00	1.00
	NC	1.00	1.00	1.00	1.00	1.00	1.00
	SIZE	38634	30881	35309	27323	25845	22666
SVD-U	PNSR	Inf	Inf	Inf	Inf	Inf	Inf
	SSIM	1.00	1.00	1.00	1.00	1.00	1.00
	NC	1.00	1.00	1.00	1.00	1.00	1.00
	SIZE	38634	30881	35309	27323	25845	22666
SVD-U	PNSR	Inf	Inf	Inf	Inf	Inf	Inf
	SSIM	1.00	1.00	1.00	1.00	1.00	1.00
	NC	1.00	1.00	1.00	1.00	1.00	1.00
	SIZE	38634	30881	35309	27323	25845	22666

When $\alpha = 1$, the results reveal a sharp degradation in image quality, with very low PSNRs (down to –47.54 dB) and low SSIMs, watermaking the images unusable for clinical use. In contrast, for $\alpha = 0.001$, PSNRs increase considerably, reaching up to 38.49 dB, with SSIMs close to 1.0, ensuring excellent preservation of visual quality while maintaining optimum watermark robustness (NC =

1.0). This shows that this α value offers an ideal compromise between image quality and watermarking robustness. Other α values, such as 0.01, offer acceptable results, but $\alpha = 0.001$ is clearly the best performer for clinical applications, where image quality and reliable watermark detection are crucial.

We set α to 0.0001 and inserted the watermark with various techniques (DCT, DFT, DWT, SVD) in several images. Table 3 compares the performance of these techniques as a function of file size, PSNR, SSIM and NC. The results show that DWT techniques, particularly with the LL and HH sub-bands, offer an excellent compromise between visual quality (PSNR of 38.49 dB and SSIM of 1.0) and reduced file size, making them particularly suitable for clinical environments where storage is a constraint. In addition, these methods maintain high robustness (NC close to 1.0), ensuring that the watermark can be detected even after image alterations. SVD methods are distinguished by infinite PSNR and perfect quality (SSIM of 1.0), but they have a greater impact on file size, which can be a limitation in terms of storage. DCT and DFT, on the other hand, deliver balanced performance with slightly larger file sizes and PSNRs around 32.46 dB, while maintaining very good visual quality. In short, each technique has its advantages: DWT for a good compromise between compression and quality, and SVD for optimum quality, but with higher storage requirements. The choice of method will depend on specific priorities, whether quality, robustness or resource management.

6 Conclusion

This paper proposes a new hybrid approach combining digital watermarking and steganography to meet the challenges of security and traceability of medical images. By creating a dataset of watermarked images, we lay the foundations for training neural networks capable of efficiently detecting watermarks while taking into account the constraints of visual quality and image size. The evaluation of different watermarking techniques shows that certain approaches offer a good compromise between robustness, imperceptibility and impact on file size. In the future, this work could be extended by exploring other watermarking techniques and integrating advances in artificial intelligence to further enhance the security of medical images in a constantly evolving digital environment.

References

1. Barni, M., Bartolini, F., Cappellini, V., Piva, A.: A dct-domain system for robust image watermarking. Signal Process. **66**(3), 357–372 (1998)
2. Bas, J.M.C.P., Chassery, J.M.: Tatouage d'images résistant aux transformations géométriques. In: Dix-septième colloque GRETSI, vol. 99, pp. 271–274 (1999)
3. Byun, S.W., Son, H.S., Lee, S.P.: Fast and robust watermarking method based on dct specific location. IEEE Access **7**, 100706–100718 (2019)
4. Cedillo-Hernandez, M., Cedillo-Hernandez, A., Garcia-Ugalde, F.J.: Improving dft-based image watermarking using particle swarm optimization algorithm. Mathematics **9**(15), 1795 (2021)

5. Chemak, C., Bouhlel, M.S., Lapayre, J.C., Kammoun, F.: Un tatouage robuste et aveugle des images pour le transfert des informations médicales. In: Proceeding of the Maghrebian Conference on Software Engineering and Artificial Intelligence (MCSEAI'06) (2006)
6. Deeba, F., Kun, S., Dharejo, F.A., Langah, H., Memon, H.: Digital watermarking using deep neural network. Int. J. Mach. Learn. Comput. **10**(2), 277–282 (2020)
7. Ernawan, F., Ariatmanto, D., Firdaus, A.: An improved image watermarking by modifying selected dwt-dct coefficients. IEEE Access **9**, 45474–45485 (2021)
8. Ganic, E., Dexter, S.D., Eskicioglu, A.M.: Embedding multiple watermarks in the dft domain using low-and high-frequency bands. In: Security, Steganography, and Watermarking of Multimedia Contents VII, vol. 5681, pp. 175–184. SPIE (2005)
9. Hoang, N.D., Nguyen, Q.L.: Metaheuristic optimized edge detection for recognition of concrete wall cracks: a comparative study on the performances of roberts, prewitt, canny, and sobel algorithms. Adv. Civil Eng. **2018**(1), 7163580 (2018)
10. Kashyap, N., Sinha, G.: Image watermarking using 3-level discrete wavelet transform (dwt). Int. J. Mod. Educ. Comput. Sci. **4**(3), 50 (2012)
11. Kaur, B., Kaur, A., Singh, J.: Steganographic approach for hiding image in dct domain. Int. J. Adv. Eng. Technol. **1**(3), 72 (2011)
12. Kaya, V.: Robust medical image watermarking using frequency domain and least significant bits algorithms. Space **9**, 12 (2018)
13. Kumar, M., Kumar, R., Yadav, J.: A robust digital speech watermarking based on least significant bit. Int. J. Innov. Technol. Explor. Eng. (IJITEE) **9**(6), 126–131 (2020)
14. Ladányi, L., Králik, M.: Automatic buildings detection using sobel, roberts, canny and prewwitt detector. J. Electr. Eng. **72**(4), 278–282 (2021)
15. Liu, J., et al.: An optimized image watermarking method based on hd and svd in dwt domain. IEEE Access **7**, 80849–80860 (2019)
16. Morkel, T., Eloff, J.H., Olivier, M.S.: An overview of image steganography. In: ISSA, vol. 1, pp. 1–11 (2005)
17. Puech, W., Dumas, M., Borie, J.C., Puech, M.: Tatouage d'images cryptées pour l'aide au télédiagnostic. In: Proceedings of 18th Colloque Traitement du Signal et des Images, GRETSI'01 (2001)
18. Setiawati, I., Hermanto, M.T., Ujianto, E.: Digital watermarking implementation of digital watermarking on images using the least significant bit method. Int. J. Eng. Technol. Nat. Sci. **5**(1), 10–18 (2023)
19. Singh, H.K., Singh, A.K.: Comprehensive review of watermarking techniques in deep-learning environments. J. Electron. Imaging **32**(3), 031804–031804 (2023)
20. Subramanian, N., Elharrouss, O., Al-Maadeed, S., Bouridane, A.: Image steganography: a review of the recent advances. IEEE Access **9**, 23409–23423 (2021)
21. Zainol, Z., Teh, J.S., Alawida, M., Alabdulatif, A., et al.: Hybrid svd-based image watermarking schemes: a review. IEEE Access **9**, 32931–32968 (2021)
22. Zhong, X., Huang, P.C., Mastorakis, S., Shih, F.Y.: An automated and robust image watermarking scheme based on deep neural networks. IEEE Trans. Multimedia **23**, 1951–1961 (2020)

Analysis of Routing Load Balancing Approaches to Optimize WSN Lifetime

Doda Afoussatou Rollande Sanou[1], Tiguiane Yélémou[2(✉)], and Hamadoun Tall[2(✉)]

[1] Université virtuelle du burkina, science du numerique, Ouagadougou, Burkina Faso
[2] Université Nazi BONI, Ecole superieure d'Informatique, Bobo-Dioulasso, Burkina Faso
tyelemou@gmail.com,tallhamadoun@gmail.com

Abstract. Wireless sensor networks (WSNs) are solicited for many communication needs. Sensor nodes are predominantly battery powered devices. For applications like environment monitoring and defense reconnaissance, they are envisaged to be deployed unfriendly environment where it is diffcult to replace them after their deployment. This constitutes an obstacle for the use of these networks in low income countries. The effcient management of the energy of these nodes becomes a real challenge for the vulgarization of these solutions for these countries. Energy consumption of the nodes must be properly managed in order to prolong the network lifetime. Different energy-effcient have been proposed in literature over the years. Many of these solutions seek to optimize the overall energy consumption in the network. Depleting the energy of a single node may render the system ineffcient. We investigate energy-balanced routing approaches. We implement an approach based on taking into account number of foreign data flows to be supported by intermediate nodes in order to minimize their energy consumption and then extend network lifetime. This approach is compared to those taking into account intermediate nodes residual energy in the choice of the next hop to the sink.

Keywords: WSN · routing protocol · energy-efficient · load-balanced

1 Introduction

One of the issues for the WSN remains energy management. Several approaches have been proposed. In most cases, link quality or intermediate nodes residual energy are taken into account in the route establishing to the sink. This approach improves the overall energy consumption but the balance in this residual energy is not always guaranteed. In some situations like intelligent surveillance, the death of a node can render the system inefficient. In this paper, we are interested in approaches based on a better distribution of overall energy consumption between the nodes. It is obvious that the energy consumption of a

A. Sere et al. (Eds.): AFRI2 2025, CCIS 2536, pp. 65–73, 2026.
https://doi.org/10.1007/978-3-031-98327-6_5

node is directly proportional to the number of messages processed or sent by this node. Thus, among solutions to optimize the energy consumption of these nodes, a fair distribution of the total energy consumption load in the network is actively investigated. Based on the RPL protocol, we propose an approach based on the choice of the node with the fewest children as the parent (intermediate neighbor node). This approach is compared to one based on better residual energy.

The rest of the document is organized as follows. In Sect. 2; we present related work. In Sect. 3, we present our approach and we compare it to that taking into account the residual energy of the potential parents. Finally, in Sect. 4, we conclude.

2 Related Work

The Limited resource nature of sensor nodes raises the problem of energy, which always requires efficient and scalable solutions. This problem is further complicated by the continuous reduction in the size of sensor nodes in order to optimize the use of electronic components and then the price of sensor nodes and users miniaturization demand. Very often, each sensor node is powered by a battery (a limited-capacity on-board power source), and because nodes are often deployed in hostile areas or in environments where human intervention is difficult or virtually impossible, any attempt to replace or recharge the battery is difficult. Thus, when a node's battery is exhausted, the node dies. When a large number of nodes die, the network becomes inefficient and may no longer be able to perform the task assigned to it. The implementation of WSNs in real-time application monitoring imposes a number of constraints in terms of transmission delay and throughput. Thus, in order to ensure an efficient use of network resources, the protocols must face energy constraints, while guaranteeing a certain quality of service. J. Ben-Othman et al. [4] have proposed a multi-channel, low-power quality-of-service routing protocol for WSNs that will balance the routing load and provide a reliable network using XOR-based Forward Error Correction (FEC) technology to ensure data redundancy and fault tolerance, with highly aggregated bandwidth, providing end-to-end delay, in order to effectively balance power consumption across multiple sensor nodes. To rebuild the path, when predicting the next jump in the route construction phase, the authors introduced two new parameters in their proposals, residual energy, available node buffer size and signal-to-noise ratio (SNR). Their proposal allows a low energy consumption network based on the quality of service.

Juuso Nurmio et al. [11] developed two objective functions based on the ETX and remaining energy metrics of parent nodes. Node'parent choice takes into account both the expected transmission count (ETX) and the remaining energy of parent nodes. A potential parent with the lowest ETX is preferred. If the ETX values of two parents are almost similar, the one with greater remaining energy is preferred. Is note as greater than a defined threshold, Their enhanced protocols obtained with these two metrics extended the lifetime of the first node to die compared to traditional rang-based protocols [7] in both dense symmetric and sparse asymmetric networks.

To provide a way to balance traffic flow, Bagula et al. [3,10] propose the Least Interference Beaconing Model (LIBP). In their approach, a node selects as a parent toward the sink, a potential one with the least traffic flow interference. LIBP extends the beaconing process with load balancing to improve the network energy efficiency.

Authors in [18] proposed a blacklisting approach to avoid a node with a low energy level being an intermediate node for source-destination transmission. For that, this node doesn't participate in to route discovery process when its remaining energy is under a certain threshold. Its low residual energy will be only used to transmit its own data. Then, it will increase its lifetime.

S. Taghizadeh et al. [14] proposed a context-aware and load balancing protocol in heavy and dynamic loads network context. In their parent selection mechanism, they take into account respectively rang, ETX, remaining energy, and number of children. We think that taking into account the number of children metric comes too late and its impact will be very limited.

N. Quang Hieu et al. [6] propose to integrate trickle timing in the routing process for energy efficiency. In their approach, when the network is stable or consistent, Trickle causes nodes to transmit very few packets and then reduce network overload. When an inconsistency is detected, the node resolves it quickly by increasing the rate of packet exchange. Their simulation results show that their enhanced protocol consumes very low energy, compared to the standard protocols.

In [12], the authors proposed a stochastic cluster head selection model aimed at improving energy balance in heterogeneous wireless sensor networks (WSNs) with multiple mobile sinks. The model uses several selection criteria, such as node density, distance, residual energy, and node capacity. Evaluation of the proposed algorithm shows better performance in terms of energy efficiency, packet delivery rate, cluster lifetime, and transmission delay, compared with the classical I_SEP, and OptGACHE algorithms. However, the paper lacks technical details on the exact implementation of these algorithms.

SEHAR et al. [15] have implemented a new cluster head selection algorithm based on the mobility level of the nodes, taking into account other criteria such as the residual energy of the nodes, the distance of the nodes from the sink, and the neighborhood density. Evaluation of their solution in terms of network stability, energy consumption, and throughput shows that their algorithm balances energy consumption and increases network lifetime compared with other algorithms such as CRPD [16], LEACH [5], and MODLEACH [8]. However, to strengthen the credibility of the proposed solution, it seems necessary to evaluate the packet delivery rate, and network latency.

The authors [9] have proposed a cluster head selection algorithm based on a balanced inter-grid system, taking into account criteria such as residual energy and node position relative to the sink. Performance evaluation of this algorithm reveals satisfactory results compared with algorithms such as LEACH, RoutingG5, and OSCH-G6, particularly in terms of energy consumption, network lifetime, and packet delivery rate. However, to guarantee true load balancing, it would be necessary to define an energy threshold beyond which a node would no longer be eligible to be selected as a cluster head.

In [13], the authors propose a data aggregation, and transmission protocol based on the clustering method. A comparison of their proposal with LEACH shows better performance. However, a comparison with other existing methods would be necessary to fully assess the effectiveness of the proposed model. In addition, it would be appropriate to implement a mechanism for selecting the collector nodes in turn, to ensure fair energy consumption.

3 A Residual Energy Aware and a Number of Children Aware Energy-Efficient Routing Protocol Approaches

3.1 Energy Aware Energy-Efficient Routing Protocol Approaches

As presented in Sect.2, for the balancing of energy consumption, several authors have proposed taking into account the remaining energy of potential intermediate neighboring nodes (parents) towards the sink. In our implemented algorithm, at network start-up, all nodes have the same amount of energy. Node's remaining energy is regularly evaluated and carried in its DIO messages. Upon receipt of these DIO messages, a node chooses as the next hop to the sink the parent node (intermediate) having the most residual energy.

Thus, just after the first exchanges, the remaining energies of the nodes are recalculated. Then, during the sectioning phase of the preferred parent, instead of proceeding as in the rpl standard, we have modified the MRHO objective function so that the best parent is the parent with the largest amount of residual energy. Thus, we compare, the residual energy of the parent nodes to decide the preferred parent each time a node is looking for a better parent. In the next section we present our approach to solving the problem.

3.2 A Number of Children Aware Energy-Efficient Routing Protocol Approaches

Our parent selection process is presented as follow.

a. *At network startup, after the DODAGs are formed, DODAG Information Object (DIO) messages are sent in multicast to all nodes on the network to allow them to select a parent (a node that transfers control messages) and to be able to reach a Destination-Oriented Directed Acyclic Graph (DODAG). In this DIO message, we will include a NB-CHIlD field initialize to zero at the start (NB-CHIlD=0);*
b. *On receipt of the DIO message, nodes send Destination Advertisement Object (DAO) to the potential parents;*

c. *Upon receipt of the DAO message from the potential child (a node that receives control messages), the parent node sends a DAO-ACK (DAO acknowledgement) in unicast to the child node and the parent node increases the number of its children (NB-CHIlD= NB-CHIlD+1). This number is included in the DIO messages;*
d. *Thus, each time a node receives a DIO message, the node compares the number of children of the potential parents and selects as preferred parent the one with the fewest children.*

The algorithm of this enhanced protocol is presented in Fig. 1.

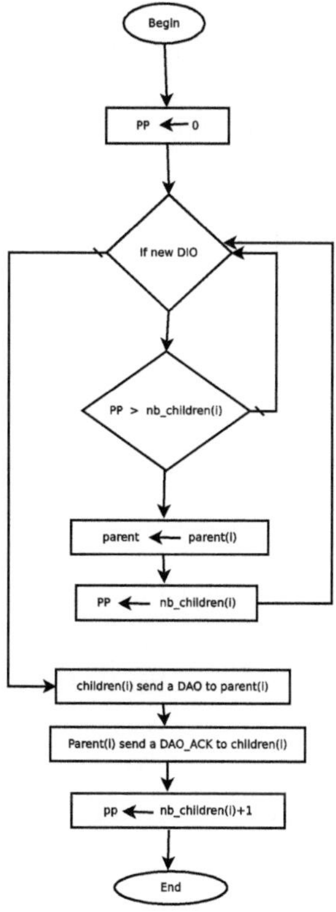

Fig. 1. Flowchart for selecting the parent according to the number of children

4 Performance Comparaison

4.1 Simulation Setup

In this section, on the one hand, we present the used simulator and the simulation conditions. On the other hand, we analyze and compare the obtained results of number of children based Routing Protocol for Low power and lossy networks (RPL) [17] to those taking into account remaining energy.

4.2 Simulation Setup

We evaluated number of children based RPL performance by means of simulations using Cooja simulator [2]. Cooja is a java-based simulator designed to simulate sensor networks running Contiki operating system [1]. In Cooja, each node is emulated with the same sensor nodes capacities as sky motes. This helps us have realistic behaviors of nodes. Simulations are performed using IEEE 802.15.4 physical layer. The medium access is governed by the well-known CSMA/CA algorithm.

In the different simulations, we used a queue length of 10 data packets with a 50-byte packet size which corresponds to the storage capacity of the packet queue of sky motes.

We compared this number of children based RPL with remainging energy based one.

We used a simulation area of $100 \times 100\ m^2$ where sensor nodes are randomly scattered. For each topology we ensure that the network is connected (no isolated nodes) before starting the evaluation process. For each iteration, the same topology is used for the 2 protocols. We used the Unit Disk Graph radio Medium(UDGM) provided in Cooja simulator as the radio propagation model.

In the presented results, each value is an average of ten different simulations for each scenario. We evaluated the performance of our contribution according to 3 metrics: network lifetime, packet delivery ratio and data packets end-to-end delay.

The Table 1 summarizes the simulation parameters.

Table 1. Simulation parameters.

Parameters	Values
Medium access	IEEE 802.15.4 CSMA/CA
Duty-Cycle	Disabled
Radio model	UDGM
Packet queue size	10 packets
Packet size	50 bytes
Nodes energy source	2 $\times$ AA batteries
Each node energy budget	15,390 J
Simulation surface	100×100 m^2
Topology	Random
Number of nodes	10 and 40
Packet generation rate	$\{1, 5\}$ packets/s/node
Number of repetitions	10 iterations

4.3 Simulation Results Analysis

In this paper, the network lifetime is defined as the time until the first node exhausts its energy in the network. The simulation results show us that the network lifetime is longer with number of children aware RPL compared to RPL with residual energy. When the node transmits 5 packets of data per second, the first node dies for lack of power at 23 h in our proposal, 17 h for the RPL with residual energy and 6 h for the standard RPL. It is also observed that with our proposal, all the nodes die at almost the same time. This approach helps to balance the load between the nodes and then balance the energy consumption. To evaluate protocol robustness, we have measured the packet delivery rate for de 3 protocoles. Packet delivery ratio (PDR) is defined as the number of packets successfully received at the destination relative to the number of packets sent to the destination. The results of our simulations show that when each node generates 5 packet per second, delivery ratios of the two protocols are high (more than 98%) and very close. But, the protocol include number of children selection achieved more% delivery ratios (Figs. 2, 3, 4 and 5).

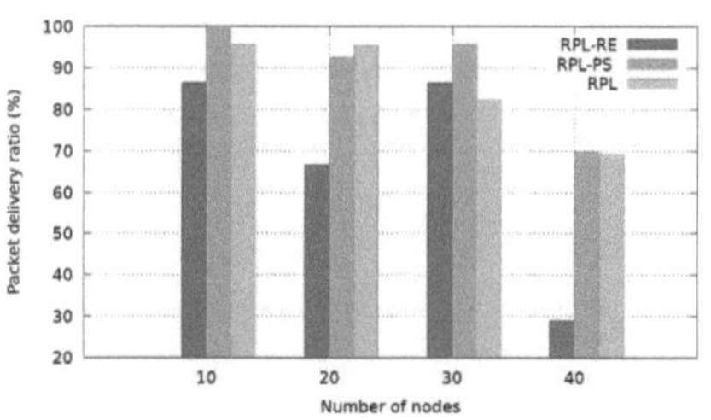

Fig. 2. PDR: generation 1p/sec/node with 20, 40 and 60 nodes scenarios.

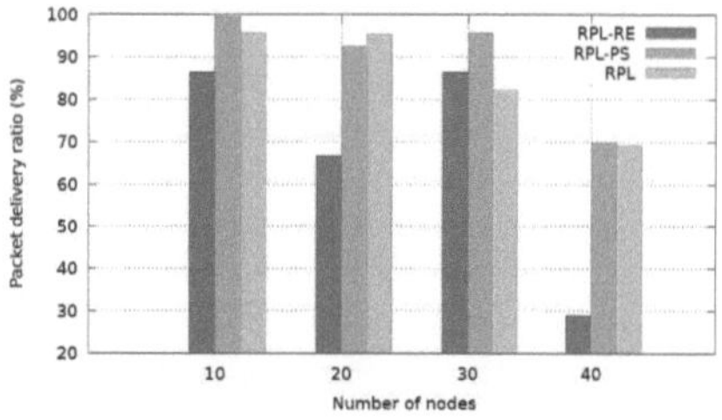

Fig. 3. PDR: generation 5p/sec/node with 20, 40 and 60 nodes scenarios.

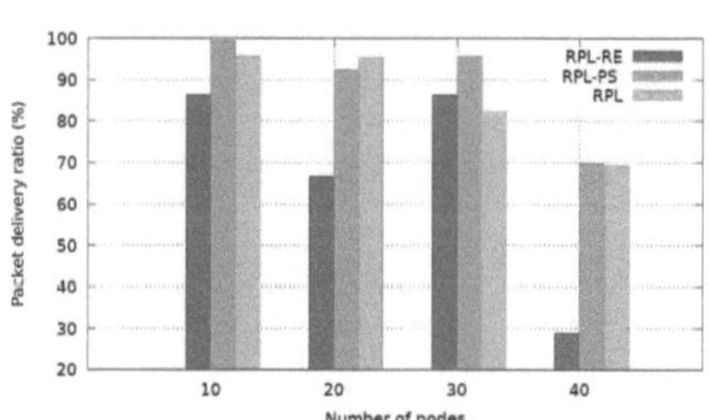

Fig. 4. Network lifetime: generation 1p/sec/node with 20, 40 and 60 nodes scenarios.

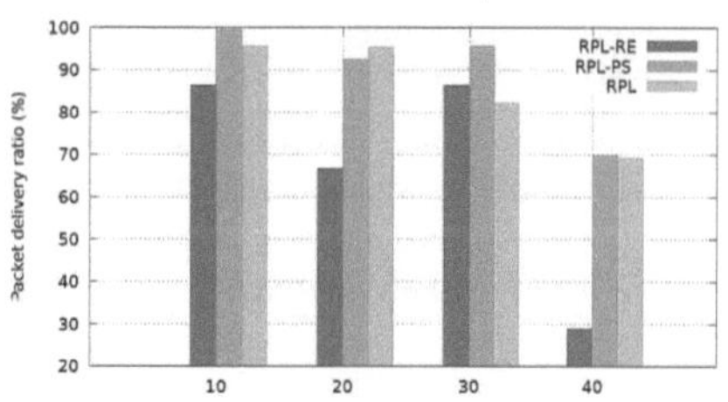

Fig. 5. Network lifetime: generation 1p/sec/node with 20, 40 and 60 nodes scenarios.

5 Conclusion

WSNs are increasingly used for data collection in different domains. The sensor nodes that compose it are very often equipped with batteries which are difficult to replace. In some critical context such as danger monitoring, the death of a node may render the system inefficient. The efficiency of these solutions lies in efficient management of the energy of these nodes. We investigated an energy management approach based on taking into account the number of children of potential parents (gateways to the sink) in the route establishment process. In this approach, a node selects as next hop to the sink, potential intermediate with higer remaining energy. This permit better energy consuption balance. The simulation results of this approach show that we succeed in improving the lifetime of the network which we summarize to the lifetime of the first one which would exhaust its energy.

References

1. Dunkels, A., Gronvall, B., Voigt, T.: Contiki a lightweight and flexible operating system for tiny networked sensors. In: IEEE LCN, pp. 455–462 (2004)
2. Osterlind, F., Dunkels, A., Eriksson, J., Finne, N., Voigt, T.: Cross-level sensor network simulation with COOJA. In: IEEE LCN (2006)
3. Bagula, A., Djenouri, D., Karbab, E.: Ubiquitous sensor network management: the least interference beaconing model. In: 2013 IEEE 24th Annual International Symposium on Personal, Indoor, and Mobile Radio Communications (PIMRC), pp. 2352–2356 (2013). ISSN: 2166-9589
4. Ben-Othman, J., Yahya, B.: Energy efficient and QoS based routing protocol for wireless sensor networks. J. Parallel Distrib. Comput. **70**(8), 849–857 (2010)
5. Heinzelman, W.R., Chandrakasan, A., Balakrishnan, H.: Energy-efficient communication protocol for wireless microsensor networks. In: Proceedings of the 33rd Annual Hawaii International Conference on System Sciences, p. 10. IEEE (2000)
6. Hieu, N.Q., Thanh, N.H., Huong, T.T., Thu, N.Q., Quang, H.V.: Integrating trickle timing in software defined WSNs for energy efficiency. In: 2018 IEEE Seventh International Conference on Communications and Electronics (ICCE), Hue, July 2018, pp. 75–80. IEEE (2018)
7. Levis, P., Gnawali, O.: The Minimum Rank with Hysteresis Objective Function (2012)
8. Mahmood, D., Javaid, N., Mahmood, S., Qureshi, S., Memon, A.M., Zaman, T.: Modleach: a variant of leach for wsns. In: 2013 Eighth International Conference on Broadband and Wireless Computing, Communication and Applications, pp. 158–163. IEEE (2013)
9. El Idrissi, N., Abdellah, N., et al.: Energy-aware clustering and efficient cluster head selection. Int. J. Smart Sens. Intell. Syst. **14**(1), 1–15 (2021)
10. Ngqakaza, L., Bagula, A.: Least path interference beaconing protocol (LIBP): a frugal routing protocol for the internet-of-things. In: Mellouk, A., Fowler, S., Hoceini, S., Daachi, B. (eds.) WWIC 2014. LNCS, vol. 8458, pp. 148–161. Springer, Cham (2014). https://doi.org/10.1007/978-3-319-13174-0_12
11. Nurmio, J., Nigussie, E., Poellabauer, C.: Equalizing energy distribution in sensor nodes through optimization of RPL. In: 2015 IEEE International Conference on Computer and Information Technology; Ubiquitous Computing and Communications; Dependable, Autonomic and Secure Computing; Pervasive Intelligence and Computing, pp. 83–91 (2015)
12. Pravin, R.A., Murugan, K., Thiripurasundari, C., Christodoss, P.R., Puviarasi, R., Lathif, S.I.A.: Stochastic cluster head selection model for energy balancing in IoT enabled heterogeneous WSN. Meas. Sensors **35**, 101282 (2024)

13. Singh, J., et al.: Energy efficient data aggregation and density-based spatial clustering of applications with noise for activity monitoring in wireless sensor networks. Eng. Sci. **19**(7), 144–153 (2022)
14. Taghizadeh, S., Bobarshad, H., Elbiaze, H.: CLRPL: context-aware and load balancing RPL for Iot networks under heavy and highly dynamic load. IEEE Access **6**, 23277–23291 (2018)
15. Umbreen, S., Shehzad, D., Shafi, N., Khan, B., Habib, U.: An energy-efficient mobility-based cluster head selection for lifetime enhancement of wireless sensor networks. IEEE Access **8**, 207779–207793 (2020)
16. Wang, S., Jiguo, Yu., Atiquzzaman, M., Chen, H., Ni, L.: Crpd: a novel clustering routing protocol for dynamic wireless sensor networks. Pers. Ubiquit. Comput. **22**, 545–559 (2018)
17. Winter, T.: RPL: IPv6 Routing Protocol for Low-Power and Lossy Networks (2012)
18. Yeiemou, T., Tall, H., Sanou, D.A.R.: BAIWL: blacklisting approach to improve wireless sensor network lifetime. In: 2020 IEEE International Conf on Natural and Engineering Sciences for Sahel's Sustainable Development - Impact of Big Data Application on Society and Environment (IBASE-BF), Ouagadougou, Burkina Faso, February 2020, pp. 1–5. IEEE (2020)

Data Analytic and Decision Making

Design of a Big Data Architecture for Precision Agriculture in Burkina Faso

Ghislain Wend-Puire Seghda(✉), Pasteur Poda, and Abdoulaye Sere

Laboratoire d'Ananalyse, de Mathématiques Discrètes et d'Informatique, Université Nazi BONI, Bobo Dioulasso, Burkina Faso
gseghda@hotmail.com

Abstract. The advent of Big Data technology in agriculture has precipitated a paradigm shift in the manner by which farmers oversee the operations of their farms. The paper delineates the influence of Big Data on enhancing agricultural productivity, highlighting the global tendency to leverage data from satellites, sensors, and drones for yield prediction, disease prevention, and resource optimisation. This article examines the various Big Data architectures employed in the agricultural sector and their respective applications. In light of the specific challenges posed by limited data, a lack of digital infrastructure, and reliance on traditional agricultural knowledge, our objective is to design a Big Data architecture tailored to the agricultural sector in Burkina Faso. The proposed architecture is based on a centralised data lake, a processing layer using machine learning algorithms, and a straightforward visualisation interface, facilitating the utilisation of the information by farmers. This architecture is designed to be accessible to small-scale farmers, taking into account both the lack of digital infrastructure and the literacy levels of producers.

Keywords: Precision agriculture · architecture · big data · endogenous knowledge

1 Introduction

Despite its importance to the national economy, the agricultural sector in Burkina Faso is facing significant challenges. The combined effects of population growth, urbanisation, and climate change reduce the amount of arable land and damage soil quality, which could have serious implications for food security [1] [2]. In contrast to developed countries, where agriculture is more mechanised and less dependent on labour and weather fluctuations, Burkina Faso, like many other African countries, has a large proportion of its working population employed in this sector [3,4]. The need for innovative solutions to ensure food self-sufficiency is becoming increasingly urgent. Digital technologies and Big Data may prove to be the keys to optimising production and improving the resilience of agricultural systems in the face of environmental challenges [5].

A. Sere et al. (Eds.): AFRI2 2025, CCIS 2536, pp. 77–93, 2026.
https://doi.org/10.1007/978-3-031-98327-6_6

The global agricultural sector has derived considerable benefit from the adoption of Big Data. Data, gathered from a multitude of sources (including satellites, sensors, and drones), are used to improve the understanding of agricultural ecosystems, anticipate yields, optimise input use, and diagnose crop diseases at an early stage [6]. A considerable number of countries have already established ambitious initiatives with the objective of exploiting the potential of Big Data in the agricultural sector. The initiatives mentioned above have produced positive results. These successes can be attributed to substantial investment in research and development, as well as close collaboration between researchers and farmers. Numerous researchers from various countries have been involved in this field of study. Their efforts have culminated in the formulation of an architectural framework for monitoring agricultural campaigns. Two recent studies, conducted by Alex et al. [7] and Fenu et Malloci [8], illustrate the potential of Big Data architectural designs to improve crop management practices.

In their study, Alex et al. [7] focused on the prediction of yields and the assessment of the risks associated with excessive fertiliser use. The model, which is based on convolutional neural networks, is capable of classifying crops into three categories based on weather and soil data, namely healthy growth, required alert, and emergency alert. The originality of the study lies in its decomposition of the fertiliser components, which allows a more detailed understanding of their impact on crops. This approach enables not only the optimisation of fertiliser use but also a reduction in their environmental impact.

In a similar vein, Fenu and Malloci [8] have developed a more comprehensive crop monitoring system. The system comprises a data collection apparatus, a data management module, and a mobile application, which enables farmers to monitor the health of their crops in real time and detect diseases early. This preventive approach helps limit yield losses and reduce the use of pesticides.

Both studies share the objective of improving agricultural productivity through the analysis of massive data. However, they differ in their approach. Alex et al. favour a predictive approach, while Fenu and Malloci focus on real-time monitoring. In addition, the data used and the models developed are specific to each study.

Although Big Data opens up new opportunities for agriculture, it faces major obstacles in developing countries such as Burkina Faso [9]. The main challenges are the lack of reliable and comprehensive data, particularly in the agricultural sector, and limited digital infrastructure, especially in rural areas. These limitations hinder the optimal use of information technologies.

The potential of big data to revolutionise agriculture in Burkina Faso is undeniable. However, the lack of reliable and comprehensive data and the limited digital infrastructure, especially in rural areas, are major obstacles. Paradoxically, the endogenous ancestral knowledge of farmers, the fruit of centuries of adaptation to often difficult environments, is an invaluable source of knowledge about crops, soils, climates, and farming practices. The key is to find a way to integrate this endogenous knowledge with agricultural data to optimise farming practices, despite the limited amount of data available. The main research question is therefore what big data architecture should be implemented in order to monitor agricultural campaigns in Burkina Faso, based on data which, although insufficient, integrate endogenous knowledge?

In this paper, we therefore propose a scalable and flexible Big Data architecture, which is designed to operate on small datasets and which should remain so when these become larger. It should also make it possible to exploit the endogenous knowledge of local producers. In order to propose and present such an architecture, our paper will follow the following plan. We will begin by presenting the concepts of Big Data and Big Data architectures in the agricultural sector. These concepts will lead to the proposal of a design method for a Big Data architecture. We then describe the proposed architecture and its components. Finally, we will discuss the relevance of such an architecture in the agricultural context of Burkina Faso.

2 The State of Art and Method Description

2.1 The Concept of Big Data in Agriculture

The term "big data" is used to describe datasets that are extremely large and complex and that exceed the processing capabilities of traditional relational database management systems. The data in question are distinguished by five key characteristics: exponential volume, increased velocity, considerable variety, veracity, and a value that requires particular attention.

- **Volume:** The term "volume" is used to describe the amount of data that is generated. The sheer amount of data generated necessitates the implementation of distributed storage and computing infrastructures capable of managing petabytes or even exabytes of information. This expansion is attributed to the proliferation of connected devices (IoT), social media, online transactions, and scientific data.
- **Velocity:** The generation of data is occurring at an unprecedented rate, requiring the processing of information in real time or near real time to extract value. Continuous data flows originating from a multitude of sources, including sensors, social networks, and financial markets, require the implementation of streaming architectures and incremental algorithms.
- **Variety:** The variety of data formats that make up big data is considerable. The term "big data" encompasses a multitude of data formats, including structured data (relational databases), semistructured data (e.g., XML, JSON) and unstructured data (e.g., text, images, video, audio). This diversity requires the use of analytical tools and techniques that are tailored to the specific characteristics of each type of data.
- **Veracity:** Data quality is an important concern. Raw data may contain errors, inconsistencies, biases, and missing values. Data cleansing, integration, and validation techniques are crucial for ensuring the reliability of analyses.
- **Value:** Big data analysis can be used to extract hidden knowledge, identify trends, optimise processes, personalise customer experiences, and make

informed decisions. The applications are numerous and widespread across all sectors of activity.

In the agricultural sector, the application of Big Data has been demonstrated to be an effective approach in numerous countries, facilitating the support and monitoring of agricultural production [10]. Using data on soil conditions, meteorological forecasts, and crop health, farmers can make well-informed decisions about planting, irrigation, and the application of fertilisers and pesticides. This results in optimised yields and a reduction in production costs. Secondly, analytical tools can predict extreme weather events, pest invasions, and other agricultural risks. This capacity for prediction enables farmers to adopt measures aimed at the mitigation of potential losses. Furthermore, the utilisation of Big Data facilitates the management of resources, including water, fertilisers, and energy, ensuring the efficient and sustainable use of these resources. In conclusion, the integration of Big Data within the agricultural sector signifies a paradigm shift in the management of farming enterprises. It empowers decision-making processes through the analysis of accurate data, thereby enhancing the efficiency and profitability of contemporary agricultural practices.

2.2 Examples of Big Data Applications in Agriculture

The integration of Big Data technologies in agriculture has led to many innovative applications that optimise production and increase profitability [11].

- **Precision agriculture:** Precision agriculture is defined as a set of techniques and practices designed to minimise the direct utilisation of inputs in agricultural plots [12]. It uses comprehensive data sets to facilitate optimal decision-making in agricultural operations, and the use of data obtained from sensors, satellites, and drones facilitates more precise and efficient crop management [13]. Precision farming involves the rational use of fertilisers and pesticides, adapted to the specific requirements of crops, thus reducing costs and mitigating environmental impact [7,14]. Precision farming is a term used to describe agricultural practices that are focused on increasing the efficiency and productivity of farming operations. One of the key elements of precision farming is the use of soil sensors, which enable the precise measurement of soil humidity and salinity. This, in turn, facilitates the improvement of crop health. Furthermore, the implementation of field mapping facilitates the identification of regions that require particular attention, thus ensuring that the most efficient and effective agricultural practices are employed in every area.
- **Yield forecasting:** Agricultural yield prediction models use historical data, current weather conditions, and soil characteristics to estimate future crop yields [7,15]. These forecasts help farmers plan their activities and make strategic decisions. Thanks to simulation models, farmers can now anticipate their yields by combining historical data, weather, and soil characteristics. These tools make it possible to assess the impact of climate change and make strategic decisions to optimise production and adapt to natural hazards.

- **Water Resources Management:** Water is very important for good agricultural production. In countries that are irrigated for an average of 3 to 4 months of the year by rainwater, optimising irrigation is crucial. Big Data technologies enable precise water management, minimising wastage and ensuring efficient distribution through intelligent irrigation and optimal management of water reserves. Smart irrigation [16] is an irrigation system that automatically adjusts the water quantities according to the specific needs of plants, weather conditions, and soil moisture [4].
- **Disease and Pest Monitoring:** In agriculture, Big Data plays a crucial role in disease prevention and crop monitoring. By analysing images captured by satellites and drones, Deep Learning models detect the first signs of stress in plants, often linked to disease or insect attacks [4]. In addition, by combining historical data with information on climatic conditions, predictive models can anticipate epidemics [8]. Farmers are alerted in real time via their mobile devices, giving them the opportunity to intervene quickly and effectively.

2.3 Typical Big Data Architectures in Agriculture

Big Data architecture in agriculture encompasses several components designed to manage, process, and analyse massive volumes of data from a variety of sources. The most common architectures are as follows.

- **Lambda architecture:** The lambda architecture [17] represents a pivotal component within the broader field of big data systems. It is the architecture most frequently employed to facilitate the concurrent processing and management of substantial datasets, both in real time and in batches. It boasts scalability and fault-tolerance, thus ensuring its effectiveness in high-pressure environments. The lambda architecture integrates real-time processing (streaming) and batch processing, thereby ensuring comprehensive data analysis within big data systems [18]. The Lambda architecture is characterised by the operation of two distinct processing pipelines: a real-time processing pipeline (speed layer) and a batch processing pipeline (batch layer). These two pipelines function independently of each other and process data in parallel, with the results of both pipelines being combined in the service layer to yield the final result [19].
  The Lambda architecture has been demonstrated to be ideal for real-time weather monitoring, irrigation management, and historical analysis of crop yields.
- **Kappa architecture:** The Kappa architecture constitutes an alternative approach to the Lambda architecture in the processing of real-time data streams in Big Data systems [20]. It has been proposed as a simplification of the Lambda architecture, with the result that the need for two separate processing pipelines (one for real-time processing and another for batch processing) is eliminated. The Kappa architecture proposes the use of a single pipeline to process real-time data, thus simplifying the overall system architecture. In a Kappa architecture, real-time data processing is carried out

continuously and data in transit and historical data are stored in the same system.
The Kappa architecture finds application in real-time monitoring of agricultural equipment, instant detection of extreme weather conditions, and rapid management of agricultural inputs.
- **Microservices and Containers:** This architecture is really impressive! It breaks applications down into independent services that communicate with each other via APIs [21]. Containers, such as Docker, make it a breeze to deploy and run these services in an isolated and portable way. It's absolutely perfect for agricultural management systems where different modules (e.g. irrigation, fertilisation, yield forecasts) can be updated, deployed or scaled independently.

The architectures presented above are an interesting advance in themselves, but there is still room for improvement. They do not make it possible to harness farmers' endogenous knowledge, which represents a tremendous opportunity for future development. This knowledge can supplement the data, which is often incomplete and unsuitable for decision-making in the context of Burina Faso. Moreover, the need for data is insatiable for each of the architectures presented above, and access to vast sets of agricultural data in Burkina Faso remains a luxury.

2.4 Design Stages of Big Data Architecture

Designing a Big Data architecture for agriculture is a rigorous process that involves several key stages. These steps are presented in the Fig. 1.

Firstly, a comprehensive examination of the particular requirements of agricultural enterprises is imperative. This requires a precise identification of the desired outcomes, which can include the optimisation of water usage, the prediction of yields, or the improvement of product quality. The comprehensive examination of the requirements yielded two significant challenges. The initial challenge is to monitor producers. This requires the establishment of a system for the collection of data related to farming practices, yields, and the constraints encountered [22]. This information is vital for the evaluation of the impact of interventions, the adaptation of strategies according to findings, and the identification of new, more optimal approaches. The second challenge pertains to the selection of seeds. The adaptation of seed varieties to local conditions represents a pivotal factor in determining the success of any given endeavour. It is essential that farmers have access to the tools required to select seeds that are optimal for their plots and climatic conditions. The specific features of the Burkina Faso context can be summarised as follows. First, there is a low level of literacy, which means that simple and intuitive digital tools must be made available to all users. Secondly, the dearth of data necessitates the development and proposal of methods tailored to the field, based on traditional knowledge and farmers' observations. Lastly, climate variability makes forecasting yields a challenging undertaking. One of the distinctive features of the project is the

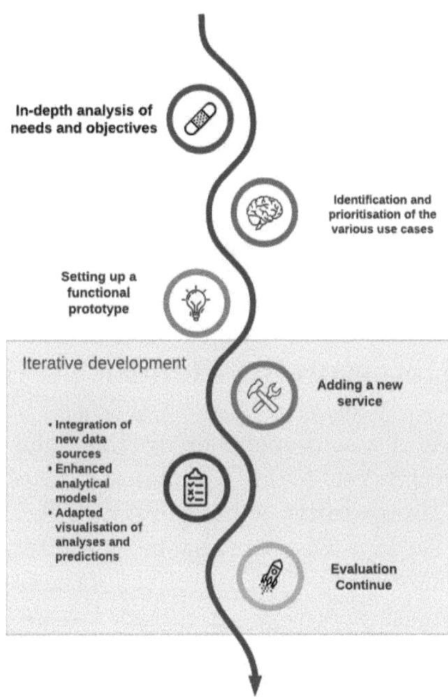

Fig. 1. Architecture design stages.

integration of traditional knowledge of farmers. Farmers possess a deep understanding of soils and crops, acquired over generations. It is therefore imperative to engage them in all phases of the project and to validate the models with them.

In the second stage, a prototype is constructed in order to test the selected technologies and validate the overall architecture. The objective is to create a simplified version of the system that can process a limited set of data and execute the fundamental functions. This phase is vital to ensure that the solution aligns with the identified needs and refines the technological choices.

Finally, the development of the Big Data architecture is an ongoing process that occurs in an iterative manner. New functionalities are incorporated step by step, commencing with the most straightforward and impactful. The application of artificial intelligence and machine learning is facilitating the refinement of analytical models, resulting in the generation of increasingly accurate results. Specific consideration is given to the visualisation of data, with the objective of facilitating the interpretation of results by farmers. In addition, an ongoing evaluation of the solution is conducted to ascertain its impact on productivity, with any necessary adjustments subsequently made. This iterative approach ensures the scalability of the solution, allowing it to be adapted to the evolving needs of farmers. The initial priority functionality is designed to help the farmer identify the optimal crop. It is crucial to determine which seeds are most conducive to achieving optimal yields in a given soil. To illustrate, consider a farmer who seeks to identify the optimal crops for his land. After collecting data in the field, the techniques and tools employed in the analysis layer enabled the detection of the prevailing weeds. The agricultural ontology established connections between soil fertility and the grasses that flourish in it with weather conditions. By entering the predominant weeds into the ontology, the system can determine the most suitable crop for a given soil type and identify any soil deficiencies.

This iterative approach makes it possible to design a Big Data architecture tailored to the specific needs of each farm, while guaranteeing long-term scalability and flexibility.

3 Big Data Architecture to Monitor Agricultural

From the initial stages of soil preparation to the final stages of harvest, the agricultural monitoring process demands a high degree of precision and responsiveness. Therefore, it is imperative to carry out an effective monitoring of agricultural campaigns in Burkina Faso to enhance agricultural productivity, ensure food security, and promote sustainability of the agricultural system. The proposed Big Data architecture provides a robust framework for the collection, storage, processing, analysis, and visualisation of small amounts of data from a variety of sources, thereby providing valuable information for decision-making at all levels of the agricultural system.

The first step to achieving improved agricultural yields is to select a crop that is well suited to the soil. Previous studies on this topic have indicated the potential benefits of using soil data for this purpose. However, in developing countries such as Burkina Faso, it can be challenging for producers to access these data, limiting their ability to make informed decisions. Our proposed architecture, in its initial form, aims to address this challenge by providing information on the suitability of different crops for specific soil types. The data used in this process include meteorological data and images of plants and soil conditions.

The architecture consists of five main components. It is shown in Fig. 2.

3.1 Data Ingestion Layer

Data ingestion is the process of integrating data from different sources, with the aim of making it accessible and usable for future analysis [23]. This process plays a fundamental role in providing the information needed to generate detailed and relevant descriptions of the data. Data ingestion has several key objectives to facilitate the creation of metadata [24]. Firstly, it enables the structure, format and content of the data to be analysed and understood, by identifying data types, fields, the relationships between them, and the associated validation rules. Secondly, it enables the data to be enriched by adding contextual information and additional metadata, such as the origin of the data, the date it was created, the conditions under which it was collected, or the licences under which it is used. Finally, data ingestion facilitates data indexing, making it easier to find and retrieve information.

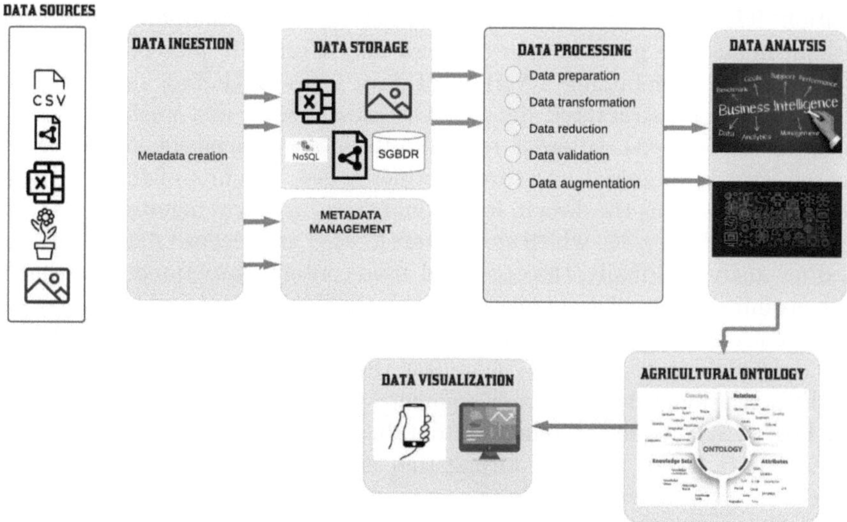

Fig. 2. Big Data Architecture to monitor agricultural campaigns.

Various tools and technologies are available for data ingestion. Some, such as Talend, Informatica, and AWS Glue, offer integrated functionality for ingesting, processing, and enriching data. Other tools, such as Informatica PowerCenter and IBM InfoSphere DataStage, can connect and integrate data from disparate sources. However, their learning curve and limited performance for processing small volumes of data made them less suitable solutions for our architecture. Instead, we opted for custom pipelines created using programming languages such as Python or R, enabling more flexible automation of the data ingestion process. This approach was chosen for our data ingestion project.

Data ingestion offers a number of advantages for the creation of metadata [3]. Accurate and complete metadata are essential to optimise the use of data. Data ingestion therefore makes it possible to generate high-quality metadata that provides an in-depth understanding of the data itself. This enriched and descriptive metadata facilitates the discovery of relevant data for specific analyses or applications. It is also easily searched and understood by users. Well-structured metadata are also essential for data governance. It enables effective management of the data lifecycle and the application of access control policies. In this sense, data ingestion contributes to the creation of metadata used to support data governance.

3.2 Data Storage Layer

The data storage layer is the entity responsible for the storage of the collected data [25]. It is essential that the data repository is capable of managing large amounts of data in different formats, which makes the data lake an optimal solution. This layer serves as a vast repository for information that is stored without immediate processing or organisation, in order to preserve its integrity. It is capable of containing a variety of data types, including structured data (databases), semi-structured data (JSON files, XML), and unstructured data (images, videos, text). In order to facilitate data management and access, the storage layer is organised into three distinct zones. The first of these is the raw zone, which contains the data in its original state, as it was ingested. The second is the intermediate zone, which stores transformed and cleaned data, ready to be used for analysis. Finally, the organised zone contains structured data that has been optimised for analytical queries. The technologies employed in this layer are contingent on the particular requirements and the volume of data in question. The most prevalent solutions encompass the Hadoop Distributed File System (HDFS), relational database management systems (RDBMS) such as MySQL and PostgreSQL, and non-relational databases (NoSQL). The HDFS typically stores data in 64MB blocks, a format that is not optimal for architectures that process small data sets.

In the context of our project, a basic file system is used for the storage of raw data. A graph-orientated DBMS is used to represent the relationships between the metadata present within the data lake. A document-orientated database management system (DBMS) is used to store refined versions of text documents. Subsequently, a relational database management system is used to store refined representations of tabular documents and images. Sore et al. [24] propose a raw storage zone, which retains all the raw data collected. In our architectural framework, this storage zone can also be used to replenish processed data in other zones, ensuring its availability for future utilisation. This guarantees that it can be reused in subsequent analyses.

3.3 Data Processing Layer

Once stored in a data lake, raw data must undergo a series of processing stages prior to utilisation for analytical or business applications [26]. These stages facilitate the transformation of raw data into a form that is fit for purpose and of high quality. In the case of our primary use case, which is primarily concerned with images, the data undergo a series of phases. The initial stage comprises image preprocessing, including resizing, normalising, and rectification of geometric distortions. To illustrate, the lenses of smartphones can introduce barrel or pincushion distortions. Geometric correction algorithms, such as homography, are employed to rectify these distortions. Moreover, certain machine learning algorithms, such as convolutional neural networks (CNN), require images with uniform dimensions. It is therefore imperative that the images be resized and scaled to ensure that they have the same widths and heights prior to processing. The second stage is to enhance the quality of the image, which involves the reduction of noise and the optimisation of contrast. Noise in images may originate from a number of sources, including the acquisition, transmission, or compression processes. There are numerous types of noise, including salt-and-pepper noise and Gaussian noise. To address this, specific algorithms, such as adapted filters, are employed to reduce noise according to its nature. The third stage is image segmentation, which involves the grouping of pixels according to predefined criteria. This segmentation allows the image to be divided into distinct regions, thus constituting a partition. The application of image segmentation can facilitate the separation of the foreground from the background, or alternatively, the grouping of areas together based on similarities in colour or shape. This step is essential to simplify the complexity of an image by extracting the relevant objects it contains, thereby facilitating its subsequent analysis.

The selection of appropriate tools and technologies depends on the specific requirements and available resources. The most prevalent are Hadoop and Spark, which are distributed processing platforms capable of handling substantial amounts of data [27]. In addition, there are Python and R, which are programming languages that are used for data manipulation and analysis. However, despite the considerable capabilities of Hadoop and Spark in handling large data sets, there are inherent limitations when utilising these tools for smaller datasets, particularly in the context of developing countries. Firstly, Hadoop necessitates the possession of specific technical skills and expertise in system administration, which can prove problematic for less experienced technical teams. Secondly, although Hadoop can run on inexpensive hardware, the initial investment required to set up a cluster, even a small one, can be significant. Finally, using Hadoop to process small amounts of data is akin to using a jackhammer to swat a fly, resulting in unnecessary overload in terms of resources and processing time.

In order to achieve the objectives of our project, we have elected to utilise a range of programming languages, including Python, which incorporates specific libraries for data processing. These have been selected to align with the volumes of data that we are required to handle.

3.4 Data Analysis Layer

The data analysis layer is of central importance in any Big Data architecture, particularly in the field of agriculture. It facilitates the formulation of well-informed decisions aimed at optimising yields and crop management. The application of predictive modelling techniques represents a crucial means of anticipating future occurrences within the domain of agricultural practice. Such techniques may be used to predict yields [15]. Using linear or logistic regression models to estimate future yields as a function of factors such as weather conditions, soil quality, and cultivation practices. In addition, decision trees can be used for the detection of diseases. Such trees may be used in the construction of decision rules for the identification of disease risks based on disparate indicators. The analysis of images constitutes an indispensable element of precision agriculture. The use of satellite imagery facilitates the monitoring of crops. It is possible to monitor the health of crops, identify areas exhibiting signs of stress, and evaluate the overall growth of plants. The application of image analysis with object detection allows the precise localisation and identification of plants, grasses, and insects within images, thereby facilitating targeted crop management.

Several tools are available for the purpose of performing these analyses. Programming languages such as Python, with specialist libraries such as Pandas, NumPy, and Scikit-learn, offer considerable flexibility and computing power. Although Big Data platforms such as Hadoop and Spark are highly capable of processing large amounts of data, they are not always optimally suited to the needs of agriculture, where data volumes are often more modest. In this context, transfer learning emerges as a promising alternative. This technique involves repurposing deep learning models that have previously been trained in extensive databases to adapt them to specific tasks, such as the classification of agricultural images. This approach enables the achievement of high-quality results with limited data.

3.5 Agricultural Ontology Layer

Ontology is of crucial importance in the fields of information science and data management, providing a formal representation of concepts and relationships within a given domain. By modelling knowledge, it creates a unified structure that allows data to be understood and exploited effectively, especially in complex contexts such as Big Data [28]. Ontologies facilitate the integration of endogenous data and knowledge by establishing a unified framework that explicitly defines the meaning of concepts and the relationships between them. The use of a common language to describe the data enables the integration of information from disparate sources, facilitating the comparison and compatibility of the data. In addition, they facilitate more precise queries and sophisticated reasoning. In addition, they facilitate communication between disparate systems and applications, ensuring a uniform understanding of data and metadata.

To illustrate, consider the case of a farmer seeking to optimise the crops to be sown on his land. Once data on the field in question have been collected and predominant weeds have been identified, an agricultural ontology can be employed to link data on soil fertility and weeds. To achieve this, it is necessary to include concepts such as soil types, weed species, and their relationships with climatic conditions in the ontology. Subsequently, the system could be used to recommend crops. In fact, by entering data on the predominant weeds and soil characteristics into the ontology system, it is possible to determine which crops would be best suited to the terrain. To illustrate, if the ontology indicates that a specific weed flourishes in nitrogen-deficient soils, this may indicate a nutrient deficiency in the soil. Consequently, the ontology may recommend crops that enrich the soil in nitrogen or are adapted to such conditions. Furthermore, the ontology could be used to identify soil deficiencies, such as a lack of essential nutrients, and to recommend specific treatments or improvements.

3.6 Data Visualisation Layer

The Big Data architecture proposed in this study has been developed with direct producers (farmers) in mind, who may not possess the skills of data scientists or agronomists and therefore face challenges in interpreting complex graphs.

The objective of the study is to facilitate the development of intuitive interfaces that enable a wide audience to swiftly comprehend key information. The primary criteria for ensuring the effective visualisation of data and knowledge are simplicity, clarity (through the use of explicit legends, consistent colours and accessible vocabulary), interactivity and contextualisation. There are several appropriate types of display:

- Customised dashboards provide an overview of key indicators, are customisable and can be updated in real time. Dashboards can be used to monitor yield trends by crop, plant health and weather forecasts.
- Geographic maps show the spatial distribution of phenomena (e.g. crop zones, drought risk zones) using heat maps to represent yields and disease distribution maps.

The process of visualising agricultural data for a non-specialist audience requires a tailored approach, including the selection of appropriate tools and adherence to the principles of data visualisation. Several libraries can be used to build such interfaces. For this study, the following libraries will be used: D3.js and Chart.js. These open-source libraries offer a high degree of flexibility for the creation of customised visualisations.

4 Discussion

The proposed Big Data architecture for monitoring agricultural campaigns in Burkina Faso aims to integrate limited data, a constrained digital infrastructure, and the indigenous knowledge of farmers. This conceptual framework raises several points for discussion, particularly when compared to existing architectures in similar contexts.

Several studies [7,8,13,29] have demonstrated the effectiveness of using Big Data in agriculture, especially to predict yields and manage crop diseases. However, the architecture presented here stands out due to its adaptation to data-limited contexts, which is a significant challenge in developing countries like Burkina Faso. Unlike architectures [13], which are based on complex neural networks and large amounts of data, our approach focusses on creating scalable and modular systems that work with small volumes of data while integrating the ancestral knowledge of farmers.

One of the main limitations in implementing Big Data systems in rural areas remains the lack of stable Internet connections and robust digital infrastructure. Traditional Big Data architectures, such as Lambda and Kappa, which are often deployed in advanced agricultural environments, require sophisticated technological infrastructure to manage real-time and batch data processing. However, these infrastructures are not realistic for small-scale farmers in countries such as Burkina Faso, where access to technology is limited and cost is a key factor.

The proposed architecture addresses this challenge by employing a centralised data lake, offering a simpler and more suitable approach to local realities. The choice of a data lake allows the storage of large volumes of data from various sources (such as weather data, satellite images, and user input) without the need for an expensive real-time infrastructure. This enables farmers and local cooperatives to access the data asynchronously.

The architecture includes an innovative decision-making mechanism based on the indigenous knowledge of farmers, rather than complex soil chemical analyses. This choice is appropriate for Burkina Faso, where traditional practices and farmers' observations of soil characteristics (colour, presence of certain grasses, etc.) play a crucial role in crop selection. Unlike agricultural models in developed countries, which rely on sophisticated scientific data regarding soil nutrients and chemical composition, this architecture suggests using local visual indicators, such as soil colour or grass types, to help determine the optimal crop.

For example, a farmer could use this approach to identify the best crop to plant at the beginning of the season. This system combines local data with traditional knowledge, making the decision-making process accessible even to farmers without scientific training.

The architecture consists of several technical layers, each playing a key role in data processing. Although there are specialised tools, in this architecture, customised pipelines written in Python are used to automate the data ingestion process flexibly. These tools allow the architecture to adapt to small data volumes. Since Hadoop is suitable for very large data volumes, simple file systems are used in this architecture to maximise efficiency according to the needs. For processing, Python and its specialised libraries, such as Pandas for data manipulation and Scikit-learn for machine learning models, enable efficient handling of small amounts of data. In later stages, frameworks like Apache Spark could be introduced to ensure scalability as data volumes increase. The data analysis layer uses machine learning algorithms to predict agricultural yields, detect diseases, and optimise resource use. The constraint of data size directs the use of transfer learning models, which offer better results on small datasets.

5 Conclusion and Perspectives

In conclusion, this document has presented the main stages in the design of a Big Data architecture adapted to the specific characteristics of agriculture in Burkina Faso. We have highlighted the urgent need to adopt innovative solutions to meet the challenges of food security, exacerbated by climate change, demographic pressure, and urbanisation. The use of digital technologies and Big Data is proving to be a valuable opportunity to optimise agricultural production and strengthen the resilience of local systems.

Existing research has demonstrated the positive impact of Big Data architectures in the agricultural sector, particularly in terms of yield forecasting and real-time crop monitoring. These architectures are based on very large volumes of data and real-time information sources. However, these solutions face significant obstacles in developing countries such as Burkina Faso, due to the lack of reliable data and limited digital infrastructure. The originality of this proposal lies in the integration of farmers' endogenous knowledge, making it possible to combine traditional knowledge with modern technologies. In addition, unlike traditional Big Data architectures, which are aimed primarily at expert users, our solution has been designed to be accessible to everyone, including small-scale farmers.

The proposed architecture is based on a centralised data lake, a processing layer using machine learning algorithms, and a simple visualisation interface, which makes it easy for farmers to use the information. However, challenges remain, particularly in terms of connectivity and end-user training.

This approach represents a first step towards sustainable and accessible precision agriculture, while paving the way for future improvements, such as the implementation of an agricultural ontology and the development of applications tailored to the specific needs of farmers in Burkina Faso. The prospects offered by advances in technology and data will enable this architecture to be refined and extended in the years to come.

References

1. Agriculture and food security (2022). https://www-2021.usaid.gov/burkina-faso/agriculture-and-food-security. Accessed 10 Oct 2024
2. Agriculture and food security | Burkina Faso. U.S. Agency for International Development (2023). https://www.usaid.gov/burkina-faso/agriculture-and-food-security. Accessed 10 Oct 2024
3. Trawina, H., Diop, I., Malo, S., Traore, Y.: Architecture of a platform on sharing endogenous knowledge to adapt to climate change. In: Mejia, J., Muñoz, M., Rocha, Á., Quiñonez, Y. (eds.) CIMPS 2020. AISC, vol. 1297, pp. 131–141. Springer, Cham (2021). https://doi.org/10.1007/978-3-030-63329-5_9
4. Zougmoré, R.B., Läderach, P., Campbell, B.M.: Transforming food systems in Africa under climate change pressure: role of climate-smart agriculture. Sustainability **13**(8), 4305 (2021). https://doi.org/10.3390/su13084305, https://www.mdpi.com/2071-1050/13/8/4305. Accessed 09 Mar 2024. ISSN 2071-1050
5. Sonhaye, K.N.: L'intelligence artificielle, une opportunité pour l'agriculture au togo. ctd, no. 11 (2022). https://doi.org/10.4000/ctd.7219, http://journals.openedition.org/ctd/7219. Accessed 06 Sept 2023. ISSN 2491-1437
6. Karunathilake, E.M.B.M., Le, A.T., Heo, S., Chung, Y.S., Mansoor, S.: The path to smart farming: innovations and opportunities in precision agriculture. Agriculture **13**(8), 1593 (2023). https://doi.org/10.3390/agriculture13081593, https://www.mdpi.com/2077-0472/13/8/1593. Accessed 10 Oct 2024. ISSN 2077-0472
7. Anna Alex, M.S., Kanavalli, D.A., Head of Computer Science Department of M S Ramaiah Institute of Technology: Intelligent computational techniques for crops yield prediction and fertilizer management over big data environment. IJITEE **8**(12), 3521–3526 (2019). https://doi.org/10.35940/ijitee.L2622.1081219, https://www.ijitee.org/portfolio-item/L26221081219/. Accessed 03 Feb 2024. ISSN 22783075
8. Fenu, G., Malloci, F.M.: An application of machine learning technique in forecasting crop disease. In: Proceedings of the 2019 3rd International Conference on Big Data Research, Cergy-Pontoise, France, pp. 76–82. ACM (2019). https://doi.org/10.1145/3372454.3372474, http://dl.acm.org/doi/10.1145/3372454.3372474. Accessed 06 Mar 2024. ISBN 978-1-4503-7201-5

9. Degila, J., Tognisse, I.S., Honfoga, A.-C., et al.: A survey on digital agriculture in five west African countries. Agriculture **13**(5), 1067 (2023). https://doi.org/10.3390/agriculture13051067, https://www.mdpi.com/2077-0472/13/5/1067. Accessed 10 Oct 2024. ISSN 2077-0472
10. Jones, M.: IBM is acting on an agricultural data mass. TechHQ (2019). https://techhq.com/2019/05/ibm-is-acting-on-an-agricultural-data-mass/. Accessed 15 Mar 2023
11. Cravero, A., Bustamante, A., Negrier, M., Galeas, P.: Agricultural big data architectures in the context of climate change: a systematic literature review. Sustainability **14**(13), 7855 (2022). https://doi.org/10.3390/su14137855, https://www.mdpi.com/2071-1050/14/13/7855. Accessed 01 Feb 2024. ISSN 2071-1050
12. Bricout, M., Roussel, R., Monteil, C.: Agriculture de précision : Définition. In: INRAE (2022). https://doi.org/10.17180/VJVJ-2G81. https://dicoagroecologie.fr/dictionnaire/agriculture-deprecision/. Accessed 06 Aug 2024
13. Zheng, Y.-Y., Kong, J.-L., Jin, X.-B., Wang, X.-Y., Zuo, M.: CropDeep: the crop vision dataset for deep-learning-based classification and detection in precision agriculture. Sensors **19**(5), 1058 (2019). https://doi.org/10.3390/s19051058, https://www.mdpi.com/1424-8220/19/5/1058. Accessed 07 Sept 2023. ISSN 1424-8220
14. Semlali, B.-E.B., El Amrani, C., Ortiz, G.: Hadoop paradigm for satellite environmental big data processing. Int. J. Agric. Environ. Inf. Syst. **11**(1), 23– 47 (2020). https://doi.org/10.4018/IJAEIS.2020010102, https://services.igi-global.com/resolvedoi/resolve.aspx?doi=10.4018/IJAEIS.2020010102. Accessed 14 Mar 2024. ISSN 1947-3192, 1947-3206
15. Ramos, P., Prieto, F., Montoya, E., Oliveros, C.: Automatic fruit count on coffee branches using computer vision. Comput. Electron. Agric. **137**, 9–22 (2017). https://doi.org/10.1016/j.compag.2017.03.010, https://linkinghub.elsevier.com/retrieve/pii/S016816991630922X. Accessed 13 Mar 2024. ISSN 01681699
16. Feng, Y., Peng, Y., Cui, N., Gong, D., Zhang, K.: Modeling reference evapotranspiration using extreme learning machine and generalized regression neural network only with temperature data. Comput. Electron. Agric. **136**, 71–78 (2017). https://doi.org/10.1016/j.compag.2017.01.027, https://linkinghub.elsevier.com/retrieve/pii/S0168169916306275. Accessed 08 Aug 2024. ISSN: 01681699
17. Kanjilal, J.: An introduction to the lambda architecture. Developer.com. (2021). https://www.developer.com/design/intro-to-lambda-architecture/. Accessed 13 Mar 2024
18. Roukh, A., Fote, F.N., Mahmoudi, S.A., Mahmoudi, S.: Big data processing architecture for smart farming. Procedia Comput. Scie. **177**, 78–85 (2020). https://doi.org/10.1016/j.procs.2020.10.014, https://linkinghub.elsevier.com/retrieve/pii/S1877050920322791. Accessed 01 Feb 2024. ISSN 18770509
19. Kumar, Y.: Lambda architecture - realtime data processing (2020). https://doi.org/10.13140/RG.2.2.19091.84004, http://rgdoi.net/10.13140/RG.2.2.19091.84004. Accessed 12 Mar 2024
20. An optimized kappa architecture for IoT data management in smart farming. JUSPN **17**(2) (2022). https://doi.org/10.5383/JUSPN.17.02.002, https://iasks.org/articles/juspn-v17-i2-pp-59-65.pdf. Accessed 08 Aug 2024. ISSN 19237332, 19237332
21. Yang, X., Shu, L., Chen, J., et al.: A survey on smart agriculture: Development modes, technologies, and security and privacy challenges. IEEE/CAA J.

Autom. Sinica **8**(2), 273–302 (2021). https://doi.org/10.1109/JAS.2020.1003536, https://www.ieee-jas.net/en/article/doi/10.1109/JAS.2020.1003536. Accessed 18 May 2024. ISSN: 2329-9266, 2329-9274

22. López, I.D., Grass, J.F., Figueroa, A., Corrales, J.C.: A proposal for a multi-domain data fusion strategy in a climate-smart agriculture context. Int. Trans. Oper. Res. **30**(4), 2049–2070 (2023). . https://doi.org/10.1111/itor.12899, https://onlinelibrary.wiley.com/doi/10.1111/itor.12899. Accessed 01 Feb 2024. ISSN 0969-6016, 1475-3995
23. Alwidian, J., Rahman, S.A., Gnaim, M., Al-Taharwah, F.: Big data ingestion and preparation tools. MAS **14**(9), 12 (2020). https://doi.org/10.5539/mas.v14n9p12, http://www.ccsenet.org/journal/index.php/mas/article/view/0/43572. Accessed 08 Aug 2024. ISSN 1913-1852, 1913-1844
24. Sore, S., Traore, Y., Bikienga, M., Ouedraogo, F.T.: An architecture of a data lake for the sharing, agricultural knowledge in Burkina Faso. In: Saeed, R.A., Bakari, A.D., Sheikh, Y.H. (eds.) AFRICOMM 2022. Lecture Notes of the Institute for Computer Sciences, Social Informatics and Telecommunications Engineering, vol. 499, pp. 209–218. Springer, Cham (2023). https://doi.org/10.1007/978-3-031-34896-9_13. ISBN 978-3-031-34896-9
25. Trawina, H., Malo, S., Diop, I., Traore, Y.: Towards a social and semantic web platform for sharing endogenous knowledge to adapt to climate change. In: 2020 15th Iberian Conference on Information Systems and Technologies (CISTI), Seville, Spain, pp. 1–5. IEEE (2020). https://doi.org/10.23919/CISTI49556.2020.9141028, https://ieeexplore.ieee.org/document/9141028/. Accessed 10 Oct 2023. ISBN 978-989-54-6590-3
26. Ouafiq, E.M., Saadane, R., Chehri, A.: Data management and integration of low power consumption embedded devices IoT for transforming smart agriculture into actionable knowledge. Agriculture **12**(3), 329 (2022). https://doi.org/10.3390/agriculture12030329, https://www.mdpi.com/2077-0472/12/3/329. Accessed 13 Mar 2024. ISSN: 2077-0472
27. Journal, I.: Big data: An analytic architecture and prediction using spark for e-agriculture. https://www.academia.edu/37604418/Big_data_An_analytic_architecture_and_prediction_using_spark_for_E_agriculture. Accessed 30 July 2023
28. Lavelle, L.: Introduction À L'Ontologie. Editions du Félin (2008)
29. Lottes, P., Khanna, R., Pfeifer, J., Siegwart, R., Stachniss, C.: UAV based crop and weed classification for smart farming. In: 2017 IEEE International Conference on Robotics and Automation (ICRA), Singapore, Singapore, pp. 3024–3031. IEEE (2017). https://doi.org/10.1109/ICRA.2017.7989347, http://ieeexplore.ieee.org/document/7989347/. Accessed on 12 May 2023. ISBN 978-1-5090-4633-1

Edge-AI and IoT Based Smart Agriculture: Challenges and Use Cases

Babacar Mbaye Faye(✉), Fatou Diop, and Ibrahima Niang

Mathematics and Computer Science Department, Cheikh Anta Diop University, Dakar, Senegal
{babacarmbaye.faye,fatou110.diop,ibrahima1.niang}@ucad.edu.sn

Abstract. In order to make agriculture a more productive and sustainable sector, intelligent farming makes use of cutting-edge technology like artificial intelligence (AI) and the Internet of Things (IoT). These developments give farmers the ability to optimize irrigation, fertilization, and pest management by enabling the real-time collecting and analysis of data on crop health, soil quality, and climate. While about 25% of big farms are implementing IoT, the increasing use of Edge-AI is making applications like animal monitoring, weed identification, and crop disease detection possible even in areas with poor connectivity.

Although these technologies have transforming power, more general adoption is hampered by issues including high costs and accessibility constraints for small-scale farmers. This paper explores how Edge-AI and IoT are revolutionizing agriculture by examining their applications, addressing their challenges, and evaluating their role in enhancing decision-making, resource efficiency, and sustainability. With advancements in 5G and lightweight AI models, these technologies hold the promise of redefining farming practices and ensuring food security in an increasingly resource-constrained world.

Keywords: Smart Agriculture (SA) · Artificial Intelligence (AI) · Internet of Things (IoT) · Edge Computing (EC) · Edge-AI

1 Introduction

It is predicted that by 2050, there will be 9.7 billion people living on the planet, putting enormous pressure on the agricultural industry, which will need to increase food production considerably to meet demand [1]. The problem is made even more difficult by persistent hazards such as harsh weather conditions and the negative consequences of climate change, which interfere with conventional farming methods and reduce crop yields. To tackle these difficulties, researchers are using modern technological advances, which offer a promising future for improving farming practices and making them smarter, more sustainable and better adapted to the climate [2].

A. Sere et al. (Eds.): AFRI2 2025, CCIS 2536, pp. 94–104, 2026.
https://doi.org/10.1007/978-3-031-98327-6_7

The agricultural landscape is being transformed by the introduction of a network of interconnected devices capable of producing, exchanging and processing vast quantities of data. In agriculture, Internet of Things technologies such as sensors, drones and automated systems offer the possibility of real-time monitoring of crop health, soil conditions and environmental elements [3]. Not only does this connectivity simplify precise farm management and reduce resource wastage, it also opens up new prospects for remote farming techniques, which play a key role in optimizing today's extensive farming operations [4]. Edge computing refers to the processing of data at the edge of the network, as close as possible to its source, rather than relying solely on a centralized data center. In the field of intelligent agriculture, artificial intelligence at the edge can significantly improve decision-making processes by providing immediate data analysis, which is essential for time-sensitive agricultural decisions such as irrigation management and pest control. By integrating Edge artificial intelligence, farmers can use automated, intelligent systems that react immediately to changing conditions in the field, improving crop yields and reducing operating expenses. Collaboration, IoT and Edge-AI not only address traditional farming challenges, but also pave the way for innovative practices that are set to transform the field [5].

This article explores the integration of Edge-AI and IoT technologies in agriculture, focusing on real-life use cases and the challenges they present. First, it highlights key applications that demonstrate the transformative potential of these technologies. Secondly, it looks at the technical, economic and operational challenges that need to be overcome to fully exploit their benefits. By examining these aspects, this study aims to provide a global perspective on the future of smart agriculture.

The remainder of the paper is organized as follows: Sect. 2 presents the technological foundations of smart agriculture, focusing on Edge-AI and IoT. Section 3 highlights key use cases, including real-time monitoring, water management and warning systems. Section 4 explores the challenges associated with implementing these technologies, such as cost, data security and interoperability. Finally, Sect. 5 concludes the paper with a summary of the results and an outlook on future advances.

2 Background

2.1 Technological Evolution in Agriculture

From the Green Revolution to today's Gene Revolution, agricultural technology has undergone significant advancements over the course of its history [6]. These revolutions have not only increased food production globally but have also reshaped agricultural practices, making them more reliant on technology and data-driven insights to address modern challenges. These transformations have made agriculture an automated and data-driven industry, integrating technologies such as artificial intelligence (AI), Edge Computing, and the Internet of Things (IoT).

During the mechanization phase, machines replaced human power, leading to increased capacity, reduced labor costs, and improved product quality [7]. This phase was followed by increased automation and streamlined management. However, these advancements also resulted in the development of more complex, capital-intensive production systems. Recent advances in biotechnology, such as genome editing and recombinant DNA technology, have further improved crop resistance, quality, and yield. This ongoing technological evolution in agriculture can be understood through the prism of technological trajectories within a complex technological regime. These advancements set the stage for the exploration of specific technological innovations, such as drones, robotics, and biotechnology, which are reshaping agricultural practices in unique and impactful ways.

- Drone: also known as unmanned aerial vehicles UAVs, drones are becoming increasingly important in modern agriculture and are not just for photography or delivery services [8]. Drone technology in agriculture aims to create new opportunities and efficiencies rather than replace outdated methods. Although the initial investment has been significant, it has been offset by long-term savings. Reduced labor costs, targeted application of resources and improved crop yields all contribute to a positive return on investment.
- Robotics: has enabled the automation of irrigation, harvesting and field monitoring systems. Known as "agribots" or "agrobots", agricultural robots help farmers not only to carry out labor-intensive activities, but also to practice precision farming, ensuring that resources are used as efficiently as possible [9]. For example, some agrobots combined with sensors and artificial intelligence are used for selective harvesting of high-value fruit crops to identify ripe fruit and minimize waste. As a result, agricultural exploitations are becoming hi-tech centers due to this technological evolution.
- Biotechnology: is an important factor in agriculture, offering creative ways to increase crop production, improve nutritional value and reduce environmental impact. The presence of plant pests and diseases results in a significant loss of crop yield. Even if they are used in agriculture, agrochemicals may not be the best option in terms of sustainability these days. The use of biotechnology in agriculture, on the other hand, improves the exceptional quality of plants and livestock [10]. The evolution of flowers can be identified using scientific techniques such as genetic engineering, hybridization, tissue-engineering and plant breeding. The genome-editing technology known as CRISPR-Cas9 enables high target specificity at progressive speed and precision. It makes it possible to create transgenic flowers with desirable characteristics such as resistance to pests, drought and disease, and excessive yield capacity [11].

2.2 IoT, Edge Computing and Artificial Intelligence in Agricultural

IoT in Agriculture: IoT sensors, drones and automated machines collect huge amounts of data on crop health, soil conditions and environmental factors. They enable real-time monitoring and control through interconnected devices. What's more, the arrival of 5G has enhanced IoT capabilities by enabling lower latency in data transmission. This connectivity facilitates precision farming, resource optimization and waste reduction. The introduction of 5G technology has further enhanced IoT capabilities, enabling faster data transmission and lower latency [12]. The Fig. 1 shows the different sensor parameters in the agricultural sector.

Edge Computing: Edge computing pushes back the latency and cost limits of cloud computing. Indeed, Cisco's Edge Computing, introduced in 2014, bridges the gap by bringing cloud computing capabilities closer to end users [13]. In agriculture, Edge Computing enables real-time resource optimization, precise crop monitoring and improved decision-making processes. With Edge Computing, IoT systems have become more comprehensive, allowing IoT data to be processed as close to its source as possible, thus reducing latency [14].

Artificial Intelligence Applications: artificial intelligence techniques have enabled advanced data analysis and predictive modeling in agriculture. Deep learning, which simulates cognitive functions using interconnected neurons, facilitates sophisticated data processing and pattern recognition [15,16]. The collaboration of IoT, Edge computing and AI enables local data processing, improving crop, soil and water resource management, as well as weather monitoring. The Fig. 1 gives an overview of AI applications in agricultural practices.

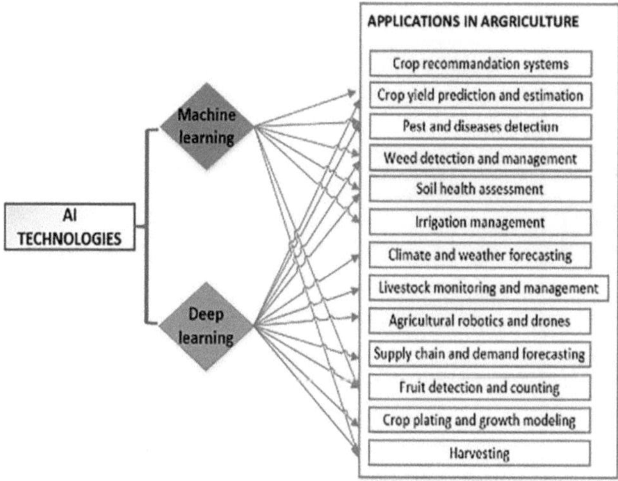

Fig. 1. AI application in agricultural practices

2.3 Current Adoption Trends

The integration of previous research and advancements provides a foundation for understanding the current adoption of IoT, Edge Computing, and AI in agriculture. For example, studies have shown how IoT-based systems with sensors and actuators improve soil monitoring and water management, enabling resource-efficient practices [17]. Similarly, research on Edge Computing highlights its role in reducing latency and bandwidth costs, making real-time decision-making feasible even in remote areas [18]. These advancements align with AI's capabilities in predictive analytics, as demonstrated in studies focused on pest identification and yield forecasting [19]. The adoption of IoT, Edge Computing, and AI in agriculture is accelerating, driven by the need for real-time decision-making and efficient resource management. IoT sensors are increasingly deployed to monitor soil moisture, weather conditions, and livestock health. Edge Computing addresses the limitations of cloud-based systems by providing localized data processing, which is especially beneficial in remote areas with limited connectivity.

AI applications are expanding, with farmers leveraging predictive analytics for optimizing irrigation schedules, detecting pests early, and forecasting yields. These technologies are transforming agricultural production models from being human-centered to information- and software-centric [20,21]. Smart systems powered by AI and IoT facilitate irrigation, weed control, and crop health monitoring in real time, offering significant benefits for both farmers and consumers. However, challenges persist in task allocation, data processing, privacy protection, and service stability. Addressing these barriers will be key to fully realizing the potential of these transformative technologies (Fig. 2).

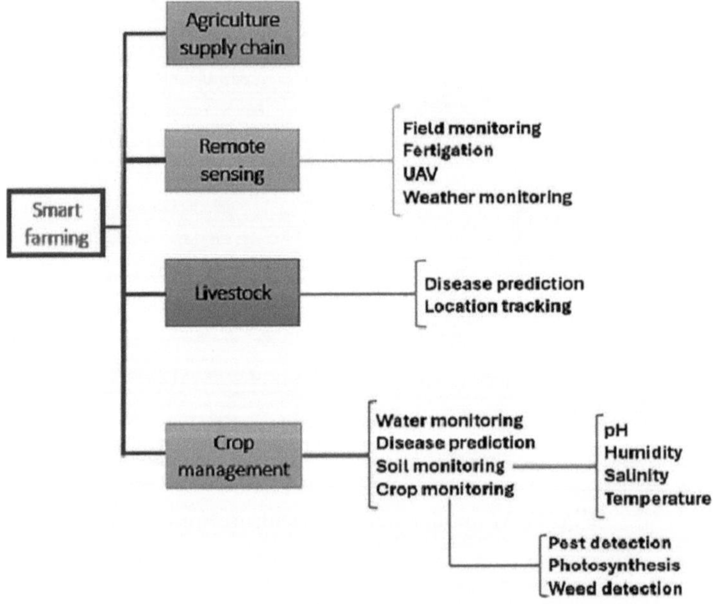

Fig. 2. Applications of smart agriculture

3 Use Cases

To better understand the potential of IoT and Edge-AI technologies in agriculture, in this section we look at specific use cases that highlight their real-world applications and benefits.

3.1 Managing Conflicts Between Herders and Farmers

In rural areas, problems between herders and farmers are increasingly frequent in Africa, particularly in Senegal, where deaths and injuries have been deplored. They are generally caused by the activities of shepherds in search of pasture and water. These conflicts threaten social cohesion and the objectives of development and economic integration. The origins of these conflicts are multiple, but the most common are the destruction of fields due to reduced grazing and occupation of dry-season pastures, poor animal maintenance and animal occupation points around water [22]. To address these challenges, a new technological solution is to use RFID (radio frequency identification) technology combined with Edge-AI and mobile applications to create a guided grazing system for herders. This system can help herders access watering points without encroaching on cultivated fields, thus reducing conflicts and improving resource management. The first step is to install RFID tags at watering points and at key points along designated paths leading to the watering points. These tags will emit unique identifiers that can be read by compatible devices, such as smartphones equipped with RFID readers.

Edge-AI devices locally analyze data from RFID readers and information on routes to water points from geolocation systems to dynamically update routes based on water point availability, quality and usage. This analysis is carried out locally, reducing latency and improving decision-making speed. A mobile application connected to the Edge-AI system can be used as a navigation tool to display optimized routes to the nearest water point, for example. The application needs to be designed so that it remains functional in areas with poor connectivity, exploiting offline maps and locally stored data.

In Ethiopia, the Livestock Data for Decisions (LD4D) initiative has eased conflicts between herders and farmers. Using IoT sensors, geographic information systems (GIS) and decision support tools, LD4D maps critical resources, guiding herders to less congested areas to reduce tensions. The integration of Edge-AI could enhance the effectiveness of this system by enabling local data analysis and real-time alerts, improving conflict prevention and resource management.

3.2 Managing Water Availability

In rural and agricultural environments, effective management of water availability is essential to safeguard animal welfare and optimize resource use. Monitoring water levels in tanks and troughs is essential to avoid water shortages, which can lead to dehydration and harm animal welfare. A system combining IoT and

Edge-AI can be used to prevent water shortages and ensure a continuous supply of water through monitoring and automation.

Water level sensors can be installed on platforms to provide real-time data on the amount of water available. And thanks to Edge-AI devices, water level forecasts can be made on a seasonal basis. This proactive approach means that immediate action can be taken before water supply becomes critical. Automating the replenishment of water tanks can significantly improve the efficiency of water management on farms. Based on data received and analyzed by water level sensors, the Edge-AI system decides when to activate water pumps or open valves to replenish water tanks. The system can be programmed with specific rules, such as maintaining certain water levels at different times of the day, or adjusting water levels according to weather conditions and livestock needs.

The intelligent Edge-cloud framework proposed in [23] for water quality monitoring has demonstrated the potential of these technologies. Their approach uses sensors that collect and transmit environmental data (chlorine, pH, turbidity, etc.) to Edge devices for near real-time pre-processing and detection. Edge servers use the MLP model to detect contaminants, while the cloud is used for intensive tasks such as pattern training and long-term storage. This collaboration guarantees efficient, scalable water management.

3.3 Alert Systems

A system integrating IoT sensors and Edge-AI devices can also be used as a real-time alert system for critical issues such as sudden drops in water quality or quantity, which can have a significant impact on livestock health if not dealt with quickly. Indeed, data collected by IoT sensors will be analyzed locally by Edge-AI devices, and analysis can include identifying trends and detecting anomalies that could indicate potential problems, such as contamination events or leaks causing rapid drops in water levels. When a potential problem is detected, the system will immediately send alerts to operations managers or janitors. These alerts can be sent by SMS, e-mail or push notifications via a dedicated application, ensuring that information reaches the parties responsible as quickly as possible. In certain situations, not only will alerts be sent, but automated responses can also be triggered. For example, if a significant drop in water quality is detected, the system can automatically divert water from a reserve reservoir or shut down a contaminated source to prevent damage.

Such a system can improve resource management, reduce latency and ensure efficient, proactive operations, making it an essential tool for livestock management (Fig. 3).

4 Challenges

Despite the promising use cases for IoT and Edge-AI technologies in agriculture, several challenges need to be addressed to ensure.

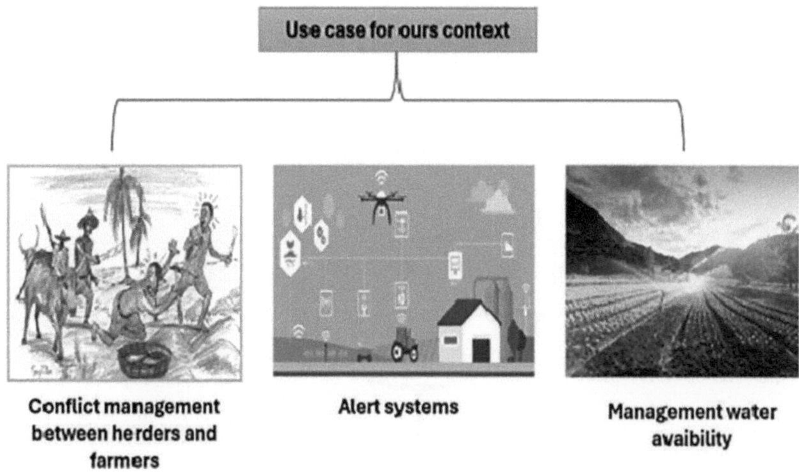

Fig. 3. Use cases

4.1 Technical Challenges

Many agricultural regions, particularly in developing countries, face limited or unreliable Internet connectivity, which can hamper the performance of IoT devices and Edge-AI systems dependent on data transmission and cloud integration. What's more, integrating IoT and Edge-AI into existing agricultural systems can be complex due to the diversity of equipment, legacy systems and different technology standards [24]. Added to this is the limited computing power and storage capacity of Edge devices, which restricts their ability to handle complex AI models or large volumes of data. Indeed, IoT devices generate large volumes of data that can be difficult to process and secure, particularly in decentralized configurations. These problems can be solved by developing offline functionalities, such as those using Edge-AI for local processing, to alleviate this problem by reducing dependence on continuous Internet access. The establishment of universal protocols and the adoption of modular systems can also enable progressive integration without disrupting existing processes. Regarding the limited capacity of Edge devices, the use of lightweight AI models optimized for Edge devices, such as TinyML or other resource-efficient machine learning frameworks can guarantee efficient local data processing without overloading the system (Fig. 4).

4.2 Economic Challenges

Deploying IoT devices, Edge-AI systems and supporting infrastructure requires significant investment, which can be an obstacle for small-scale farmers. In addition, IoT sensors, Edge devices and associated technologies require regular maintenance, which adds ongoing costs and necessitates technical expertise [25]. Government subsidies, cooperative models and scalable solutions tailored to small-

Fig. 4. Smart agriculture challenges

holder needs and budgets can reduce this burden by providing training programs for local technicians, and establishing cost-sharing mechanisms can improve system accessibility and longevity.

4.3 Social and Cultural Challenges

While technologies such as RFID and GIS can mitigate conflicts, the success of these solutions depends on cooperation between local players [26]. Indeed, farmers may be reluctant to adopt new technologies due to a lack of understanding or skepticism about their benefits. To overcome these problems, awareness campaigns and training can demonstrate tangible benefits through pilot projects involving community leaders to increase acceptance but also ensure wider adoption and sustainable use.

4.4 Environmental Challenges

IoT devices and Edge-AI systems require power, which can put a strain on energy resources in remote areas [27]. Added to this is the fact that the deployment of large-scale IoT systems can generate electronic waste over time, constituting an environmental challenge. Solutions to these problems include integrating renewable energy sources, such as solar-powered IoT devices, and implementing recycling programs and designing systems with recyclable components. These solutions can not only meet energy constraints but also reduce environmental impact.

5 Conclusion and Futures Perspectives

The use cases explored in this study show how these technologies can be applied to manage conflicts between herders and farmers, ensure efficient water use and establish robust warning systems for critical situations. Although these technologies are currently being used to improve resource management, real-time monitoring and decision-making, their implementation is still hampered by technical, economic, social and environmental challenges.

The growth of 5G infrastructure and the increasing development of lightweight Edge-AI technologies powered by renewable energies offers opportunities to reduce costs and environmental impact bringing potential solutions to these challenges. Collaboration between governments, technology providers and local stakeholders will also be beneficial in ensuring the accessibility and scalability of these innovations.

Future work should prioritize the development of modular, interoperable and secure systems, while strengthening farmer awareness and training initiatives to ensure the accessibility and long-term use of smart tools. In meeting these challenges, IoT and Edge-AI will remain essential in facilitating the transition to smart, resilient and equitable agriculture that meets the planet's growing food needs.

References

1. Author, F.: Article title. Journal **2**(5), 99–110 (2016)
2. Tao, W., Zhao, L., G., Liang, R.: Review of the internet of things communication technologies in smart agriculture and challenges. Comput. Electron. Agric. **189** (2021)
3. Heble, S., Kumar, A., Prasad, K.V.V.D., Samirana, S., Rajalakshmi, P., Dessai, U.B.: A low power iot network for smart agriculture. In: 2018 IEEE 4th World Forum on Internet of Things (WF-IoT), 17738040 (2018)
4. Quy, V.K., Nam, V.H., Linh, D.M., Ngoc, L.A., Gwanggil, J.: Wireless communication technologies for IoT in 5G: vision, applications and challenges. Wirel. Commun. Mob. Comput. (2022)
5. Elijah, O., et al.: An overview of internet of things (IoT) and data analytics in agriculture: benefits and challenges. IEEE Internet Things J. (2018)
6. Misra, S., Kumar, N.: Special issue on artificial intelligence, edge, and internet of things for smart agriculture. IEEE Micro **42**, 6–7 (2022)
7. Hamdan, M.F., et al.: Green revolution to gene revolution: technological advances in agriculture to feed the world. Plants **11** (2022)
8. Polymeni, S., et al.: The impact of 6G-IoT technologies on the development of agriculture 5.0: a review. Electronics (2023)
9. Ajay, A., Mohan, S.: UAV technology: applications, economical reliance and feasibility in Indian agriculture. Pantnagar J. Res. **22**, 1 (2024)
10. Nagalakshmi, M.V.N.: Sustainable agriculture 4.0 with 5G powered smart technology and green techniques. Available at SSRN. https://ssrn.com/abstract=4796809
11. Nautiyal, C.T., et al.: Importance of smart agriculture and use of artificial intelligence in shaping the future of agriculture. J. Sci. Res. Rep. **30**(3), 129–138 (2024)

12. Marinello, F., et al.: The path to smart farming: innovations and opportunities in precision agriculture. Agriculture (2023)
13. Ray, P.P.: Internet of things for smart agriculture: technologies, practices and future direction. J. Ambient Intell. Smart Environ. **9**, 395–420 (2017)
14. Zhang, X., et al.: Overview of edge computing in the agricultural internet of things: key technologies, applications, challenges. IEEE Access **8**, 141748–141761 (2020)
15. Bonomi, F., Milito, R., Zhu, J., Addepalli, S.: Fog computing and its role on the Internet of things. In: Proceedings 1st Edition MCC Workshop Mobile Cloud Computing, pp. 13–16 (2023)
16. Attri, I., Awasthi, L.K., Sharma, T.P.: Machine learning in agriculture: a review of crop management applications. Multimed. Tools Appl. **83**(5), 12875–12915 (2024)
17. Attri, I., et al.: A review of deep learning techniques used in agriculture. Ecol. Inform. 102217 (2023)
18. Katiyar, S., Farhana, A.: Smart agriculture: the future of agriculture using AI and IoT. J. Comput. Sci. (2021)
19. Khanna, A., Kaur, S.: Evolution of internet of things (IoT) and its significant impact in the field of Precision Agriculture. Comput. Electron. Agric. **157**, 218–231 (2019)
20. Adli, H.K., et al.: Recent advancements and challenges of AIoT application in smart agriculture: a review. Sens. (Basel Switz.) **23** (2023)
21. Farooq, M.A.A., et al.: Edge-AI for precision agriculture: applications and challenges (2022)
22. Saif, S., et al.: Smart e-agriculture monitoring systems. AI, Edge and IoT based Smart Agriculture (2022)
23. Saleh, M.: Role of interfaith mediation centre in managing conflict between farmers and herdsmen in Bauchi State, Nigeria. J. Afr. Hist. Cult. Arts **2**(2), 110–123 (2022)
24. Shahra, E.Q., Wu, W., Basurra, S., Aneiba, A.: Intelligent edge-cloud framework for water quality monitoring in water distribution system. Water **16**(2), 196 (2024). https://doi.org/10.3390/w16020196
25. Aski, V.J., et al.: Advances on networked ehealth information access and sharing: status, challenges and prospects. Comput. Netw. **204**, 108687 (2021)
26. de Oliveira, R.C., de Souza e Silva, R.D.: Artificial intelligence in agriculture: benefits, challenges, and trends. Appl. Sci. (2023)
27. Alzubi, A.A., Galyna, K.: Artificial intelligence and internet of things for sustainable farming and smart agriculture. IEEE Access **11**, 78686–78692 (2023)
28. Meuser, T., et al.: Revisiting edge AI: opportunities and challenges. IEEE Internet Comput. **28**(4), 49–59 (2024)

Towards a Semantic Architecture for Data Lakes

Aboubacar Sione(✉), Yaya Traore, and Julie Thiombiano

LAboratoire de Mathématiques et d'Informatique, Université Joseph KI-ZERBO, Ouagadougou, Burkina Faso
{aboubacar.sione,yaytra}@ujkz.bf, thiombianojulie@gmail.com

Abstract. Data lakes are a storage system for large volumes of raw heterogeneous data, adopting an area-based architecture. The main challenge of this architecture is the extraction and storage of raw data without any content monitoring, making data processing and access difficult. In this paper, we propose the integration of an ontology into this architecture, particularly in the data extraction and access areas. In the data extraction area, the role of the ontology is to eliminate ambiguities and terminological confusion to ensure reliable data extraction. In the data access area, the ontology will transform simple queries into semantic data access queries. This architecture improves the data preparation and data access stages, which are essential for leveraging stored data.

Keywords: Data lake · Architecture · Ontology · Area · Semantic

1 Introduction

With the boom in data in terms of volume and diversity [2], companies and institutions are facing unprecedented data management challenges. Traditionally, data warehouses have been used to store structured data from variety of sources. However, their rigidity and prior structuring requirements make these solutions less suited to current needs, where data is increasingly heterogeneous, unstructured, and derived from multiple formats and sources. This complexity makes access difficult and efficient reuse of data. In response to these challenges, data lakes, generally organized in data ponds [1] or areas [4], have emerged as centralized storage solutions for keeping raw format data. Nevertheless, this approach raises new problems: without a clear organization and semantic framework, data lakes can easily become "data swamps", where the abundance of unstructured raw data complicates their exploitation. The absence of semantics also makes data extraction, access, and integration more complex, limiting their usefulness to end users. The aim of this work is to propose a semantic architecture for data lakes, by integrating an ontology into the data ingestion and access processes. This approach aims to improve raw data management and exploitation on the one hand by eliminating terminological ambiguities and confusions during data extraction, to guarantee the quality and reliability of ingested data. And on

A. Sere et al. (Eds.): AFRI2 2025, CCIS 2536, pp. 105–116, 2026.
https://doi.org/10.1007/978-3-031-98327-6_8

the other hand, to enrich user queries in the data access phase by transforming simple queries into semantic queries, thus facilitating access to more relevant data.

By integrating an ontology, our architecture seeks to make data lakes more accessible, improve their organization, and enable richer, more precise data exploitation. This study lays the foundations for a generic data lake architecture organized into areas, where semantics plays a central role in the data ingestion and access stages, thus reinforcing their value for the user.

The rest of the paper is organised as follows: Sect. 2 gives an overview of the state of the art on data lake architectures. Then, in Sect. 3, we present our approach. In Sect. 4, we discuss our architecture and we end with a conclusion and perspectives in Sect. 5.

2 State of the Art

In this section, we will present the area-based architectures used for building a data lake and the work on these architectures.

2.1 Area-Based Architecture

In area-based architecture, data are allocated according to their degree of reorganization [5]. To present an area-based architecture, we rely on the one from [3] in Fig. 1. Their architecture proposes four areas, namely:

(1) **Ingestion area:** It involves the entry of data into the data lake. This area allows extracting data from its source and ingesting it into the data lake. This can be done in batches or streams.
   - **Data extraction:** This involves transferring data from its source and ingesting it into the data lake. This can be done by using tools such as talend Open Studio for Data integration, Sqoop, Flume, Flink, Samza, etc. Data transfer protocols such as HTTP and FTP can also be used for data ingestion.
   - **Metadata modeling:** Metadata modeling answers the question of how to structure and organize the metadata. Notably, it is a necessary step to make the content of a data lake findable, accessible, interoperable, and reusable. The majority of proposed models are either logic-based or graph-structured. Here we categorize the existing solutions based on the types of metadata models: generic models, data vault, and graph-based models.

(2) **Maintenance area:** After data ingestion into the data lake, it becomes a vast repository of data without any information. To make the data usable, the data lake must undergo a phase of data processing and maintenance.
   - **Dataset organization:** The problem with organizing data sets is how to structure and navigate massive, heterogeneous data sets. One solution to this problem is to define new structures for grouping and organizing

datasets for easy access to a data lake. The author classifies the underlying technologies used to build a data lake, such as catalogs, classification models and directed acyclic graphs.

- **Related dataset discovery:** Data set discovery in a data lake, also known as data discovery, aims to find a subset of relevant data with similarities or complementarities to a data set, e.g. similar attribute data or overlapping instance values. As a data lake stores and manages a considerable volume of data. It is not appropriate to query or integrate all of them. In contrast, it would be advantageous to first discover which datasets are useful for a specific purpose. So the links derived from the datasets are also an essential type of metadata for exploring the data lake and also avoiding the transformation of the data lake into a data swamp.
- **Data integration:** *Data integration* (DI) addresses the problem of combining multiple, heterogeneous data sources and providing users with a single data access point. Given the breadth of data sources, the need to first discover a relevant subset of data may present itself to users, before resolving source heterogeneity in terms of data models and schemas.
- **Metadata enrichment:** *Metadata enrichment* this study focuses on metadata enrichment as the process of creating metadata implicitly from raw data in the data lake, subject to intensive computation or human effort.
- **Data cleaning:** *Data cleansing* is the mechanism for discovering and solving data quality problems. The data quality problem. The data quality problem may reside in one or more sources at schema or instance level.
- **Data provenance:** *Data provenance* also known as data lineage, this component refers to the meta-information of recorded data. It indicates their origin, use and status in the data life cycle...
- **Schema evolution:** *Schema evolution* requires managing schema changes and integrity constraints. In data lakes, possible challenges to schema evolution could be schema heterogeneity and the frequency of changes. Whereas data warehouses have a relational schema that is generally not updated very often, data lakes are more agile systems in which data and metadata can be updated very frequently.

(3) **Exploration area:** Through this area, data lake users can explore and analyze data. It is important that useful information can be retrieved from data lakes. However, this is often a challenging task due to the large number of ingested sources, and the heterogeneity of data. A user may have knowledge of one or a few data sources, but rarely, if not never, all the datasets. Thus, the existing solutions mainly solve the querying problem in data lakes in the following two directions: explore the data lakes based on the relatedness of datasets or provide a unified query interface for heterogeneous data sources.

(4) **Storage area:** An important aspect of a data lake's architecture is the storage tier, which specifies the technology used for storing data. In what follows, we show that some approaches rely on the common relational or NoSQL databases while others have developed new storage systems or combinations (polystores). The upper part depicts such diverse choices, which could be

operated on-premise or in the cloud. We classify the existing data storage solutions for data lakes by how the ingested data is stored in the lake: as files, in a single database, or using polystores. We also briefly mention industrial solutions that build data lakes on cloud platforms.

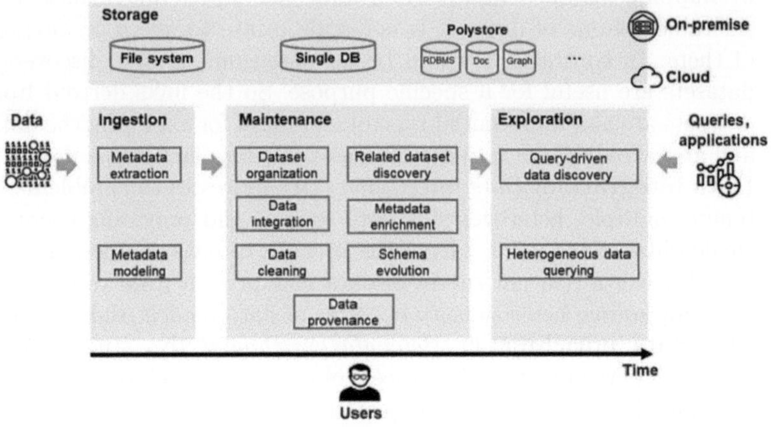

Fig. 1. Architecture of [3]

2.2 Work On Area-Based Architectures for Data Lakes

The architecture of a data lake typically consists of three layers [15]: The data sources layer, which includes all data sources in various formats. The data lake layer, which is composed of different data areas that organize the data according to their states while ensuring their storage. The commonly presented data areas are: the ingestion area, the storage area, the access area, the governance and security area... In their approach, data-related semantics are not taken into account.

In [7], the architecture of the data lakes essentially covers five areas. The personalized collection area: this allows data to be retrieved from its sources, this area also allows users to pre-process the data. Data ingestion: based on the extraction of data from its sources. Data storage: used for data persistence using a Hadoop distributed file system. Exploitation and analysis: used for data processing. Data visualization: used to learn from the data. For example, in [5], which can be seen as an area architecture, the author proposes a data lake architecture applied to medical images. According to him, the implementation of a data lake applied to medical data should be based on an architecture typical of the domain studied. However, the existing architectures and metadata management systems proposed in the literature are too generic to be applied to medical data. This is why he proposes to slightly modify HANDLE (Handling metAdata maNagement in Data LakEs) from [16], which is a graph-based metadata management system that is best suited to the case studied. The proposed architecture is therefore based on areas rather than ponds, because according to the authors, the pond-based architecture does not allow data to be stored in its raw state. The area-based architecture, on the other hand, does. The architecture is divided into four areas: the transient landing area: representing the data ingestion module. The raw data area: used to store raw data. The scenic area: dedicated to data analysis and processing. The sandbox area: used by data specialists to discover pattern associations in the data.

As data security is crucial in data management, this issue was not taken into account in the work of [5,7], however the manuscript [13] allows us to take this issue into account. In [13] Amazon Web Services (AWS) proposes an architecture with four areas, including an area dedicated to security. But in Amazon Web Services, the integration of data through semantics has not been proposed.

In the same way to [8], the data lake architecture focuses on seven areas. In this architecture, unlike the [13] architecture, data processing is divided into two areas: the refinement area and the reliable data area. In addition, we have a sandbox area: this is the access area for more advanced analyses by professional users from the reliable data area and the consumption area: this is used by professional users for analyses adapted to their needs. In this architecture, we notice a lack of semantics in the various areas.

Another way of seeing data lake architectures is the ingestion mode used to inject the data. The most popular architecture for this problem in the literature is the lamda architecture of [6]. In this architecture, a so-called lamda layer is presented, the specificity of which is that it is an additional layer to other defined structures in order to organize data into batches and flows. It consists of the data acquisition layer: which is used to acquire data from the various sources; the messaging layer: to guarantee data delivery; the data ingestion layer: used to ingest data for storage and processing; the storage layer: used to store all kinds of data; the Lambda layer: first of all, there is the batch layer (used to process data in batches. Its role is to convert raw data into modeled data), then the speed layer (used to ensure real-time processing of data from the injection layer) and the service layer (used to route data to applications dedicated to consumption). We identify four additional levels in [9], compared to [6], namely: Data governance: i) which enables users to obtain reliable data. ii) Data lineage: which presents the life cycle of data from the first to the last source. iii) Data audit: which refers to the mechanisms for accessing and modifying data. The exploitation level: which gives more details about the data after it has been retrieved by users. Data security level: used to protect data. The infrastructure and exploration management level: this level concerns the deployment of the Hadoop ecosystem for a data lake. The insights level: represents the business value that data can represent once it has been transferred, analysed and observed.

From the basis of what the lamda architecture [6] proposes, namely to be a reference to the hybrid operation of data, another hybrid processing architecture has been constructed by [10]. In this architecture, the authors propose their hybrid processing architecture, which they call BRAID. In this architecture, we have two processing engines: the batch processing engine, intended for basic data, and the stream processing engine, intended for data arriving in real time. The architecture contains three layers: the storage layer, which maintains all the data streams to prepare the data for the next layer; the processing layer, which is made up of the batch and real-time processing branches; and the results layer, where the results of data processing are stored and made available for queries (batch or stream). The special feature of this architecture is the interconnection between the storage and results layers. BRAID and the lamda architecture do not take into account the problems associated with data semantics in the data lake.

In [11], the authors give their vision of data lakes architecture through a definition that presents their architecture as an abstraction of existing architectures. Their definition is as follows: "the functional architecture of a data lake is composed of four essential areas, each containing two layers: the data processing layer and the data storage layer". The four areas in question are the data ingestion area: which injects data into the data lake, which can be done in batches, flows or hybrids; the preparation area: which enables the data to be processed; the analysis area: which is used for reporting; and the governance area: which is transversal to the other three areas. However, the different processing phases do not seem explicit to us, particularly with regard to the processing of data in the preparation or analysis areas. Also, the authors do not abode the semantics of the data in the data lake.

In [3], the authors first propose functions for each level. This describes a three level link between the users of the data lake and the storage functions which encompass several different technologies. For the ingestion area, they associate the functions of extraction and metadata modeling. At the maintenance level we have functions such as dataset organization, data integration, data cleansing, discovery of related datasets, metadata enrichment, schema evolution and data provenance. For the last area, exploration, they present the functions for discovering data using the query set and searching for heterogeneous data. The authors also address the notion of semantic enrichment, but not explicitly. This is why, based on their model, we are proposing our data lake architecture that integrates data semantics so that the data is understood, accepted and shared by everyone. This will lead to the modeling of metadata in a data lake. Metadata is structured information that explains, describes or facilitates the understanding of data in order to better explore it. The following section presents the various components of our architecture. This architectural approach seems very interesting to us, but the semantics of the data are not taken into account at the level of the access area and the exploitation area.

In [12], we mentioned PERSEUS (PERSonalised Exploration by User Support) set out to provide a computer-assisted approach to a data lake in three phases. Firstly, the co-construction of a semantic metadata catalog on top of the data lake to facilitate semantic annotation of the data lake. Secondly, the modeling of indicators and analysis dimensions using a multidimensional ontology to enable users to explore the content of the data lake. Finally, the enrichment of indicator definition with customization aspects, based on tools and user preference. Their architecture is composed of five areas: the raw area, which contains heterogeneous data sources; the normalized area, where data is extracted; the curated area, where the data sets required to calculate the necessary values are stored; and finally, the application area, where the tables in the curated area undergo an aggregation of indicators in order to display them on the graphical interface.

An architecture for semantic data lakes called *Squerall* proposed by [17]. The solution proposes distributed query execution techniques and strategies for querying varied data.

Table 1. Comparative table of different architectures.

Papers	Area architecture	Uses an ontology
Ravat and Zhao	(√)	
Hai et al.	(√)	
Sara Parente	(√)	
John and Mistra	(√)	
AWS	(√)	
Mehmood et al.	(√)	
Bianchini et al.		(√)
Dibowski et al.		(√)
Mami et al.		(√)

In Table 1, we present a few data lake architectures, checking whether they are based on area-based architecture and whether they integrate semantics. To do this, we'll use the symbol (√) for the affirmative, and no symbol if the criterion is not taken into account. We can classify the architectures in the Table 1 into two, those organized in areas but which do not integrate semantics. We also have architectures that integrate semantics but are not organized into areas. More concretely, the authors of [9] propose a semantic layer, but their approach is not based on areas architectures. We want to use ontologies in both the ingestion and access phases. The authors of [12] have taken a step in this direction, but their architecture does not contain an ingestion area. Nor does metadata modeling play a role in their approach. For this reason, [13] provides an overview of semantic-based data management and integration methods, linking them to semantic data lakes. The authors show that the community faces several challenges, highlighting the gap between data lakes and current platforms, as well as the need for semantic technologies to model the context in which heterogeneous data appears. They remain convinced that big data and semantic web technologies can reinforce each other, and that more powerful solutions for semantic data lakes will be available in the future. In the rest of our work, we will focus on the architecture proposed by [3] in Fig. 1 because it takes metadata modeling into account. The authors also propose a semantic enrichment function in the maintenance area. We believe that this function is more appropriate for the access area, as it is in this area that users will formulate SQL queries. Our aim is to improve it by adding an ontology that will replace the additional tasks users have to perform to retrieve data. In this work, we propose to replace these user tasks with an ontology that integrates the user's knowledge. This method is described in the next section, where we dissociate the metadata organization function and place it in another area called the governance and security area.

3 Our Approach

Our architecture, inspired by that of [3], is presented below in Fig. 2. Our proposal integrates an ontology into the architecture. The special feature of our approach is that the ontology will not only use semantics, but will also guide the modeling of metadata. Ontology concepts can be used as metadata. Relationships are semantic relationships that enable reasoning about the data.

This approach enriches the data collection process, enabling us to make joins and correspondences between attributes. We also use ontology in the access area to enrich semantic queries with SPARQL. The ontology being interesting, the choice of a good ontology is opposed given that the ontology is very complex to conceive. What's needed is an ontology containing the concepts of the domain.

3.1 Data Ingestion Area

This area is the first in the data lake. It includes the extraction functions, a knowledge base function of ontological type to facilitate the extraction of data from the domain concerned, which we call ontology **A**. The role of this ontology is to avoid terminological confusion right from the start of the process, and to facilitate data integration, sharing and interpretation. Indeed, as data arrives from multiple sources, there may be confusion at term level, where a term may have several synonyms or acronyms. The ontology sets up a framework to standardize concepts and the relationships between them, so as to avoid ambiguity as soon as the data is ingested into the data lake. On the one hand, this ensures better data quality within the data lake, while on the other, it avoids the need for human intervention to interpret or correct ambiguities. This area also includes a modeling function, where the concepts derived from the ontology are modeled using either graph or set methods.

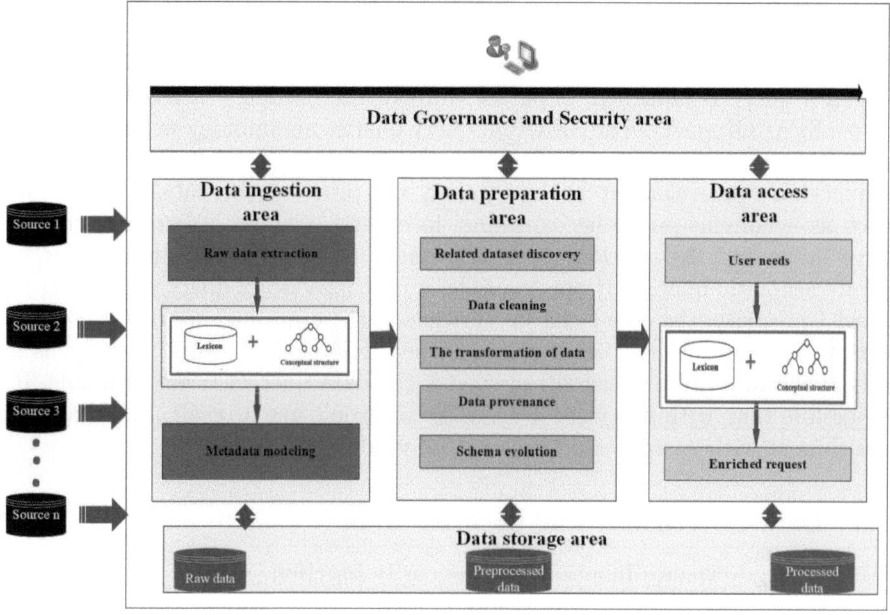

Fig. 2. Our data lake architecture

3.2 Data Storage Area

In the field of data lakes, the most fashionable technology for data storage is the Hadoop HDFS distributed file system. But just before this environment we have Relational databases and NoSQL databases. We intend to use these two technologies to set up our data lake.

Three types of data are stored in the data lake through the storage area. We have the raw data, which is the data that has been extracted after going through the ontology and modeling. Then we have the pre-processed data, which is the data that has been cleaned up, undergone missing data preparation, outlier processing, and undergone at least one transformation. We envisage an attribute *Area Indicator* to generate data polymorphism such as the simultaneous storage of multiple representations of the same data entities. Each representation corresponds to the initial data entity, modified or reformatted for a specific need. to return the area to which a data belongs. This area is intended to be transversal to the storage, processing, and access areas.

3.3 Data Preparation Area

We focus on the maintenance area described by [3] in the 2.1 section, but we don't take into account the semantic enrichment function in this area. The metadata organization function is also assigned to another area.

3.4 Data Access Area

In this area, we have functions such as data discovery using the SQL query set. When a query is launched, it passes through the ontology, which translates it into a SPARQL query. The SPARQL query queries an ontology we call **B**. When a user issues a SQL query, the **B** ontology intervenes to enrich the query. After a query on a data element X, the ontology will provide other labels on the data, such as synonyms and other concepts, in order to achieve a better result. We have integrated the ontology to enrich query terms. By enriching queries, we create semantic queries. If, for example, a user provides a query containing the word University, the query can be enriched with terms such as *Institutes*, *High school.* The word *University* is thus enriched with similar terms. This opens up other relevant search possibilities, even if the data queried is not available. It ' s possible that with the word University we won't get a result, but thanks to enrichment with *Institutes* or *High school* we do get a result.

3.5 Data Governance And Security Area

We have a governance function and a security function.

- **Data Governance And Security Area** supports the data life cycle and data quality. Thanks to this function, the data lake avoids being transformed into a data swamp.
- **Security** protects data by managing access to it. To achieve this, we opt for controlled access on two levels: authentication and authorization. We'll base our approach on that of [4]. For authentication, they use the Kerberos authentication prototype, which creates a proxy server that receives a request from the client. If the request is legitimate, the requester receives a ticket with a timestamp. Then, they use Apache Ranger for the authentication offered by HDFS.

4 Discussion

In existing approaches without ontology, within the data ingestion area, metadata modeling relies on extensive work by domain specialists and experts, who must conduct a thorough preliminary analysis to structure this metadata. With our method, this task is simplified through the use of ontology, which integrates domain knowledge and thus eases the workload of specialists.

In the data access area, our ontology, with its semantics and inference engine, enables query enrichment by adding additional terms, thereby increasing the chances of providing relevant answers to each question posed.

Thus, our approach stands out from classical methods by enabling the semi-automation of metadata modeling and simplifying data access. Acting as a domain expert, the ontology enriches queries and reduces the need for human intervention, thereby improving the efficiency and accuracy of data lake exploitation.

The ontology offers flexibility with regard to data sources and term evolution, which is very important for a data lake. This flexibility is explained by the fact that, in our approach, the ontology intervenes at two levels: first, between metadata extraction and their modeling. The concepts of the ontology can be used as entities in the metadata modeling process. Existing approaches such as [12,14,17] do not allow achieving this.

Another very important aspect of this architecture is that it enables artificial intelligence platforms to easily digest large quantities of data. This digestion is made possible by the elimination of terminological ambiguities.

As with data lakes, where data security is still maturing, our architecture is not immune to this issue. This is a limitation for our architecture.

5 Conclusion

In this paper, we discussed data lakes and their architectures to facilitate their implementation. Existing architectures in the literature range from data pond architectures to area-based architectures. The functions contained in the ingestion and access areas do not allow for leveraging knowledge of the same domain with different labels. It is in this context that we propose our data lake architecture. This architecture is inspired by that of [3], integrating an ontology to encompass all themes of a domain. Our architecture includes a total of five areas: the ingestion area, the preparation area, the access area, the storage area, and the governance and security area. We discussed the benefits of adding an ontology to a data lake architecture. This will help avoid terminological confusion on the one hand, and on the other hand, the ontology will enrich user queries.

In our future work, we plan to propose algorithms to implement each function of each area in our architecture. Finally, a metadata modeling method based on ensemble methods will be proposed after our ontology has capitalized on domain knowledge, particularly that of agricultural data in Burkina Faso.

References

1. Inmon, B.: Data Lake Architecture: Designing the Data Lake and Avoiding the Garbage Dump. Technics Publications (2016)
2. Madera, C.: L'évolution des systèmes et architectures d'information sous l'influence des données massives: les lacs de données. Thèse de doctorat. Université Montpellier (2018)
3. Hai, R., Koutras, C., Quix, C., Jarke, M.: Data lakes: a survey of functions and systems. IEEE Trans. Knowl. Data Eng. (2023)
4. Rangarajan, S., Liu, H., Wang, H., Wang, C.-L.: Scalable architecture for personalized healthcare service recommendation using big data lake. In: Beheshti, A., Hashmi, M., Dong, H., Zhang, W.E. (eds.) ASSRI 2015/2017. LNBIP, vol. 234, pp. 65–79. Springer, Cham (2018). https://doi.org/10.1007/978-3-319-76587-7_5
5. Parente, S.: The design of a data lake architecture for the healthcare use case: problems and solutions (2020)

6. John, T., Misra, P.: Data Lake for Enterprises: Leveraging Lambda Architecture for Building Enterprise Data Lake. Packt, Birmingham (2017)
7. Mehmood, H., et al.: Implementing big data lake for heterogeneous data sources. In: 2019 IEEE 35th International Conference on Data Engineering Workshops (ICDEW), pp. 37–44 (2019)
8. LaPlante, A., Sharma, B.: Architecting data lakes data management architectures for advanced business use cases (2016)
9. Panwar, A., Bhatnagar, V.: Data lake architecture: a new repository for data engineer. Int. J. Organ. Collect. Intell. (IJOCI) **10**(1), 63–75 (2020)
10. Giebler, C., Stach, C., Schwarz, H., Mitschang, B.: Braid. In: Proceedings of the 7th International Conference on Data Science, Technology and Applications, pp. 294–301 (2018)
11. Ravat, F., Zhao, Y.: Data lakes: trends and perspectives. In: Hartmann, S., Küng, J., Chakravarthy, S., Anderst-Kotsis, G., Tjoa, A.M., Khalil, I. (eds.) DEXA 2019, Part I. LNCS, vol. 11706, pp. 304–313. Springer, Cham (2019). https://doi.org/10.1007/978-3-030-27615-7_23
12. Bianchini, D., De Antonellis, V., Garda, M.: A semantics-enabled approach for personalised Data Lake exploration. Knowl. Inf. Syst. **66**(2), 1469–1502 (2024)
13. Hoseini, S., Theissen-Lipp, J., Quix, C.: A survey on semantic data management as intersection of ontology-based data access, semantic modeling and data lakes. J. Web Semant. **81**, 100819 (2024)
14. Dibowski, H., Schmid, S., Svetashova, Y., Henson, C., Tran, T.: Using semantic technologies to manage a data lake: data catalog, provenance and access control. In: SSWS@ ISWC, pp. 65–80 (2020)
15. Janssen, N., Ilayperuma, T., Jayasinghe, J., Bukhsh, F., Daneva, M.: The evolution of data storage architectures: examining the secure value of the data lakehouse. J. Data Inf. Manage. 1–26 (2024)
16. Eichler, R., Giebler, C., Gröger, C., Schwarz, H., Mitschang, B.: HANDLE - a generic metadata model for data lakes. In: Song, M., Song, I.-Y., Kotsis, G., Tjoa, A.M., Khalil, I. (eds.) DaWaK 2020. LNCS, vol. 12393, pp. 73–88. Springer, Cham (2020). https://doi.org/10.1007/978-3-030-59065-9_7
17. Mami, M.N., Graux, D., Scerri, S., Jabeen, H., Auer, S., Lehmann, J.: Uniform access to multiform data lakes using semantic technologies. In: Proceedings of the 21st International Conference on Information Integration and Web-Based Applications & Services, pp. 313–322 (2019)

New Metric Procedure for Better Decision-Making in the Case of Votes

Rasmané Pagbelguem(✉) and Zoïnabo Savadogo

Joseph KI-ZERBO University, Ouagadougou, Burkina Faso
rasmane_pagbelguem@ujkz.bf, serezenab@yahoo.fr

Abstract. In any voting process, one of the most important steps is the aggregation of individual preferences into a collective preference. For the approval voting system, aggregation is performed using aggregation operators or metrics, which are mathematical functions that combine and summarize multiple numerical values into a single one, such that the final result accounts for all individual values. The aggregation of preferences using metric procedures is highly regarded in the literature. However, some of these procedures often yield outcomes with multiple ties and are challenging to implement in practice, particularly in the African context. To address these shortcomings, we propose in this work a voting method based on the principle of approval voting and a metric procedure. The new method allows for the evaluation of all candidates, reduces compensatory effects, and produces a result without ties. We have applied this metric procedure to examples, and we observe that our results outperform those produced by some existing metric procedures in the literature.

Keywords: Approval Voting · Metric Procedure · Aggregation Function · Profile

1 Introduction

Voting systems (or electoral procedures) can be defined as mechanisms that derive a collective decision (the election of one or more candidates) from individual preferences. These mechanisms are often formalized and analyzed in an ordinal context: each individual is assumed to be able to express their preferences by choosing or ranking, without contradiction, the set of options from the one they deem best to the one they like the least [7]. According to [1], three main families of voting systems can be distinguished: majority systems, proportional systems, and mixed systems. Each family of methods has its advantages and disadvantages, which largely depend on the principle of aggregating individual preferences. Aggregation methods (or decision rules) are mathematically represented by functions that, for each combination (or profile) of individual preferences, yield a ranking (or selection) of the options under collective judgment. But how can we find an operator that aggregates individual preferences

A. Sere et al. (Eds.): AFRI2 2025, CCIS 2536, pp. 117–129, 2026.
https://doi.org/10.1007/978-3-031-98327-6_9

into a collective preference that most faithfully represents the individual preferences?

Borda [3] and Condorcet [4] demonstrated as early as the late 18th century that the majority principle, well-known and widely used, could lead to paradoxes and controversial outcomes. As for mixed systems (approval or evaluation), the operators used (arithmetic mean, weighted mean, median, etc.) are not without criticism. In fact, mean-type aggregators allow for compensatory effects, and the median often results in multiple ties.

Thus, the previous concern remains a challenge for both practitioners of social choice theory and mathematicians.

In this work, we propose a voting method based on the principle of approval voting, where the aggregation function is a metric procedure. This means a function that evaluates the distances, also known as disagreements, between voters on a given profile. The consensus will then be the profile with the least disagreements. The main objective is to perform an aggregation that evaluates all candidates, reduces compensatory effects, and provides a result with broad voter agreement.

Before explicitly describing this new approach, we will present some aggregation operators used in voting systems and then review a few metric procedures already existing in the literature.

2 State of the Art

2.1 Some Preference Aggregation Operators

An aggregation operator can be considered as a mathematical function that takes an input, called the argument, and produces a unique output representing the overall score of the input. Each input has a unique output associated with it. The aggregation function is generally denoted by $y = f(x)$, where x the argument and y is the aggregated value. The argument x can be a vector of size n: $x = (x_1, x_2, ..., x_n)$,and $x_1, x_2, .., x_n$ are referred to as the components of x. There are several aggregation operators in the literature, but we will limit ourselves in the following to presenting the most commonly used operators, without claiming to be exhaustive. We refer the reader to the following references for a more in-depth study: [2,5,6].

2.2 Weighted Sum and Average Operators

The weighted sum or weighted arithmetic mean is defined by:

$\psi(a_1, ..., a_n = \sum_{i=1}^{n} \omega_i a_i$, where $\omega_i \in [0, 1]$ are weights such that $\sum_{i=1}^{n} \omega_i = 1$ and ψ an agregation function.

Other types of averages exist (geometric, harmonic, etc.), which can all be expressed in the form:

$$M_f(a_1, ..., a_n) = f^{-1}\left(\sum_{i=1}^{n} \omega_i f(a_i)\right), \tag{1}$$

where f is a strictly increasing continuous function et M and M denotes weighted average. All generalized means are idempotent, continuous, and strictly monotonic. Only the weighted sum satisfies stability under linear scale change [9].

2.3 Ordered Weighted Average (OWA)

The OWA (Ordered Weighted Average) operator was introduced by Yager [12]. It is defined by:

$$OWA_{\omega}(a_1, ..., a_n) = \sum_{i=1}^{n} \omega_i a_{(i)} \tag{2}$$

with $\omega = (\omega_1, ..., \omega_n)$ a weight vector, $\omega_i \in [0, 1]$ such that $\sum_{i=1}^{n} \omega_i = 1$ and where the notation (.) indicates a permutation of the indices such that $a_{(1)} \leq ... \leq a_{(n)}$.

Thus, the weight is not applied to the sources but to the rank of the quantities. The following special cases are important:

- $\omega_1 = 1$ (and therefore $\omega_i = 0, i > 0$): minimum operator;
- $\omega_n = 1$: maximum operator;
- $\omega_i = 1$ for a given i: order statistic of rank i;
- if n is odd, $\omega_{\frac{n+1}{2}} = 1$: median, and if n is even, the median is defined by $\omega_{\frac{n}{2}} = \omega_{\frac{n}{2}+1} = \frac{1}{2}$ Generally, we have:

$$OWA_{\omega}^{f}(a_1, ..., a_n) = f^{-1}\left(\sum_{i=1}^{n} \omega_i f(a_{(i)})\right) \tag{3}$$

where f is a continuous, strictly increasing function.

Symmetric Sums. They were introduced by Sylvert in 1979 [7]. Symmetric sums are defined as continuous, non-decreasing, neutral operators that satisfy $\psi^{(2)}(0, 0) = 0$, $\psi^{(2)}(1, 1) = 1$, and are stable for scale intersection, i.e. $\psi(a_1, a_2) = 1 - \psi(1 - a_1, 1 - a_2)$. They are of the form:

$$\psi(a_1, a_2) = \left(1 + \frac{g(1 - a_1, 1 - a_2)}{g(a_1, a_2)}\right)^{-1} \tag{4}$$

where g is an increasing, continuous function with $g(0, 0) = 0$.

2.4 The Majority Grade

From [15].

Let c_i be a candidate or competitor with the grades or assessments $g_{i1}, g_{i2}, ...g_{in}$ with n the number of judges or voters and such that $g_{i1} \succcurlyeq g_{i2} \succcurlyeq ... \succcurlyeq g_{in}$. The notation $a \succcurlyeq b$ means that *a is at least as good as b*.

$f : \mathcal{L}^n \times \mathcal{A} \rightarrow \mathcal{L}$ a ranking function which associates a unique rank (in the same language) for each candidate with each voting method, where $\mathcal{A}$ is the set of candidates. Then the majority evaluation or majority rank $f^{maj}(c_i)$ is by definition :

$$f^{maj}((g_{i1}, g_{i2}, ..., g_{in}), c_i) = \begin{cases} \pi_{\frac{n+1}{2}}(g_{i1}, g_{i2}, ..., g_{in}) & \text{if } n \text{ is odd} \\ \pi_{\frac{n+2}{2}}(g_{i1}, g_{i2}, ..., g_{in}) & \text{if } n \text{ is even} \end{cases}$$

where π_j is the orthogonal projection onto the jth component of the vector $(g_i1, g_i2, ..., g_in)$.

For example, if 5 judges award the grades 4, 8, 7, 9, 5 à c_i, we have; $f^{maj}((9, 8, 7, 5, 4), c_i) = \pi_3(9, 8, 7, 5, 4) = 7$.

3 Metric Procedures

Metric procedures are decision support methods that aggregate preferences or permutations. Their main aim is to introduce a quantitative dimension (measurement) into decision-making processes.

The aggregation of preferences using metric procedures is very popular in the literature. We present here the most frequently used.

3.1 Blin's Metric

In 1976 Blin proposed a model [10] which consists of determining a linear consensus ordering from linear individual rankings (strict order relations). The rankings are represented in matrix form:

$$P^t = [p_{ir}^{(t)}], t \in T, \text{ where}$$

$$p_{ik}^{(t)} = \begin{cases} 1 & \text{if } x_i \text{ occupies rank } r \in \{1; 3/2; 2; ..., m-1; m-1/2; m\} \\ 0 & \text{sinon} \end{cases}$$

Blin's approach consists in determining a consensus of arrangements noted here $Q = [q_{it}]$ and showing the minimum of disagreements with the matrix: $P^t = [p_{ir}^t], t \in T$. So we need to solve :

$$\min \left\{ \sum_{t=1}^{s} \sum_{i=1}^{m} \sum_{k=1}^{m} |q_{ik} - p_{ik}^t| : Q \in SO \right\} \tag{5}$$

With:

- ◇ **SO:** The set of strict order relations,
- ◇ **s:** the set of decision-makers,
- ◇ **m:** is the number of candidates.

Noting:

$$\delta_{BL}(Q, P^t) = \sum_{i=1}^{m}\sum_{k=1}^{m} |q_{ik} - p_{ik}^t| \tag{6}$$

The problem is written:

$$\min\left\{\sum_{t=1}^{s} \delta_{BL}(Q, P^t) : Q \in SO\right\}. \tag{7}$$

The problem is thus transformed into an assignment problem whose optimal solution is obtained by applying a classic solution algorithm: the Hungarian method.

3.2 The Kemeny-Snell Metric

The individual rankings are represented in matrix form by $M^{(t)} = [m_{ik}^{(t)}], t \in T(\text{set of voters})$ with

$$m_{ik}^{(t)} = \begin{cases} 1 & \text{if}\, x_i succ^{(t)} x_k \\ 1/2 & \text{si}\, x_i \approx^{(t)} x_k \\ 0 & \text{si}\, x_k succ^{(t)} x_i \end{cases}$$

The aggregation consists in determining a transitive matrix $B = [b_{ik}]$ which is the most representative of the matrices $M^{(t)} = [m_{ik}^{(t)}], t \in T$. Consensus is obtained by minimising the number of disagreements between B and $M^{(t)}$ i.e.:

$$\min\left\{\sum_{t=1}^{s}\sum_{i=1}^{m}\sum_{k=1}^{m} |b_{ik} - m_{ik}^{(t)}| : B \in WO\right\} = \left\{\min\sum_{t=1}^{s} \delta_{KS}(B, M^{(t)}) : B \in WO\right\} \tag{8}$$

where WO is the set of complete pre-orders. The optimal matrix B^* corresponds to the matrix representation of a complete pre-order. This optimisation problem cannot be solved by classical mathematical programming methods because of the transitivity of the matrix B; but various solution algorithms have been proposed by Leese, Norman and Cook & Saipe (see [13] and [11]).

3.3 The New Metric Procedure for Multi-Decider Makers Choice (NMPMMC)

It was proposed in 2016 by Zoïnabo Savadogo et al. [14]. This procedure uses the approval voting system but with a multi-choice preference with four indifference levels. The idea is to rank the candidates with the possibility of having more than two candidates in the same class. In this method:

- The individual rankings are represented in matrix form by: $M^t = [m_{ir}^{(t)}]$, $t \in T$ (set of voters) with:

$$m_{ir}^t = \begin{cases} 1 & \text{if } c_i \text{ is the } 1^{st} \text{ choice,} \\ 1/2 & \text{if } c_i \text{ is the } 2^{nd} \text{ choice,} \\ 0 & \text{if } c_i \text{ is at the } 3^{rd} \text{ choice,} \\ -1/2 & \text{if } c_i \text{ is at the } 4^{th} \text{ choice,} \\ -1 & \text{elsewhere} \end{cases} \qquad (E)$$

- The minimum distances of disagreement are calculated in the same way as in Blin's method.
- The best choice (solution) is the arrangement which gave the minimum distance of disagreement.

4 Presentation of the Strict Ranking Metric Procedure (SRMP)

4.1 Description of the Procedure

Let m denote the number of candidates or alternatives or objects; n the number of voters or decision-makers.

Principle

Step 1 Each voter or decision-maker ranks the candidates or alternatives in order of preference. This gives n rankings, also called profiles.
Let $\prod = \{\pi_1, \pi_2 ..., \pi_n\}$ be the set of these n preference profiles. We are trying to find a π^* that would be closest to all the π_i. In other words, $d(\pi^*, \pi_i) = \min d(\pi, \pi_i)$, where d is a distance and π is any profile. We propose to use the distance of the symmetric difference which can be interpreted as a *the distance* of two matrices [10] and in the case of voting this is understood as *disagreement.*

Step 2 Writing preferences in matrix form. Let $\tilde{rg}_{ij}$ be the rank (in numbers) of the candidate c_i in the profile π_j, $i = 1, ..., m$ and $j = 1, ..., n$. So if $\tilde{rg}_{11} > \tilde{rg}_{21}$ then $c_2 \succ c_1$ in the π_1 profile.and if $\tilde{rg}_{11} = \tilde{rg}_{21}$ then $c_2 \approx c_1$ in the π_1 profile.
– The rank matrix noted $\tilde{Rg}$ is written as:

$$\tilde{R}_g = \begin{pmatrix} & c_1 & c_2 & \cdots & c_n \\ \pi_1 & \tilde{r}_{g_{11}} & \tilde{r}_{g_{12}} & \cdots & \tilde{r}_{g_{1n}} \\ \pi_2 & \tilde{r}_{g_{21}} & \tilde{r}_{g_{22}} & \cdots & \tilde{r}_{g_{2n}} \\ \vdots & \vdots & \vdots & \ddots & \vdots \\ \pi_m & \tilde{r}_{g_{m1}} & \tilde{r}_{g_{m2}} & \cdots & \tilde{r}_{g_{mn}} \end{pmatrix}$$

– From the data of $\tilde{Rg}$ we write the evaluation or performance matrices of the voters noted M^t and defined by:$M^t = [m_{ik}^{(t)}]$, $t \in T$ (set of voters) where $M^t = [m_{ik}^{(t)}]$, $t \in T$ (set of voters) with:

$$m_{ik}^{(t)} = \begin{cases} 1 & \text{if } c_i \succ^{(t)} c_k \\ 0 & \text{if } c_i \approx^{(t)} c_k \\ -1 & \text{if } c_k \succ^{(t)} c_i \end{cases}$$

Step 3 We then generate all the possible permutations that can be formed with the m candidates. Let us denote Q the set of all these random permutations.

Step 4 We calculate the mismatches using the following formulae:
→ The distance between two pairs of arrangements is calculated as follows:

$$\delta(Q^{(t)}, M^{(t)}) = \sum_{i=1}^{m}\sum_{k=1}^{m} |q_{ik}^{(1)} - m_{ik}^{(1)}| \tag{9}$$

→ The disagreement also called Delta Blin (δ_{BL}) of the voters on any order Q is calculated as follows:
$\delta_{BL}(Q, M^{(t)}) = \sum\limits_{t=1}^{s}\sum\limits_{i=1}^{m}\sum\limits_{k=1}^{m} |q_{ik} - p_{ik}^{t}|$, where $t \in T$.
This means, for example, that:
$\delta_{BL}(Q, M^{(t)}) = \delta(Q, M^{(1)}) + \delta(Q, M^{(2)}) + ... + \delta(Q, M^{(s)})$
For m candidates, we will have a set of K disagreements of cardinal $m!$

Step 5 Once the disagreements are known, we identify the ranking $Q^* \in Q$ which allowed us to obtain the minimum number of disagreements. This choice constitutes a ranking of candidates on which there is less disagreement.

4.2 Applications on Examples

To better test our method on various cases, we programmed it in the Python language. The programme obtained works perfectly even for a large number of candidates and voters.

-**Example 1:** The following rankings are the preferences of three voters out of five candidates.

$$V_1 : c_4c_5c_1c_2c_3$$
$$V_2 : c_1c_5c_3c_4c_2$$
$$V_3 : c_5c_2c_3c_4c_1$$

We are looking for the median or consensus ranking. Using our method we have successively:

▶ *Matrix of rows*

$$\tilde{R}_g = \begin{pmatrix} & c_1 & c_2 & c_3 & c_4 & c_5 \\ \pi_1 & 3 & 4 & 5 & 1 & 2 \\ \pi_2 & 1 & 5 & 3 & 4 & 2 \\ \pi_3 & 5 & 2 & 3 & 4 & 1 \end{pmatrix}$$

▶ *Voter Evaluation Matrix*

$$M^{(1)} = \begin{pmatrix} 0 & 1 & 1 & -1 & -1 \\ -1 & 0 & 1 & -1 & -1 \\ -1 & -1 & 0 & -1 & -1 \\ 1 & 1 & 1 & 0 & 1 \\ 1 & 1 & 1 & -1 & 0 \end{pmatrix} \quad M^{(2)} = \begin{pmatrix} 0 & 1 & 1 & 1 & 1 \\ -1 & 0 & -1 & -1 & -1 \\ -1 & 1 & 0 & 1 & -1 \\ -1 & 1 & -1 & 0 & -1 \\ -1 & 1 & 1 & 1 & 0 \end{pmatrix} \quad M^{(3)} = \begin{pmatrix} 0 & -1 & -1 & -1 & -1 \\ 1 & 0 & 1 & 1 & -1 \\ 1 & -1 & 0 & 1 & -1 \\ 1 & -1 & -1 & 0 & -1 \\ 1 & 1 & 1 & 1 & 0 \end{pmatrix}$$

▶ *The possible permutations with these five candidates*;

$$Q = \begin{pmatrix} 1\,2\,3\,4\,5 \\ 1\,2\,3\,5\,4 \\ \cdots\cdots \\ \cdots\cdots \\ 5\,4\,3\,2\,1 \end{pmatrix}; \; Q \text{ is of size } 5! = 120 \text{ permutations.}$$

Each permutation of Q can be represented in matrix form $Q^t = [q_{ir}^{(t)}]$ using the relation (E).

▶ *For the other steps, we have introduced the data into our python program and after execution we obtain the following result* (Fig. 1)*:*

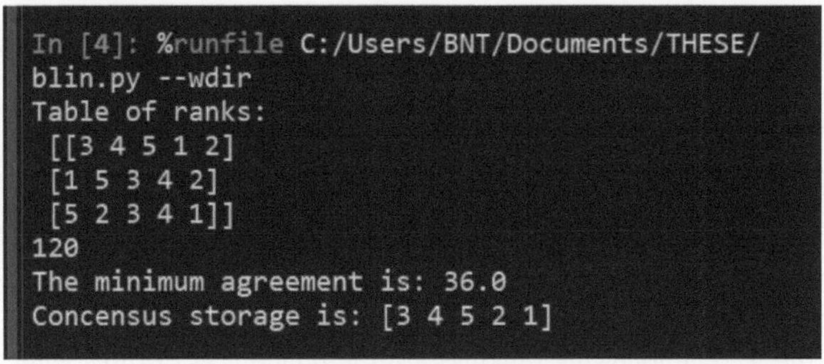

```
In [4]: %runfile C:/Users/BNT/Documents/THESE/
blin.py --wdir
Table of ranks:
 [[3 4 5 1 2]
 [1 5 3 4 2]
 [5 2 3 4 1]]
120
The minimum agreement is: 36.0
Concensus storage is: [3 4 5 2 1]
```

Fig. 1. Results for 3 voters and 5 candidates

That is to say: $\pi^* = [c_5, c_4, c_1, c_2, c_3]$ and The winner is therefore c_5 (Table 1).

Table 1. Ranking of candidates in the consensus ranking

Candidate	c_1	c_2	c_3	c_4	c_5
rank	3rd	4th	5th	2nd	1st

We obtain the same result as that proposed in [11] using the Kemeny-Young coefficient method.

-Example 2: Consider a vote where three voters rank four candidates according to their choice (Table 2).

Table 2. Preferences of 3 voters out of 4 candidates

	1st choice	2th choice	3th choice	4th choice
$V^{(1)}$	c_1	c_2	c_3	c_4
$V^{(2)}$	$\{\}$	c_1, c_2	$\{\}$	c, c_4
$V^{(3)}$	c_4	c_1	c_3	c_2

$\Leftrightarrow$

	c_1	c_2	c_3	c_4
$V^{(1)}$	1	2	3	4
$V^{(2)}$	2	2	4	4
$V^{(3)}$	2	4	3	1

Integrating this data into the program gives the following results (Fig. 2):

```
In [6]: %runfile C:/Users/BNT/Documents/THESE/
blin.py --wdir
Table of ranks:
 [[1 2 3 4]
 [2 2 4 4]
 [2 4 3 1]]
24
The minimum agreement is: 20.0
Concensus storage is: [1 2 3 4]
```

Fig. 2. Results for 3 voters and 4 candidates

That is: The winner is therefore c_1 (Table 3)

Table 3. Results given by SRMP

Candidates	c_1	c_2	c_3	c_4
rank	1st	2nd	3rd	4th

Solving this example using New Metric Procedure of Multi-decision Makers Choice (NMPMMC) and Blin's method gives the following results respectively (Table 4):

Table 4. Results given by NMPMMC and the Blin method

Candidates	c_1	c_2	c_3	c_4
Best_choice	0,5	0,5	0	-0,5.
rank	1st	1nd	3rd	4th

Candidates	c_1	c_2	c_3	c_4
Best_choice	2	2	3	4
rank	1st	1st	3rd	4th

-**Example 3:** Consider a vote where three voters have ranked five candidates according to their choice (Table 5).

Table 5. Preferences of 3 voters out of 5 candidates

	1st choice	2th choice	3th choice	4th choice
$V^{(1)}$	c_2, c_3	c_1	c_4	c_5
$V^{(2)}$	c_2	c_1	c_4	c_3, c_5
$V^{(3)}$	c_1	c_3	c_2, c_4	c_5

$\Leftrightarrow$

	c_1	c_2	c_3	c_4	c_5
$V^{(1)}$	2	1	1	3	4
$V^{(2)}$	2	1	4	3	4
$V^{(3)}$	1	3	2	3	4

By integrating this data into the program we obtain the following results (Fig. 3):

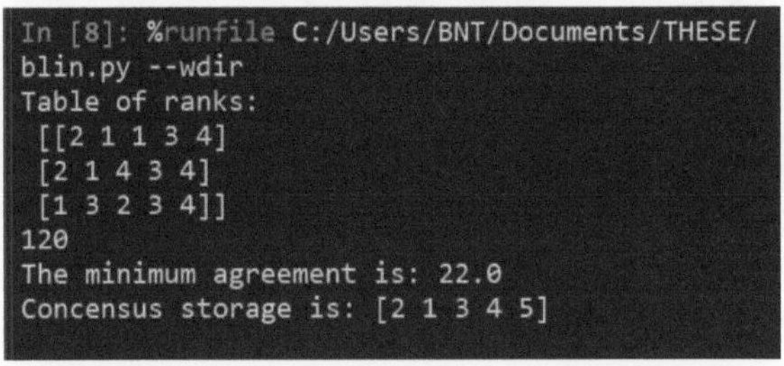

```
In [8]: %runfile C:/Users/BNT/Documents/THESE/
blin.py --wdir
Table of ranks:
 [[2 1 1 3 4]
 [2 1 4 3 4]
 [1 3 2 3 4]]
120
The minimum agreement is: 22.0
Concensus storage is: [2 1 3 4 5]
```

Fig. 3. Results for 3 voters and 5 candidates

That is: The winner is therefore c_2 (Table 6)

Table 6. Results obtained with SRMP.

Candidate	c_1	c_2	c_3	c_4	c_5
rank	2nd	1st	3rd	4th	5th

Solving this example using NMPMMC and Blin's method respectively gives the following results (Table 7).

Table 7. Results obtained with Blin's method and NMPMMC.

Candidates	c_1	c_2	c_3	c_4	c_5
Bestchoice	0,5	1	-0,5	0	-0,5.
rank	2nd	1st	4th	3rd	4th

Candidates	c_1	c_2	c_3	c_4	c_5
Bestchoice	2	1	2	3	4
rank	2nd	1st	2nd	3rd	4th

4.3 Comparison and Discussion

From the last two examples we have the following comparison tables (Table 8):

Table 8. Comparison of rankings for the three methods.

Example 2				
Candidates	c_1	c_2	c_3	c_4
NMPMMC	1st	1st	3rd	4th
Blin	1st	1st	3rd	4th
SRMP	1st	2nd	3rd	4th

Example 3					
Candidates	c_1	c_2	c_3	c_4	c_5
NMPMMC	2nd	1st	4th	3rd	4th
Blin	2nd	1st	2nd	3rd	4th
SRMP	2nd	1st	3rd	4th	5th

For these examples, we see that we have the same winners using the three methods. In example 2, the two methods (Blin and NPMCMD) declare c_1 and c_2 to be ex æquo, but from the data we can see that c_1 beats c_2, which is what our procedure proposes. In these examples, our metric procedure gives a complete ranking of the candidates from first to last. This is easily explained by the fact that in our method, the set Q is made up of permutations and the consensus $Q^* \in Q$. Also for practical application, we think that our method would be more practical and realistic. Indeed, in our approach, the voter is simply asked to rank the candidates in order of preference, without any intermediate rank as in Blin's method, or category ranking as in the multi-decider choice metric.

4.4 Contributions and Limitations of the SRMP

The Strict Rankings Metric Procedure aims to improve decision-making in voting contexts, by introducing an innovative approach to quantifying and comparing voters' preferences. Major contributions include the proposal of a robust methodology that eliminates ties, guaranteeing clear and unambiguous results. Greater flexibility thanks to its applicability to all types of storage, whether partial or total. Beyond the context of voting, the new metric procedure can solve the permutation median problem, which is an existential problem in the field of Operational Research. However, this procedure has certain limitations, including increased complexity in its implementation due to its NP nature, a characteristic shared with all permutation-based methods, which may limit its adoption on a large scale. It also depends on the quality of the input data and requires further validation in more diverse contexts to confirm its generalizability. These findings pave the way for future research to simplify the procedure and extend its applicability.

5 Conclusion

In this paper we have proposed a new metric procedure called the Strict Ranking Metric Procedure(SRMP). This method offers a robust solution for aggregating individual preferences into a collective preference in voting contexts. Unlike some existing methods, this procedure guarantees tie-free results, providing a clear and unambiguous ranking of candidates, from best to last, whatever the type of ranking (partial or total order). The results obtained are not only more expressive, but also better adapted to real-life scenarios, where clarity and precision in decision-making are essential. The Metric Strict Ranking Procedure represents a significant advance in preference aggregation, offering a reliable and flexible tool for decision-making in voting systems. Its potential applications extend to various fields, such as political science, economics and artificial intelligence.

However, it's important to note that this procedure, while innovative, shares the NP complexity inherent in permutation-based methods, which may limit its large-scale applicability.

As future perspectives, we plan to explore the properties of the social choice functions satisfied by this metric procedure, to extend its application to multi-decider multicriteria problems, and to study algorithmic optimizations to reduce its computational complexity. These steps will strengthen both the theoretical foundations and the practical applicability of the proposed method.

References

1. Baujard, A., et al.: Compte-rendu de l'expérimentation «VOTER AUTREMENT ». Working Papers (Groupe d'Analyse et de Théorie Economique Lyon St-étienne (GATE Lyon St-Étienne)), p. 48 (2017)
2. Alinezhad, A., Khalili, J.: New Methods and Applications in Multiple Attribute Decision Making (MADM). Springer (2019). https://doi.org/10.1007/978-3-030-15009-9
3. Borda, J.C.: Mémoires sur les Élections au Scrutin. Hist. l'Acad. Roy. Sci. (1781)
4. Schandeler, J.P.: Condorcet: the universalism of the Enlightenment in question (1963-2008). Hal-03751250. https://hal.science/hal-03751250v1.14-4-2022
5. Soumana, F.: Décision multicritère: un système de recommandation pour le choix de l'opérateur d'agrégation. Capitole.fr (2018)

6. Smaoui, H., Lepelley, D.: LE Système de vote par note à trois niveaux: Etude d'un nouveau mode de scrutin. Rev. d'Econ. Polit. **131** (2021)
7. Grabisch, M., Perny, P.: Multicriteria aggregation, fuzzy logic, principles, decision support. Eur. J. Oper. Res. 81–120 (2003)
8. Milosz, R., Hamel, S.: Mediane of 3 permutations, 3-cycles and 3-hitting set problem. J. Discrete Appl. Math. (2018)
9. Marichal, J.L.: Aggregation operators for multicriteria decision aid. Ph.D. thesis, University of Liège (1998)
10. Jean-Marie, B.L.I.N.: Alinear assignment formulation of the multiattribute decision problem. Rev. franç aise d'autom. inform. recherche opér. tome **10**(V2), 21–32 (1976)
11. Kemeny, J.G.: Mathematics without numbers. Manage. Sci. **24**, 1721–173224 (1978)
12. Yager, R.R.: On ordered weighted averaging aggregation operators in multicriteria decision making. IEEE Trans. Syst. Man Cybern. **18**, 183–190 (1988)
13. Slim, B.K.: L'aide multicritère à la décision de groupe: L' du surclassement de sythèse. Thèse. UNIVERSITÉ LAVAL Quebec (1998)
14. Savadogo, Z., Ouedraogo, P.O.F., Some, K., So, O., Ulungu, B., Somé, B.: New metric procedure of multi-decisions makers choice. Far East J. Appl. Math. **95**(5), 329–341 (2016)
15. Savagogo, Z., Takougang, S.A.M., Somé, B.: Méthode de Vote basée sur une Distance d'Evaluation des Préférences par rapport au Candidat Idéal .Int. J. Appl. Math. Res. 243–264 (2021)

Beyond the Social Relations Based Contact List: Integrating Context

Pasteur Poda(✉) and Issaka Kiemdè

Université Nazi BONI, Laboratoire d'Algèbre, de Mathématiques Discrètes et d'Informatique, Bobo-Dioulasso, Burkina Faso
pasteur.poda@u-naziboni.bf

Abstract. The ability of smartphone Contact List (CL) to extend the user's memory has been pushed to its limit by research carried out in the 2010 decade in Ubiquitous Computing. Developed algorithms have been implemented by industrials to facilitate the retrieval of contacts, namely based on recency or frequency and more recently based on social relations. In this paper, we investigate how to push back the existing limits of the CL ability to extend the user's memory. We adopt the MOM (Modeling, Organisation, Middleware) approach for context-aware systems development and design a new CL based on social relations with the novelty of adding a modeling of the context, so to capture the essence of the context that motivates every new entry in the CL. We have developed the new CL application using W3C standard technologies of semantic web and React Native mobile development framework. We succeeded in testing a variety of functions, from the more traditional to those taking advantage of the new design, including extended contact search and context-aware functions.

Keywords: Contact List · contact retrieval · context-aware · MOM approach

1 Introduction

As technologies and means of storing contact lists develop, the size of contact lists is inevitably increasing. Several studies, e.g.: those of [2,3,5], had already shown a continuous increase in the size of the Contact List: 92 contacts in 2012 [3], 308 in 2015 [2], probabily over a thousand today depending on the societies and the individuals. This reality is first and foremost the result of the social relations that give rise to the need to register a contact in one's Contact List, as noted by Poda et al. [11] in relation to sub-Saharan African communities. As a consequence of contact lists size increase, fast contact retrieval could become a difficult task.

Also, as the Contact List size increases continuously, the existence of rarely even never called contacts becomes obvious. In works reported in [3] and [6], the authors also found that almost 47% of contacts in modern smartphones have

A. Sere et al. (Eds.): AFRI2 2025, CCIS 2536, pp. 130–142, 2026.
https://doi.org/10.1007/978-3-031-98327-6_10

not been contacted for at least 6 months or have never been contacted at all. It is also reported that more than 90% of communications occur with just the top 10 contacts [2].

Driven by the well-argued observations of [2,3] and [6], techniques have been developed to help in retrieving a relevant contact in the Contact List. Mekh et al. [1] classified these techniques into two categories of approaches: design based approach and call prediction based approach.

In the design based approach, the traditional alphabetical order way of displaying contacts is rethought. The techniques that have been developed aimed to make contact retrieval quicker and easier. Can be cited as an example the work of Bergman [3] that results in placing rarely used contacts at the bottom of the screen and in a smaller font. In the call prediction based approach, the idea is to use temporal and contextual data in order to predict the contact the user is likely to call. So, the most likely contacts a user will call at a given time are calculated and displayed. Many solutions already proposed include that of [5,7] and [8]. As an example, the algorithm proposed in [5] used contact recency and frequency as inputs and achieved an average prediction accuracy of 80%. Let's consider a user profile where the size of the Contact List is at least a thousand contacts, with several dozen contacts called daily. In the context of sub-Saharan Africa, such a user profile can easily be encountered, especially for people with a certain social and/or political responsibility. For such a user profile, the two categories of approach can easily present limitations and give the user no other choice than a blind or keyword search. Indeed, what happens if the contact we're looking for isn't among the top 10 or 20? The retrieval of a rarely called contact becomes an even more difficult task, especially as there is an even greater probability of not remembering any of his contact information in order to perform a keyword-based search. The user could have another trick up his sleeve if the context surrounding the registration of the contact sought had been memorised in his Contact List.

A third category of approach introduced by Poda et al. [9–11] have tried to mitigate the above mentioned limits. An approach consisting of an extension[1] of the user memory by integrating the social ties that can exist between the contacts, that is to say some of the multiple factors that can motivate the recording of a contact in the Contact List. An approach that makes it easy to search for any contact, whether frequent, recent or rarely contacted, or even forgotten. A common feature of all these approaches proposed in the literature is that they aim the smartphone user's memory extension in order to make contacts retrieval easier.

In spite of the milestone made in this third category of approach, all the potential of the user's memory extension is not exploited. That's why we are wondering if the smartphone Contact List can be redesigned in such a way to fully ease contact retrieval independently of if the desired contact is recently,

[1] In reference to the MEMEX (MEMory EXtension) presented in the paper "As we may think" by Vannevar Bush, the precursor of the World Wide Web.

frequently or rarely called, and simultaneously render it context-aware through the same redesign.

Our objective is mainly to redesign the Contact List so that it can incorporate contextual information, including the information that motivate a contact to be added to the list.

2 Methods: The MOM Approach

To achieve our double objective for efficient contact retrieval and for availability of context-aware functionalities, the recipe is herein in the redesigning of the Contact List so to integrate additionnal data to classical contact information. These additionnal data have to help describe the context that characterises the entry of a new contact input in the Contact List. These data are intended to carry information on circumstances mainly. They are intended to enable context-aware functions.

It follows that the redesigned Contact List is devoted to become a central part of a context-aware system. The fundamental building blocks to develop a robust context-aware system are gathered in the MOM (Modeling, Organisation, Middleware) approach [12]. The MOM approach for context-aware systems comprises three complementary steps: a context Modeling to effectively capture the context, a context Organisation to organise and store the context model without losing the semantics, and a Middleware to serve as an integration platform, given that once captured, organised and stored, the context needs to be accessed and shared by applications.

2.1 Context Modeling

Context modeling is the first step of the MOM approach. It is the underlying foundation in the building of context-aware system. It results in a model of the context. "A context model is a set of contextual factors that characterise a situation" [15]. Several techniques are available for the modeling of context. A sample of those techniques include graphical techniques like UML (Unified Modeling Language), Key value methods that describe context information in the form of a list of pairs attributes and their values, logic-based methods using logic concepts to define context, markup scheme techniques based on technologies such as XML and JSON, object-based design, ontology-based techniques. Ontology-based approach consists of specifying concepts and their relationships. W3C standards technologies like OWL and RDF are illustrative of this category of context modeling methods. Some hybrid approaches also exist and usually consist of the combination of several of the above-mentioned modeling tools.

Context modeling makes a context model available. Although a context model can be queried (e.g. from an application), it remains limited if there is no possibility of inference. Nor would it make it easy to develop context-aware functionality. **Context reasoning** is the underlying layer of context modeling, enabling reasoning to be performed on a context model. So, the context reasoning makes it possible to derive new contextual information such as contextual factors or cues from the existent context model for context-aware systems [12]. A formal definition of context reasoning found in the literature is as follows: "context reasoning is deducing new and relevant information to the use of application(s) and user(s) from the various sources of context-data" [16].

As with context modeling, there are many different approaches to context reasoning ranging from classical methods like fuzzy-logic or rule-based to up-to-date tools like supervised/unsupervised learning using algorithms such as Decision Tree or Support Vector Machine.

2.2 Context Organisation

Once the context modeling is complete, the next step in the MOM approach is the context organisation. During this phase, answer is given to the question of how to efficiently organise and store the context model within a computer system environment. Several ways for the context model organisation exist. They include ontological organisation and storing but also many other ways such as object-oriented, relational database, tuple-based, distributed hash table, etc. The ontological way of organising the context model is one of the well-known approaches. It matches very well for context-aware systems where the context is captured in the form of a graph. As mentioned in [12], the ontological way for the context organisation is convenient for keeping in place the links between contextual information and for implementing concepts of rules and facts used in reasoning. It would also be effective for storing complex data structure with densely linked data. To achieve context organisation and storing using the ontological approach, standards exist for the development of the ontology. They are mainly composed of semantic web ontology languages (OWL, RDF, RDFS, TRIPLE, SPARQL, etc.). From a profusion of other tools useful in the implementation of an ontology, we can mention Protege, OilEd, SWOOP, SMORE, etc.

2.3 Context Middleware

In classical software engineering, middleware is the software layer in a client-server architecture that enables fruitful collaboration between the application (the client) and the data access layer (the server). In this context of context-aware systems, it retains the same role of enabling an application to interact with the organised and stored context model. So, without middleware, the organised and stored context model would be useless. A brilliant definition made available in the literature is that of Krishnamoorthy which says that: "a context-aware middleware acts as an integration point that compiles the context for the given situation, enabling applications, subscribed to it, to be context-aware" [13]. Common implementations of middleware include among others API (applications programming interface), RPC (remote procedure call) and application servers.

2.4 New Contact List: MOM Implementation and Development APIs

We applied the MOM approach to design and develop the Contact List application proposed herein. The context modeling was based on a graph representation so that contact-to-contact and contact-to-context relationships are explicit. To facilitate context reasoning as well reasoning with relationships between contacts, we adopt a rule-based technique that easily works with ontological approach of context organising and storing. Therefore, as relationships linking contacts to each other or to their contexts can be easily translated to RDF triplets, W3C standard technologies, namely RDF, OWL and SPARQL are used. The middleware to choose in order to enable effective exploitation of the organised and stored graph of contacts and context should meet the main criterion that is the user application must be simple as possible to run in a mobile environment. We also made the option for the application not to be distributed. For this, various APIs exist including Apache Jena or Javascript RDF, messaging and call APIs, smartphone sensor attack APIs, etc.

To develop the application, we chose React Native, one of the most popular frameworks. Specific libraries were used to implement communications (calls and messaging), data persistence, context inference, etc. These include:

- react-native-community/voice: used to manage the audio sensor (microphone), which captures audio and translates it into text;
- react-native-tts: used to translate audio into text;
- react-native-fs: for data persistence in files;
- react-native-push-notification: for notifications handling;
- react-native-background-actions: to run tasks in the background when the application is closed.

2.5 A Voice Interaction Context-Aware Feature

To implement this context-aware feature of voice interaction, proprietary APIs that can be integrated with React Native are available. However, they are expensive to acquire, so we have turned to two open source APIs: react-native-tts and react-native-community/voice. We then defined the algorithm described in Table 1 to implement the voice interaction feature.

3 Results

3.1 New Contact List Model

As a result of the Contact List designing with context model integrated, we are led to the graph given in Fig. 1. The nodes of the graph represent the contacts each with its classic contact information (names, phone number, email,...). Two types of the nodes have to be distinguished: the node noted «Me» represents the owner of the smartphone, the other nodes are noted «C_j» and represent different

Table 1. Implemented Algorithm for Voice Interaction feature.

```
Variables
    vocal, vocalnumber, vocalcharacter, vocalmessage: voice message
    request, number, character, message: text
    playText, listen, searchlistContactcontaining, sendmessage: function
begin
  vocal ⟵ listen()
  request ⟵ vocal.toText()
  if(request="call") then
    playText ("dictate the number to call ")
    vocalnumber ⟵ listen()
    number ⟵ vocalnumber.toText()
    call(number)
  else
    if(request="search") then
      playText("dictate the characters to search")
      vocalcharacter ⟵ listen()
      character ⟵ vocalcharacter.toText()
      searchlistContactcontaining (character)
  else
    if(request="send message") then
      playText("dictate the number to send the message ")
      vocalnumber ⟵ listen()
      number ⟵ vocalnumber.toText()
      playText("dictate the message to send")
      vocalmessage ⟵ listen()
      message ⟵ vocalmessage.toText()
      sendmessage(message, number)
  else
    playText("Vocal misunderstood ")
end
```

contacts stored in the Contact List. Two types of arcs in the graph represent relationships between contacts: of type «*Is my...*» when the contact is directly tied to the «Me» node, and «*Is the... of...*» between other contacts. These arcs reflect social ties (e.g.: *is the classmate of*, *is the friend of*, etc.) that can exist between contacts. A third type of arc, noted «*has the context*», associates each node to its context if necessary.

The context is captured by providing answers to four main questions. The answers will enable us to identify a set of keywords that will constitute the con-

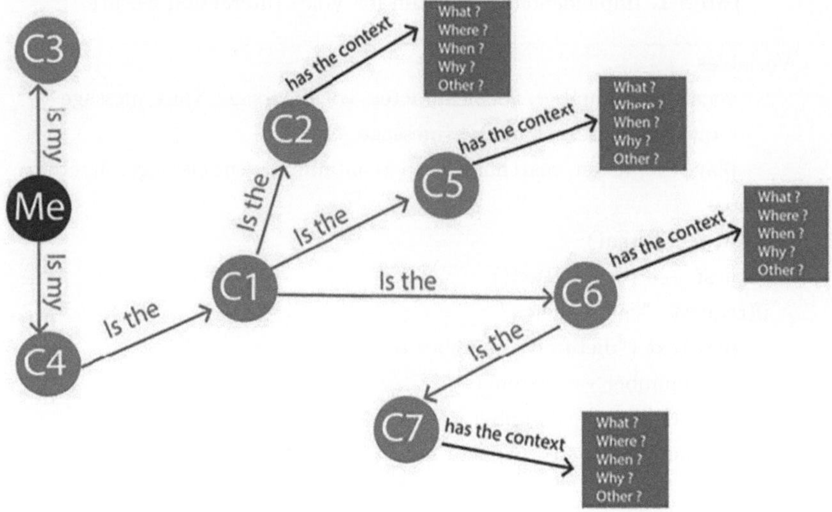

Fig. 1. Graph of Contact List With Context Model

textual information to be represented, organised and stored for use in context reasoning and for its interrogation by more targeted queries in retrieval procedures for instance. The first question is related to the object of the context. It is formulated by "***what*** is it about?" and results in a short description of the event or the actual situation that motivates the decision to record the contact. As an example of answer: the wedding of John. The second question relates to the location and is set as "***where*** does it take place?". Following the logic of the previous example, a possible answer would be: "*the wedding takes place at the* ***Splendid Hotel in Koudougou***". The key terms "*Splendid Hotel, Koudougou*" will serve as contextual information to be integrated to the context model. The third question concerns time, i.e. the date or, more vaguely, the moment when the event takes place. The question is then in the form "***when*** does it take place?". An example of answer could be: "*Thursday, December 18, 2015*" or more vaguely in the form of "*Spring 2015*". One of these two answers formats (date or season in the example) will represent the contextual information to capture here. The fourth question is about the "***why***" in order to know the motivation behind the decision of adding the given contact in the Contact List. An example of information to provide as answer here could be the following: "*in his role of Master of Ceremony (MC), he (the recorded contact) was extraordinarily awesome and I may need his services one day*". The information to be captured as the contextual information in this example could be summarised to these three words: "*extraordinarily awesome MC*". In addition to these four questions that help the discovery of context data, other information at the user's discretion can be noted to enrich the context. This could be, e.g., the social tie that exists between the recorded contact and another contact already present in the Contact List, or a description of the contact (e.g.: his home town/village) that has not been taken into account with the four questions.

Beyond this first result that derives from the modeling step, we applied the organisation step and got the Contact List in the form of an RDF file.

3.2 New Contact List App

Architecture. To make the Contact List usable by an application, we implemented the middleware step and got the application architecture as given in Fig. 2. Several features have been developpped and successfully tested based on the proposed architecture.

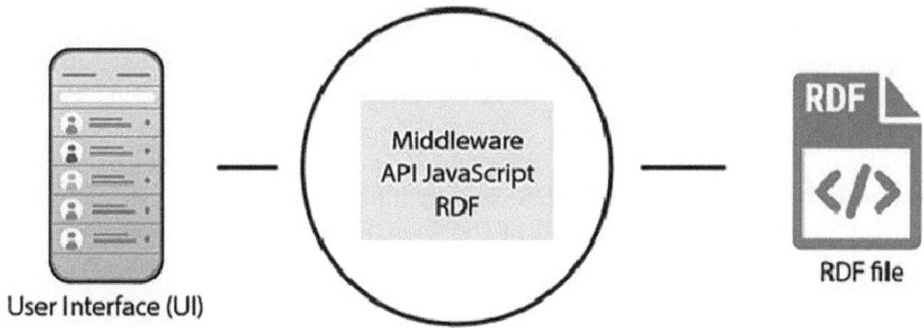

Fig. 2. Android-based Contact List implementation Architecture.

Classical Features. The classical CRUD (Create, READ, Update and Delete) functions but adapted to the new design of the Contact List allow to add a new contact with its specific context in the List, to display both contact and context information, to proceed with contact or context information update and the possibility to remove a contact from the Contact List. Moreover, the search function is extended to enable efficient contact retrieval even in case of oblivion or in the presence of homonyms. In any situation, keywords based search can be used about not only classical contact information but also about context information or social ties existing between contacts.

We have just noted that the new Contact List enables the context to be used in keyword based search. This should be viewed as a preliminary outcome. Indeed, the integration of context model is expected to enable the Contact List to support a variety of context-aware features.

Context-Aware Features. Numerous context-aware functions can be designed and implemented, from those already available in the related literature to new ones yet to be invented. From this perspective, location-based functions of this kind like those presented in the work of [4] can easily be implemented herein to exploit the user's location as a contextual information.

Beyond the classical features, we have successfully developed and tested a context-aware function consisting of a **voice interaction**. It works in a similar way to *Siri* on the Apple's personal computers. *Siri* is an intelligent voice assistant that can converse with the Macbook user. Indeed, our context-aware function works in such a way that the application is able to detect contextual information from the user's environment. This can happen, e.g., while the user is having a phone conversation. The user can also intentionally dictate some precise contextual information (a place, a date, an event, ...) to the application in order to trigger the context-aware feature. As soon as a contextual information is detected by the application, it triggers a search procedure that can result in the display of contacts likely to be of interest to the user. In this way, the context-aware function reads the context and anticipates the user's needs. Illustration in Fig. 3 shows a search triggered by our application (named Mitinsi), where "ali" represents the detected context information (in this case, a specific contact named "ali"). At the end of the search, contacts containing the string "ali" are listed.

4 Discussions

To ease the contact retrieval in the Contact List, different approaches consisting of the user's memory extension have been developed but remained limited to face the continuous increase of the Contact List size. So, we herein consider a redesigning of the Contact List so that, on the one hand to fully ease contact retrieval independently of if the desired contact is recently, frequently or rarely called, and on the second hand to render it context-aware through the same redesign. We adopted the MOM approach for context-aware system and then developed the redesigned Contact List app using React Native framework for mobile app development. Among the main results obtained, it should be noted that a new Contact List model is obtained. It integrates traditional contact information, as well as contact-to-contact social relationships and context modeling. It should also be noted that the proposed new Contact List model has been implemented on android with multiple and diverse features covering traditional functions, their extended versions taking advantage of the new design, various contact search functions based on keywords extended to key expressions introduced with the context modeling. A context-aware feature enables the user to find a contact by interacting vocally with the app.

The innovations we have made to the Contact List in this paper represent a consolidation of the existing with an opening to enable more context-aware use cases. If we look at the Contact List as a data structure, we can describe the new design as a 3rd-generation Contact List. The 1st generation is the one that only

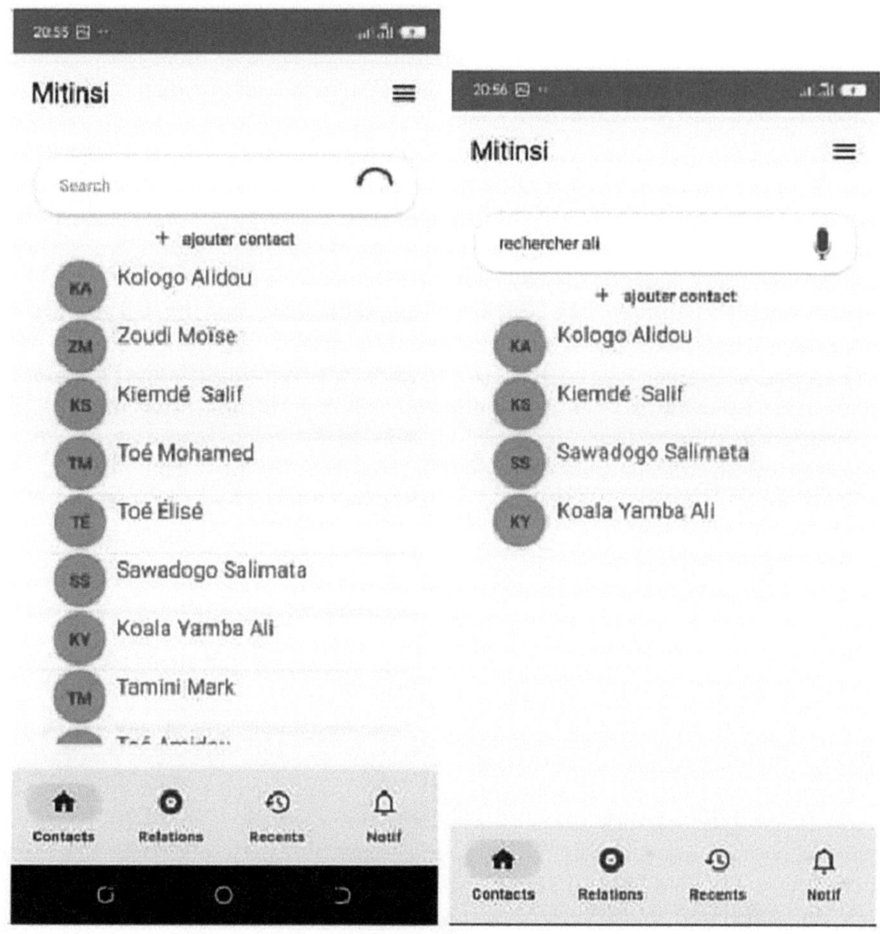

Fig. 3. Voice interaction based context-aware feature.

allows the recording of classic contact information. The 2nd generation is the one based on social relations introduced by Poda et al. [11]. With this 2nd generation, contacts are no longer isolated structures, but rather linked together to form a graph; the nodes of the graph containing classic contact information while the arcs carry knowledge about the social relationship that may exist between one contact and another. With the 3rd generation of Contact List, the graph of the 2nd generation is extended to offer, in addition to contact-to-contact relationships, contact-to-context relationships; the context mainly storing information on the situation that prevailed when a given contact was registered. A great deal of work carried out over the 2000 and 2010 decades has focused on 1st generation Contact List, notably to address recommendation-type functions or context-aware functions, e.g., [4] and [6], but also functions for sorting the display of the Contact List according to an order based on recency and/or frequency. The 2nd generation has favored a systematic search deemed more relevant with the ever-increasing size of the Contact List. When the default display based on alphabetical order or recency/frequency becomes inoperative, a search must be used that requires the user to remember the contact sought. Search algorithms have therefore been enriched with a richer palette of keywords. Social relations between contacts are also used to facilitate the retrieval of rarely called contacts, even not called at all for some time. With the 3rd generation, we consider that the recency/frequency display is quickly inoperative with a particularly populated Contact List of at least a thousand contacts. The new innovation further strengthens that introduced with the 2nd generation. The range of keywords used to find a contact has been further enriched, extending the user's memory even further by recording contextual information in addition to that provided by previous generations. Manually, it will be more likely to find a contact by opting to search by any of the classic contact information, or by social relations, or by contextual information. Moreover, context reasoning offers a greater possibility of supplementing the user's failure to remember. The numerous context-aware functionalities that can be implemented, such as contact search via voice interaction, demonstrate that this innovation is capable of significantly impacting the quality of experience of the user regarding contact retrieval.

Given the ever-increasing availability of storage capacity in smartphone memory and in the cloud, a key strong point of the innovation proposed here is that it can be easily implemented both locally on each smartphone and in a distributed environment on the cloud. In the latter case, a boulevard of innovations is opened up to drive the development of distributed service platforms, particularly for mobile network users. These distributed services could be based on recorded context information and, e.g., on certain user preferences. At this stage of the study reported here, it should be noted that it could be further enhanced by a study oriented towards the design and development of a variety of context-aware contact retrieval features to be evaluated by users from the point of view of their user experience. These additional studies could take advantage of Machine Learning techniques to add value to the wealth of data stored in the Contact List.

5 Conclusion

To make it easier to find contacts in increasingly crowded Contact List, many different works have been done in Ubiquitous Computing, albeit with the limitations that certain Contact List sizes can impose. As existing developments have consisted in a kind of extension of the user's memory, we ask ourselves how we could further extend it in order to facilitate contact retrieval and at the same time make the Contact List further context-aware. We investigated this question using the MOM (Modeling, Organisation, Middleware) approach for context-aware system development, and succeeded in integrating context modeling into the Contact List. This modeling allowed additional information to be stored when a new contact has to be added, enabling a larger contact search base. We implemented the new version of the Contact List using W3C standards for semantic web technologies, as well as React Native framework for mobile development with a number of specialised libraries. We have shown that well-established functions can be extended to take into account contextual information, thus facilitating and further extending the probability of finding a contact quickly. We have noted that the new design obtained opens up both to the implementation of existing context-aware algorithms and to the design of new context-aware use cases. This was illustrated with the voice interaction feature. Our contribution is important to the social memory of the user. It's to encourage users to store their memories, and to enable them to store memories of other people in society with whom they share an experience. This new development of the Contact List will form the basis for the development of a whole range of context-aware functionalities to enhance human well-being and make the phone a real companion that complements the user's memory. It also provides sufficient input for engineering and research in this field. In terms of research, an interest is thus created in upgrading existing context-aware algorithms, but also in creating new ones. For engineering, it's so provided a basis for the development of notification services platforms to be integrated into the 5G mobile technology ecosystem.

References

1. Fatima, M., Rextin, A., Hayat, S., Nasim, M.: Exploiting contextual information to improve call prediction. PLoS ONE **14**(10), e0223780 (2019)
2. Bentley, F.R., Chen, Y.Y.: The composition and use of modern mobile phonebooks. In: Proceedings of the 33rd Annual ACM Conference on Human Factors in Computing Systems, pp. 2749–2758. CHI'15. New York, NY, USA, ACM, 2015
3. Bergman, O., Komninos, A., Liarokapis, D., Clarke, J.: You never call: demoting unused contacts on mobile phones using DMTR. Pers. Ubiquit. Comput. **16**(6), 757–766 (2012)
4. Plessas, A., Georgiadou, O., Stefanis, V., Komninos, A., Garofalakis, J.: Assessing physical location as a potential contextual cue for adaptive mobile contact lists. In: IEEE International Conference on Computer and Information Technology; Ubiquitous Computing and Communications; Dependable, Autonomic and Secure Computing; Pervasive Intelligence and Computing (CIT/IUCC/DASC/PICOM), pp. 1316–1324, 2015
5. Plessas, A., Stefanis, V., Komninos, A., Garofalakis, J.: Field evaluation of context aware adaptive interfaces for efficient mobile contact retrieval. Pervasive Mob. Comput. **35**, 51–64 (2017)
6. Komninos, A., Liarokapis, D.: The use of mobile contact list applications and a context-oriented framework to support their design. In: Proceedings of the 11th International Conference on Human-Computer Inter-action with Mobile Devices and Services, p. 79. ACM, 2009
7. Nasim, M., Rextin, A., Hayat, S., Khan, N., Malik, M.M.: Data analysis and call prediction on dyadic data from an understudied population. Pervasive Mob. Comput. **41**, 166–178 (2017)

8. Haddad, M.R., Baazaoui, H., Ziou, D., Ghezala, H.B.: A predictive model for recurrent consumption behavior: an application on phone calls. Knowl.-Based Syst. **64**, 32–43 (2014)
9. Poda, P., Zongo, R.B.A.C., Dagnogo, I., Tapsoba, T.: On a mobile phone contact list based on social relations. EAI Endorsed Trans. Smart Cities **3**(7), e6 (2018)
10. Dagnogo, I., Zongo, R.B.A.C., Poda, P., Tapsoba, T.: A novel mobile phone contact list based on social relations. In: Odumuyiwa, V., Adegboyega, O., Uwadia, C. (eds.) AFRICOMM 2017. LNICST, vol. 250, pp. 239–245. Springer, Cham (2018). https://doi.org/10.1007/978-3-319-98827-6_22
11. Poda, P., Compaoré, A.J., Somé, B.M.J.: Redesigning mobile phone contact list to integrate African social practices. In: Bissyande, T.F., Sie, O. (eds.) AFRICOMM 2016. LNICST, vol. 208, pp. 26–32. Springer, Cham (2018). https://doi.org/10.1007/978-3-319-66742-3_3
12. Pradeep, P., Krishnamoorthy, S.: The MOM of context-aware systems: a survey. Comput. Commun. **137**, 44–69 (2019)
13. Krishnamoorthy, S., Poornachandran, P., Gangadharan, S.V.: Context-aware public safety in a pervasive environment. Wirel. Public Saf. Netw. **3**, 99–111 (2017)
14. Henricksen, T.K.: A Framework for Context-Aware Pervasive Computing Applications, University of Queensland, 2003
15. Gasparic, M., Murphy, G.C., Ricci, F.: A context model for IDE-based recommendation systems. J. Syst. Softw. **128**, 200–219 (2017)
16. Nurmi, P., Floréen, P.: Reasoning in context-aware systems. Helsinki Institute for Information Technology, Position paper, 2004
17. Studer, R., Benjamins, V.R., Fensel, D.: Knowledge engineering: principles and methods. Data Knowl. Eng. **25**(1–2), 161–197 (1998)

Modeling the Spatial Dependence of Extreme Rainfall Events in West Africa: A Copula Approach for Estimating Return Levels

Remi Guillaume Bagré(✉)

Norbert Zongo University, Koudougou, Burkina Faso
remi.bagre@unz.bf

Abstract. This study examines the spatial dependence of extreme rainfall events in West Africa using copula models. The results indicate that the Frank copula provides the best fit for capturing dependencies between extreme rainfall extremes across Burkina Faso, Mali, and Niger. Return level estimates for 10-year, 20-year, and 50-year extreme rainfall events indicate substantial interdependencies among the studied regions, with the highest estimated return levels reaching up to 280 mm in some locations. These findings highlight the necessity of incorporating joint dependence structures in climate risk assessment and adaptation planning in the Sahel region.

Keywords: Extreme weather events · Copula models · Dependence structure

1 Introduction

Extreme weather events, such as intense rainfall, have become a major concern in the context of climate change. In West Africa, a particularly vulnerable region, extreme weather events such as heavy rainfall have devastating consequences for infrastructure, agriculture, and food security. Burkina Faso, Mali, and Niger, located in the Sahel region, regularly experience floods and droughts that disrupt socio-economic development. To better understand and anticipate these events, it is essential to develop statistical tools capable of modeling the frequency and intensity of extreme rainfall ([6,8]).

Modeling extreme weather events is a crucial issue for climate change adaptation and risk management. Conventional statistical modeling methods often fail to take into account the dependence between extreme events in different geographical regions ([1,9]). The simultaneous occurrence of heavy rainfall in multiple locations, often interconnected, can amplify the negative effects ([3,10]). A flexible and robust approach is therefore needed to capture these interdependencies.

A. Sere et al. (Eds.): AFRI2 2025, CCIS 2536, pp. 143–154, 2026.
https://doi.org/10.1007/978-3-031-98327-6_11

The central issue of this study is to quantify the joint dependence of extreme rainfall in three West African countries (Burkina Faso, Mali, Niger) using copulas. Copula-based approaches have been widely used to model dependencies in hydrological extremes ([2,7]), and recent studies have demonstrated their effectiveness in capturing spatial correlations in extreme precipitation events ([11,12]). How can these interdependencies be modeled while taking into account the specific climatic features of each country? What are the return levels associated with different return periods, and how can this information be used to manage hydrometeorological risks? These questions are aimed at improving our ability to predict extreme events and mitigate their impact through resilience strategies.

The main objective of this work is to apply copula-based models to extreme precipitation events and their multivariate dependencies, and to estimate return levels associated with return periods (10, 20, 50, 100 years). This modeling will provide a better understanding of climate risks in this key region, following similar methodologies applied in other parts of the world ([4,5]).

2 Methology

2.1 Introduction to Copulas

In a given region containing m stations, consider the random vector:

$$(X_1, X_2, \ldots, X_m)$$

For example, X_j represents the random variable "annual maximum rainfall at station j." We are interested in the joint distribution F of the random vector:

$$F(x_1, x_2, \ldots, x_m) = P(X_1 \leq x_1, X_2 \leq x_2, \ldots, X_m \leq x_m) \tag{1}$$

Let F_i be the marginal cumulative distribution functions (CDFs) and f_i the associated densities. In the case where the variables X_j are independent, we have:

$$F(x_1, x_2, \ldots, x_m) = F_1(x_1) \times F_2(x_2) \times \cdots \times F_m(x_m) \tag{2}$$

However, data from geographically close stations can be strongly correlated, making the assumption of independence unrealistic. An interesting approach is to use copulas, which model the dependency structure independently of the marginal distributions. In other words, copulas allow us to describe the individual behavior of each station and combine marginal distributions to obtain the joint distribution. Using copulas, one can form multivariate distributions with different marginals, where the dependence structure is governed by the copula.

According to Sklar's Theorem (1959, [9]), any multivariate distribution F, whose margins $F_1, \ldots, F_m$ are continuous, can be uniquely expressed by a CDF C concentrated on $[0,1]^m$, called a copula, which satisfies:

$$F(x_1, x_2, \ldots, x_m) = C(F_1(x_1), F_2(x_2), \ldots, F_m(x_m)) \tag{3}$$

The multivariate density of the random vector can then be written as:

$$f(x_1, x_2, \ldots, x_m) = c(F_1(x_1), F_2(x_2), \ldots, F_m(x_m)) \times f_1(x_1) \times f_2(x_2) \times \cdots \times f_m(x_m) \quad (4)$$

where c represents the copula density. The copula describes the dependence structure of the random vector.

2.2 Extreme Value Theory

Extreme Value Theory (EVT) is a branch of statistics that focuses on the behavior of the extreme tails of distributions, i.e., the rare events that occur at the far ends of the probability spectrum. In hydrology, EVT is used to model extreme phenomena such as maximum rainfall, floods, or droughts.

The Generalized Extreme Value (GEV) distribution plays a central role in EVT. It is used to model the distribution of block maxima, such as the maximum rainfall recorded each year at a station. The GEV distribution has the following form:

$$F(x) = \exp\left\{ -\left(1 + \xi \frac{x - \mu}{\sigma}\right)^{-1/\xi} \right\} \quad (5)$$

where:

- μ is the location parameter,
- $\sigma > 0$ is the scale parameter,
- ξ is the shape parameter, which determines the tail behavior.

Depending on the value of ξ, the GEV distribution converges to one of three types:

1. **Gumbel distribution** ($\xi = 0$): Models light tails and is used for distributions with exponential decay.
2. **Fréchet distribution** ($\xi > 0$): Models heavy tails and is appropriate for phenomena with large extreme values.
3. **Weibull distribution** ($\xi < 0$): Models bounded tails and is suitable for phenomena where extremes have an upper bound.

In hydrological studies, EVT is used to estimate return levels, which represent the magnitude of an event expected to occur once in a given return period (e.g., 10, 20, or 100 years). The return level $R(T)$ for a given return period T can be expressed as:

$$R(T) = \mu + \frac{\sigma}{\xi} \left(\left(-\log\left(1 - \frac{1}{T}\right) \right)^{-\xi} - 1 \right) \quad (6)$$

This formula allows the prediction of extreme events based on historical data and is widely used in risk management for natural disasters.

2.3 Parameters Estimation

The estimation of the parameters of the marginal distributions and the copula model is a crucial step in our methodology. We use a two-step procedure: first, we estimate the parameters of the marginal distributions using the Maximum Likelihood Estimation (MLE), then we estimate the copula parameters using the Inference Functions for Margins (IFM) method.

Estimation of Marginal Distributions. The extreme rainfall events are modeled using the Generalized Extreme Value (GEV) distribution, which is defined as:

$$F(x) = \begin{cases} \exp\left\{-\left[1+\xi\left(\frac{x-\mu}{\sigma}\right)\right]^{-1/\xi}\right\}, & \xi \neq 0 \\ \exp\left\{-\exp\left(-\frac{x-\mu}{\sigma}\right)\right\}, & \xi = 0 \end{cases} \tag{7}$$

where μ is the location parameter, σ the scale parameter, and ξ the shape parameter. The estimation of these parameters is performed using the Maximum Likelihood Estimation (MLE), which maximizes the log-likelihood function:

$$\ell(\mu, \sigma, \xi) = -\sum_{i=1}^{n}\left[\log\sigma + \left(1+\frac{1}{\xi}\right)\log\left(1+\xi\frac{x_i-\mu}{\sigma}\right)\right] \tag{8}$$

The numerical optimization of this likelihood is performed using the Newton-Raphson algorithm. The adequacy of the fitted GEV distribution is assessed using the Kolmogorov-Smirnov test.

Estimation of Copula Parameters. Once the marginal distributions are estimated, the next step is to fit a copula model to describe the dependence structure between the extreme rainfall events across different locations. The estimation of copula parameters is carried out using the Inference Functions for Margins (IFM) method, which consists of two steps:

1. **Estimate the marginal distributions** using MLE (as described above).
2. **Estimate the copula parameters** by maximizing the copula log-likelihood function:

$$\ell(\theta) = \sum_{i=1}^{n}\log c_\theta\left(F_1(x_i), F_2(y_i)\right) \tag{9}$$

where c_θ is the density of the copula function and θ is the dependence parameter. The estimation is performed using numerical methods such as the Broyden-Fletcher-Goldfarb-Shanno (BFGS) algorithm.

Comparison with Pseudo Maximum Likelihood Estimation (Pseudo-MLE): An alternative to the IFM method is the Pseudo Maximum Likelihood Estimation (Pseudo-MLE), where the empirical cumulative distribution functions (ECDFs) of the data are used instead of parametric marginal distributions. However, this method is less robust, particularly when marginal distributions are misspecified.

Model Selection and Goodness-of-Fit: To choose the best copula model, we use the Akaike Information Criterion (AIC) and the Bayesian Information Criterion (BIC). The best-fitting copula is selected based on the lowest AIC and BIC values. Additionally, graphical tools such as scatter plots and empirical copula comparisons are used to validate the copula fit.

3 Results and Discussion

3.1 Comparison with Existing Studies

Previous research, such as Chen et al. ([11], 2023) and Gouveia-Reis et al. ([12], 2023), have explored copula-based modeling of extreme rainfall in different regions. Our findings align with these studies in demonstrating the importance of joint dependence structures for extreme event estimation. However, our study extends these results by focusing on the Sahel region.

3.2 Data Quality Considerations

The dataset used in this study is sourced from regional meteorological agencies, and while it provides a valuable basis for modeling, potential data gaps and inconsistencies remain. Future studies should consider integrating satellite-based observations to enhance the robustness of the results.

3.3 Visualisation of Maximum Annual Rainfall

In order to analyze extreme rainfall patterns in Burkina Faso, Mali, and Niger, we focus on the statistical modeling of annual maximum rainfall. Understanding these extreme values is essential for assessing potential climate risks and dependencies between the three countries.

The analysis of maximum rainfall highlights significant variability across years, with certain periods marked by particularly intense precipitation events. While some years exhibit stable extremes, others experience notable peaks, suggesting the occurrence of extreme weather events. However, determining a clear increasing or decreasing trend requires further statistical validation.

For Mali, preliminary observations suggest a potential decrease in extreme rainfall in recent decades, which could indicate a reduction in intense precipitation events or longer drought periods. Conversely, Burkina Faso and Niger exhibit strong interannual variability, with no apparent long-term trend. These fluctuations highlight the complexity of extreme rainfall behavior in the region.

To better understand the dependencies between extreme rainfall events in these three countries, we use copula-based modeling. The 3D scatterplot (Fig. 1) represents the dependence structure between annual maximum rainfall values, using pseudo-observations derived from transformed data. This visualization provides insights into the joint behavior of extreme rainfall events across Burkina Faso, Mali, and Niger.

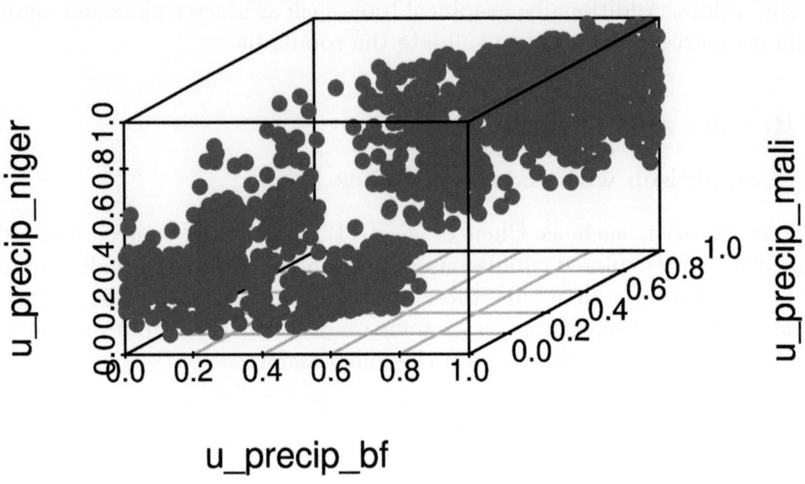

Fig. 1. Scatterplot of Rainfall Data

In the Fig. 1, the points are aligned or clustered in certain directions, suggesting a positive dependence between extreme events in these countries, i.e. extreme rainfall in one country is often associated with extreme rainfall in the others.

3.4 Copula Model Comparison

To select the most appropriate copula for modeling the dependence structure between extreme rainfall events, we tested and compared several copula families, including Normal, Student, Gumbel, Frank, Joe and Clayton. These copulas make it possible to capture different forms of dependence between extreme events, ranging from symmetrical dependence (Normal and Student copulas) to forms of asymmetrical dependence, such as those modelled by the Gumbel, Joe and Clayton copulas.

Each copula was fitted using the maximum likelihood method, and the estimated parameters for each are presented in the table below. These parameters make it possible to characterise the intensity and structure of the dependence between extreme precipitation events in the three countries, and will then be compared to identify the copula that best fits the data (Table 1).

Table 1. Comparison of parameters and AIC/BIC criteria for the different copulas

Copula	Parameter 1	Parameter 2	Log-Likelihood	AIC	BIC
Normal	0.68	–	957.02	–1912.05	–1906.85
Student	0.70	10.45	980.98	–1957.97	–1947.56
Gumbel	1.83	–	883.24	–1764.48	–1759.28
Frank	6.09	–	1095.41	–2188.82	–2183.62
Joe	2.15	–	736.61	–1471.21	–1466.01
Clayton	1.07	–	643.33	–1284.66	–1279.46

Among the tested models, the Frank copula exhibited the lowest AIC and BIC values, indicating the best fit. Unlike Clayton and Gumbel copulas, which capture asymmetric tail dependence, the Frank copula effectively models symmetric dependencies observed in extreme rainfall events across the selected locations.

The Fig. 2 shows a graphical visualisation of the copulas fitted to the maximum annual rainfall for several countries, probably Burkina Faso, Mali and Niger. This type of visualisation is essential for a visual understanding of the dependency structure between these extreme climatic events. By displaying the contours of the copulas, this image makes it possible to see how the different copulas (Student and Frank) capture the correlation and the dependency tail between the observations. The variations in the shapes of the copula contours reveal asymmetries and non-linear dependencies, making these copulas more suitable than others (Gauss, Gumbel, Joe, Clayton) for modelling extreme precipitation events.

3.5 Linking Marginal Distributions and Copulas

The marginal distributions were modeled using the Generalized Extreme Value (GEV) distribution, estimated through Maximum Likelihood Estimation (MLE). The transformed data, using the fitted GEV distribution, were then used as inputs for the copula estimation. This two-step approach ensures that the dependence structure captured by the copula is based on standardized extreme rainfall values.

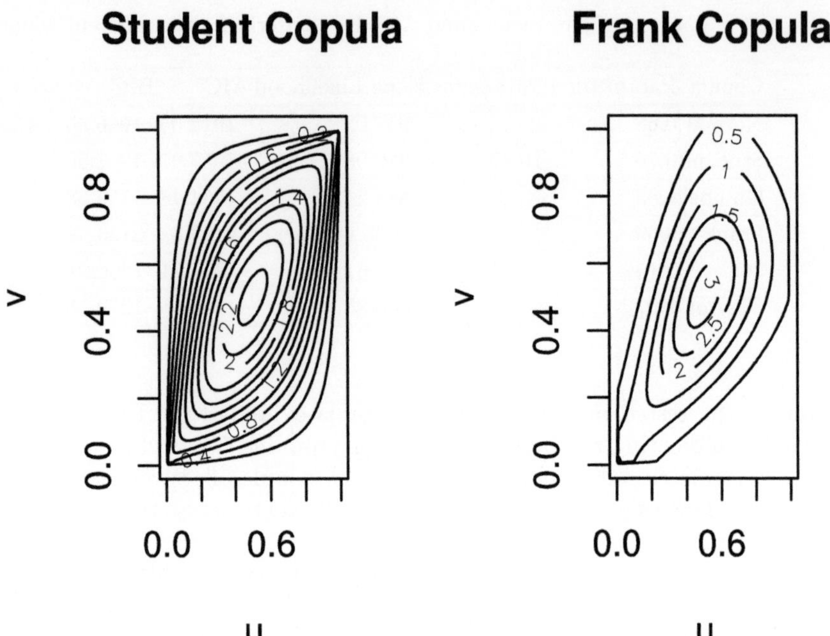

Fig. 2. Visualisation of Copulas Adjusted for Dependence on Maximum Precipitation: Graphical Comparison of Models

3.6 Precipitation Simulation Based on Selected Copula and GEV Scale Transformation

In this section, we simulate annual maximum rainfall data using the optimal copula identified in the previous analysis. This simulation is crucial for assessing the predictive performance of the selected copula model (based on the AIC or BIC criterion) and for generating hypothetical scenarios of extreme rainfall in the three regions studied: Burkina Faso, Mali and Niger.

The method involves generating uniform pseudo-observations from the fitted copula, and then transforming them into actual rainfall values via the inverse of the distribution function of the Generalized Extreme Value (GEV) distribution. This transformation process makes it possible to retain the structural dependence captured by the copula while bringing the simulations back to the original scale of precipitation, adjusted previously using the GEV margins.

Ultimately, this simulation allows us to produce precipitation scenarios for 1000 observations, representing the simulated maximum annual precipitation for each of the three regions. These results will provide a solid basis for analysing future extreme events and assessing the risks associated with precipitation in these regions (Table 2).

Table 2. Simulated rainfall data for Burkina Faso, Mali, and Niger

Observation	Simulated_BF	Simulated_Mali	Simulated_Niger
1	261.6914	132.95862	455.5868
2	268.0216	143.46058	477.6984
3	162.3080	78.53927	317.8616
4	248.9174	159.88871	545.9105
5	208.2747	107.24982	394.0262
6	186.1671	92.92606	359.6832

This table illustrates the diversity of extreme climate scenarios simulated for each country. Maximum rainfall varies considerably between countries, with potentially catastrophic events being more frequent in Niger. This simulation provides a basis for risk management analysis and climate adaptation policy planning in these regions.

The Fig. 3 helps to visually understand how simulated maximum precipitation in one region is related to precipitation in another. It provides a graphical overview of the multivariate dependency structure captured by the selected copula.

4 Calculation of Return Levels for Extreme Precipitation Events

In this section, we calculate the return levels of maximum annual rainfall for different periods (10, 20, 50, 100 years) using the GEV (Generalized Extreme Value) distribution adjusted previously for Burkina Faso, Mali and Niger. Return periods represent the quantities of rainfall associated with rare events, the probability of occurrence of which is inversely proportional to the return period. In other words, a return level for a period of 100 years corresponds to a quantity of extreme rainfall likely to be observed once every 100 years. This calculation is used to assess the future climate risks associated with extreme precipitation events (Table 3).

This graph (Fig. 4) illustrates the return levels of maximum annual rainfall for different periods (10, 20, 50, 100 years) in Burkina Faso, Mali and Niger. The coloured lines per country show the extreme rainfall levels associated with each return period, with an increasing trend, indicating that higher rainfall is expected for rarer events.

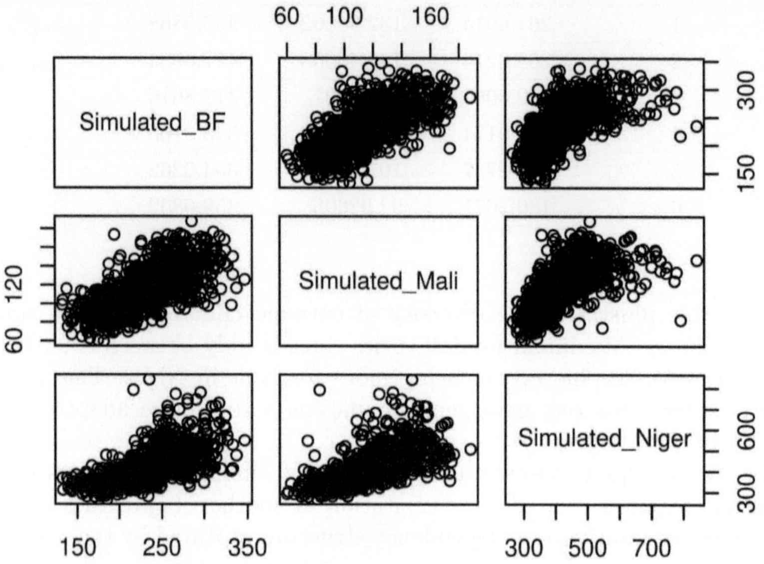

Fig. 3. Analysis of Correlations between Simulated Precipitation: Comparison between Burkina Faso, Mali and Niger using the Best Copula.

Table 3. Return levels of maximum rainfall for different periods in three countries.

Return Period (years)	Return Level (mm)	Country
10	281.4178	Burkina Faso
20	295.9188	Burkina Faso
50	311.4256	Burkina Faso
100	321.0338	Burkina Faso
10	143.9357	Mali
20	152.9505	Mali
50	162.9069	Mali
100	169.2790	Mali
10	520.8840	Niger
20	574.2710	Niger
50	648.9192	Niger
100	709.2686	Niger

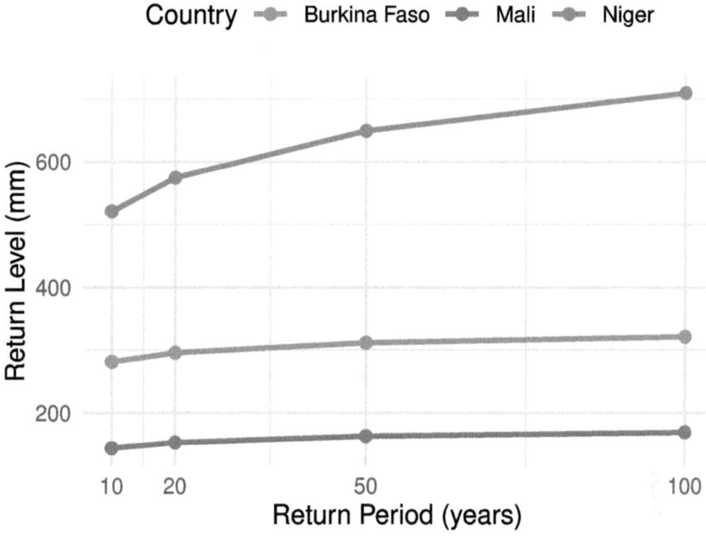

Fig. 4. Changes in Maximum Rainfall Return Levels for Different Periods in Burkina Faso, Mali and Niger

5 Conclusion

This study analyzed the dependence structure of extreme rainfall events in Burkina Faso, Mali, and Niger using copula-based modeling. By applying the Generalized Extreme Value (GEV) distribution to model marginal distributions and selecting the best-fitting copula through AIC/BIC criteria, we were able to quantify the joint behavior of extreme precipitation events across the three countries. The results indicate that the Frank copula provides the best representation of the dependence structure, capturing the symmetric relationships between extreme rainfall occurrences.

The findings highlight the strong interconnections in extreme rainfall patterns across the Sahel region, emphasizing the necessity of considering multivariate approaches when assessing climate risks. While some countries exhibit potential trends in decreasing or stable maxima, interannual variability remains dominant, reinforcing the need for continued monitoring and advanced statistical modeling.

Future research could expand this analysis by incorporating additional climate variables such as temperature and wind speed, allowing for a more comprehensive risk assessment. Moreover, integrating non-stationary copula models could enhance the ability to capture long-term climate trends and their potential impacts on extreme precipitation events.

These insights are essential for policymakers and climate risk managers in developing adaptation strategies to mitigate the impact of extreme rainfall events, particularly in a region highly vulnerable to climate variability and extreme weather phenomena.

Competing Interests. The author has no competing interests to declare that are relevant to the content of this article.

References

1. Ribatet, M., Sedki, M.: Extreme Value Copulas. A Survey. Extreme Value Modelling and Risk Analysis, pp. 67–90 (2013)
2. Schölzel, C., Friederichs, P.: Multivariate non-normal distributions for climate data using copulas. Geophys. Res. Lett. **35**(2) (2008)
3. Brunner, M.I., et al.: Dependence of floods across temporal and spatial scales: a copula-based study. J. Hydrol. Earth Syst. Sci. **23**(6), 2665–2681 (2019)
4. Zhang, L., et al.: Assessment of extreme precipitation events using copulas in South China. J. Hydrometeorol. **19**(1), 125–141 (2019)
5. Engelke, S., Hitz, A.S.: Graphical models for extremes. J. R. Stat. Soc.: Ser. B (Stat. Methodol.) **82**(4), 871–932 (2020)
6. Zscheischler, J., et al.: A few extreme events dominate global interannual variability in gross primary production. Environ. Res. Lett. **12**(3), 035001 (2017)
7. Singh, S.K., Burn, D.H.: Copula-based approach for multivariate flood frequency analysis under nonstationary conditions. J. Hydrol. Eng. **25**(2), 04019064 (2020)
8. Papalexiou, S.M., Montanari, A.: Global and regional increase of precipitation extremes under global warming. Water Resour. Res. **55**(6), 4901–4914 (2019)
9. Nelsen, R.B.: An Introduction to Copulas. Springer Series in Statistics. Springer, New York, NY (2006). https://doi.org/10.1007/0-387-28678-0
10. Yang, J., et al.: Modeling the spatial dependence of extreme precipitation in the Yangtze river basin using copula methods. Int. J. Climatol. **40**(5), 2831–2844 (2020)
11. Chen, H., Xu, Z., Chen, J., Liu, Y., Li, P.: Joint risk analysis of extreme rainfall and high tide level based on extreme value theory in coastal area. Int. J. Environ. Res. Public Health **20**(4), 3605 (2023)
12. Gouveia-Reis, D., Guerreiro Lopes, L.: A dependence modelling study of extreme rainfall in Madeira Island. Climate **9**(5), 86 (2023)

Multobjective Belugas Whale Optimizer for Pareto Optimal Solution Search

Amidou Zoungrana[1(✉)], Appolinaire Tougma[1,2], and Kounhinir Somé[1]

[1] Département de Mathématiques, Laboratoire de Mathématiques, Informatique et Applications (L@MIA), Université Norbert Zongo, BP 376, Koudougou, Burkina Faso
amidzoung@gmail.com

[2] Département de Mathématiques et Informatique Ouahigouya, Université Lédéa Bernard Ouédraogo, Ouahigouya, Burkina Faso

Abstract. This article proposes a multi-objective algorithm based on beluga whales called Multiobjective Beluga Whale Optimization (MOBWO). It is a multi-objective version of the single-objective Beluga Whale Optimization (BWO) algorithm, which is inspired by the natural behavior of beluga whales. The procedure of the MOBWO algorithm is based on the BWO algorithm, incorporating additional mechanisms. For instance, a crowding distance mechanism is used to balance exploitation and exploration phases as the search progresses. Additionally, a non-dominated sorting strategy is integrated to preserve population diversity. To verify and validate the performance of the MOBWO algorithm, we studied 22 test problems, including 10 constrained and 12 unconstrained problems. The performance of MOBWO is compared to that of MOSMA, MOWCA, and NSGA2 using various performance metrics, such as Generational Distance (GD), Inverted Generational Distance (IGD), Maximum Spread (MS), spacing (S), spread (Δ), and hypervolume (H). The quantitative and qualitative results indicate that the proposed MOBWO offers more competitive results than the other algorithms.

Keywords: Multiobjective Tests problems · metrics · Beluga Whale Optimization

1 Introduction

In most real-life problems, it is common to optimize not just a single function (criterion), but rather multiple functions (criteria) that are often in conflict with each other. These types of problems originate from various fields, such as statistics, traffic management [47], fuzzy optimization [44], location-based services [46], neural networks [48], wireless sensor networks [7,49], surveillance [8,9], computer-aided design [10], the Internet of Things [11], and many others. To solve these complex multi-objective problems, various methods are proposed in the literature. These methods can be categorized into two distinct classes: deterministic [42] and stochastic [12].

A. Sere et al. (Eds.): AFRI2 2025, CCIS 2536, pp. 155–179, 2026.
https://doi.org/10.1007/978-3-031-98327-6_12

These heuristic and metaheuristic algorithms belong to the second category, specifically to single-objective and multi-objective methods. Among the single-objective algorithms, we can cite the Genetic Algorithm (GA) [26], Differential Evolution (DE) [13], Particle Swarm Optimization (PSO) [5,25], Whale Optimization Algorithm with Nelder-Mead (WONM) [13], Slime Mold Algorithm (SMA) [39], Grey Wolf Optimizer (GWO) [21], and the African Vultures Optimization Algorithm (AVOA) [38]. In addition to these algorithms, there are Spotted Hyena Optimization [15], Seagull Optimization Algorithm [16], Henry Gas Solubility Optimization [17], Mine Explosion Optimization [18], and Butterfly Optimization [19].

Among the multi-objective algorithms, most were initially designed as single-objective algorithms and later adapted with operators to solve multi-objective problems. Examples include Evolutionary Multi-Objective Optimization (EMOO) [21], Non-dominated Sorting Genetic Algorithm (NSGA) [24], Multi-Objective Particle Swarm Optimization (MOPSO) [27], Multi-objective Evolutionary Algorithm based on Decomposition (MOEA/D) [29], Non-dominated Sorting Grey Wolf Optimization (MOGWO) [6], Multi-objective Ant Lion Optimization [22], Multi-Objective Multi-verse Optimization [20], Multi-objective Firefly Algorithm [56], Multi-objective Moth Flame Optimization (MOMFO) [32], Multi-Objective Grasshopper Optimization Algorithm (MOGOA) [34,54], Non-dominated Sorting Ion Motion Optimization Algorithm [33], Multi-Objective Grasshopper Optimization Algorithm [34], Multi-objective African Vultures Optimization Algorithm (MOAVOA) [2], Multi-objective Beluga Whale Optimization Algorithm (MOWOA) [35], Multi-objective Dragonfly Algorithm (MODA) [52], Multi-objective Slime Mould Algorithm (MOSMA) [31], Multi-objective Arithmetic Optimization Algorithm [36], and Multi-objective Plasma Generation Algorithm [37].

All these algorithm extensions for solving multi-objective problems have been developed due to the lack of a universal algorithm capable of effectively solving all optimization problems, in accordance with the "No Free Lunch" theorem [23]. This theory motivated, in this work, the development of a multi-objective version of the Beluga Whale Optimization (BWO) algorithm [51], initially designed for single-objective optimization. The BWO algorithm is an extension of the BWO algorithm, inspired by the behavior of belugas, known for their intelligence, advanced communication, and group hunting techniques. Their ability to explore their environment while collaborating efficiently helps maintain a balance between exploration and exploitation. Thus, a crowding distance (CD) and non-dominated sorting (NDS) approach was integrated into the BWO algorithm to create a multi-objective Beluga Whale Optimization (MOBWO) algorithm.

The main contributions of this study are listed as follows:

- The MOBWO algorithm was developed by introducing elitist non-dominated sorting and crowding distance (CD) mechanisms into the BWO algorithm. These additions aim to maintain optimal Pareto dominance and improve both the convergence and diversity of solutions.

- Performance indicators are listed for all multi-objective problem studies to demonstrate the effectiveness of the proposed MOBWO algorithm. These problems include (ZDT), DTLZ problems, and standard engineering problems such as CEC09 problems.
- To evaluate the effectiveness of MOBWO, comparisons were made with other algorithms sharing similar principles, such as MOSMA, MOWCA, and NSGA2. This evaluation was based on various performance metrics, measuring both the convergence of solutions to the Pareto front and their distribution.

The structure of the article is organized as follows. Section 2 presents the preliminaries. Section 3 presents the main results. Section 4 concludes the article and outlines future perspectives.

2 Preliminaries

2.1 Basic Concepts

The multi-objective optimization problem is generally defined as follows:

$$\begin{cases} \min\{f_i(x)\}, \ i = 1, 2, ..., m \\ \text{subject to} \\ g_j(x) \leq 0, \ j = 1, 2, ..., p \\ x \in \mathbb{R}^d \ ; \end{cases} \tag{1}$$

where:

- $\circ$ $x = (x_1, x_2, \ldots, x_n)$ denotes the vector of n decision variables;
- $\circ$ f_i, $i = \overline{1, m}$, are the objective functions;
- $\circ$ g_j, $j = \overline{1, p}$, are the constraints related to the optimization of f_i, $i = \overline{1, m}$.

We denote $\mathbf{D}^d$ as the admissible domain defined as follows: $\mathbf{D}^d = \{x \in \mathbb{R}^d : g_j(x) \leq 0\}$. The objective space, denoted by $\mathbf{Z}$, is the direct image of the decision space by the objective functions. It is defined as:

$$\mathbf{Z} = f(\mathbf{D^d}) = \{f(x) : x \in \mathbb{R}^d\}.$$

Definition 21 *[1, 59]. A point $x^* \in \mathbf{D}^d$ is said to be a weakly efficient or weakly Pareto-optimal solution of problem (1) if and only if there does not exist another $x \in \mathbf{D}^d$ such that:*

$$f_i(x) < f_i(x^*), \quad \forall i = \overline{1, m}.$$

Definition 22 *[59, 61]. A point $x^* \in \mathbf{D}^d$ is said to be an efficient or Pareto-optimal solution of problem (1) if and only if there does not exist an $x \in \mathbf{D}^d$ such that $f_i(x) \leq f_i(x^*)$, $\forall i = \overline{1, m}$ and for at least one $k \in \{1, \ldots, m\}$, we have $f_k(x) < f_k(x^*)$.*

We note that $Y = \{f(x^*), x^* \in \mathbf{Z}\}$ is called the Pareto front.

2.2 Beluga Whale Optimization Algorithm (BWO)

The Beluga Whale Optimization (BWO) algorithm is a single-objective algorithm proposed in 2021 by Changting Zhong, Gang Li, and Zeng Meng [51]. This algorithm is inspired by the swimming, hunting, and diving behaviors of beluga whales in the sea. The BWO optimization process primarily consists of three phases: exploration, exploitation, and whale diving.

In the exploration phase, the positions of search agents are determined by simulating the behavior of belugas swimming in pairs. The belugas' positions are updated during this phase using the following equation:

$$\begin{cases} X_{i.j}^{T+1} = X_{i.p_j}^{T} + \left(X_{r.p_1}^{T} - X_{i.p_j}^{T}\right)(1+r_1)\sin(2\pi r_2), & j \text{ is even} \\ X_{i.j}^{T+1} = X_{i.p_j}^{T} + \left(X_{r.p_1}^{T} - X_{i.p_j}^{T}\right)(1+r_1)\cos(2\pi r_2), & j \text{ is odd} \end{cases} \tag{2}$$

where T is the current iteration, $X_{i.j}^{T+1}$ is the new position for the ith beluga in the jth dimension, $p_j (j = 1, 2, \ldots, d)$ is a random number selected from dimensions d, r is arandomly selected beluga whale, r_1 and r_2 are random numbers between $(0, 1)$ and X_{i,p_j}^{T} is the position of the ith beluga in the dimension p_j.

A balancing factor B_f is defined to transition from the exploration phase to the exploitation phase. This factor is given by the following equation:

$$B_f = B_0(1 - \frac{T}{2T_{max}}) \tag{3}$$

where T is the current iteration, T_{max} is the maximum number of iterations, and B_0 randomly changes within $(0, 1)$ at each iteration. The exploration phase occurs when the balancing factor $B_f > 0.5$, while the exploitation phase occurs when $B_f \leq 0.5$.

The exploitation phase of the BWO algorithm is inspired by the predatory behavior of belugas, who move in groups and share information about their positions to hunt efficiently. This strategy is mathematically modeled as follows:

$$X_i^{T+1} = r_3 X_{\text{best}}^{T} - r_4 X_i^{T} + C_1 \cdot \text{step} \cdot \left(X_r^{T} - X_i^{T}\right) \tag{4}$$

where X_i^T and X_r^T are the current positions of the ith beluga and a random beluga, X_i^{T+1} is the new position of the ith beluga, X_{best}^T is the best position among the belugas, r_3 and r_4 are random numbers in the range $(0, 1)$, step is a random Lévy flight [45], and $C_1 = 2r_4(1 - T/T_{\text{max}})$ is the random jump intensity measuring the strength of the Lévy flight.

The third phase, which is the whale diving phase, is modeled using Eq. (5).

$$X_i^{T+1} = r_5 X_i^T + r_6 X_i^T + r_7 X_{\text{step}} \tag{5}$$

where r_5, r_6, and r_7 are random numbers within $(0, 1)$, and X_{step} represents the step size of a whale's dive, defined as:

$$X_{\text{step}} = (U_b - L_b)\exp(-\frac{C_2 T}{T_{max}}) \tag{6}$$

where U_b and L_b are the upper and lower bounds of the variables, respectively, and C_2 is the step factor related to the whale diving probability and population size. This factor is given by the formula $C_2 = 2W_f \times n$. The parameter W_f is defined as follows:

$$W_f = 0.1 - \frac{0.05T}{T_{max}} \tag{7}$$

a linear function representing the probability of whale diving.

The BWO algorithm is outlined as follows:

Algorithm 1. Pseudo-Code of BWO

Require: Algorithm parameters (population size, maximum number of iterations)
Ensure: The best solution

Initialize the population and evaluate fitness values to obtain the best solution (P*)
while $T \leq T_{\max}$ **do**
    Obtain the whale diving probability W_f using equation (7) and the balancing factor B_f using equation (3)
    for each beluga (X_i) **do**
        if $B_f(i) > 0.5$ **then**
            Exploration phase
            Randomly generate $p_y (j = 1, 2, \ldots, d)$ from the dimension
            Choose a beluga X and randomly update the new position of the ith beluga using equation (2)
        else
            if $B_f(i) \leq 0.5$ **then**
                Exploitation phase: Update the random jump intensity C_1 and calculate the Lévy flight function
                Update the new position of the ith beluga using equation (5)
            end if
            Check the boundaries of new positions and evaluate fitness values
        end if
    end for
    for each beluga (X_i) **do**
        Whale diving phase
        if $B_f(i) \leq W_f$ **then**
            Update the step factor C_2
            Calculate the step size X_{step}
            Update the new position of the ith beluga using equation (4)
            Check the boundaries of the new position and calculate the fitness value
        end if
    end for
    Find the current best solution P^*
    $T = T + 1$
end while
Display the best solution

2.3 Performance Measurement

Performance measures are used to study the effectiveness of a new proposed multi-objective optimization method. They facilitate comparison of the new method with existing methods.

Metrics Evaluating Convergence Generational Distance (GD) [1,57]
The GD metric is a convergence metric that measures the average distance between the approximate solutions and those on the Pareto front (analytical front). It is defined as follows:

$$GD = \frac{1}{|\overline{E}(P)|}(\sum_{i=1}^{|\overline{E}(P)|} d_i^p)^{\frac{1}{p}}$$

In two dimensions, we have: the parameter d_i, which is the Euclidean distance (in the objective space) between solution i and the closest point on the Pareto front:

$$d_i = \min_{k=1}^{|P|} \sqrt{\sum_{m=1}^{M} (f_m^{(i)} - f_m^{*(k)})^2}$$

where $f_m^{*(k)}$ is the mth objective function value of the kth solution on the Pareto front and $|\overline{E}(P)|$ is the area of the compromises.

Inverted Generational Distance (IGD) [36,62]
The IGD is an accurate measure for evaluating the performance of Pareto front approximations. It is calculated as follows:

$$IGD = \frac{\sqrt{\sum_{i=1}^{n} d_i^2}}{n}$$

Metrics Evaluating Diversity, Distribution, or Spacing Spacing (S) [53]
The S metric is a spacing metric that measures the total distance between candidate solutions across different sets obtained through multiple algorithms. It considers the minimum distance between each solution and the other solutions in the generated set. It is calculated as follows [6,36,54]:

$$S = \sqrt{\frac{1}{|\overline{E}(P)|} \sum_{i=1}^{|\overline{E}(P)|} (d_i - \overline{d})^2}$$

Where $|\overline{E}(P)|$ represents the trade-off surface, $d_i = \min_{k;k\neq i} \sum_{j=1}^{p} |f_j^i - f_j^k|$ corresponds to the minimum value of the sum of the positive deviations of function values between the i-th solution and all other solutions in the generated set, with

$i, k \in \{1, 2, \ldots, |\overline{E}(P)|\}$. The expression for $\overline{d}$ is given by: $\overline{d} = \frac{1}{|\overline{E}(P)|} \sum_{i=1}^{|\overline{E}(P)|} d_i$ which represents the arithmetic mean of the minimum Euclidean distances.

Spread Metric [14,58]
The SPREAD metric represents the distribution of Pareto solutions along the front. It is calculated as follows:

$$\Delta = \frac{\sum_{m=1}^{M} d_m^e + \sum_{m=1}^{N-1} |d_i - \overline{d}|}{\sum_{m=1}^{M} d_m^e + (N-1)\overline{d}}$$

where $d_i = \min_{k;k \neq i} \sum_{j=1}^{p} |f_j^i - f_j^k|$ corresponds to the minimum value of the sum of the positive deviations of function values between the i-th solution and all other solutions in the generated set, with $i, k \in \{1, 2, \ldots, |\overline{E}(P)|\}$. The expression for $\overline{d}$ is given by: $\overline{d} = \frac{1}{|\overline{E}(P)|} \sum_{i=1}^{|\overline{E}(P)|} d_i$ Where $|\overline{E}(P)|$ represents the trade-off surface.

Maximum Spread (MS) [55]
The MS metric evaluates the diversity of non-dominated solutions. It measures the length of the diagonal of a hyperbox formed by the extreme objective function values of the approximate solution set. It is calculated as follows [6,36,54]:

$$MS = \sqrt{\frac{1}{|\overline{E}(P)|} \sum_{i=1}^{|\overline{E}(P)|} \left[\frac{\min(f_i^{\max} - F_i^{\max}) - \max(f_i^{\min} - F_i^{\min})}{F_j^{\min} - F_j^{\min}} \right]^2},$$

where $f_j^{\max}$ and $f_j^{\min}$ are respectively the maximum and minimum of the j-th objective function f_j in the set of Pareto solutions, and $\overline{I} = \{1, \ldots, |\overline{E}(P)|\}$.

Metrics Evaluating Both Convergence and Diversity Hypervolume [6, 36]
The hypervolume calculates the volume in the objective space covered by the solutions in a set $\overline{E}(P)$. It is used to evaluate both the distribution and convergence of the solutions found. Mathematically, it is defined as:

$$HV = volume(\cup_{i=1}^{|\overline{E}(P)|} v_i).$$

2.4 Tests Problems

Twenty-two (22) reference functions were selected to evaluate the performance of the algorithms. Of these, sixteen (16) are two-objective optimization functions

($ZDT1$ to $ZDT4$, $ZDT6$ and $CF1$ to $CF7$) and six (6) are three-objective optimization functions (CF8 to CF10 and $DTLZ2$ to $DTLZ3$). These functions were chosen for their various characteristics, enabling a comprehensive evaluation of the algorithms' performance, particularly in terms of convexity, concavity, continuity, discontinuity, unimodality and multimodality. Table 1 presents these characteristics in detail.

Table 1. CF, ZDT and DTLZ benchmark functions

Function	Sources	T_{max}	m	d	Contraints	Characteristics
CF1	[2,4,6]	1000	2	30	$x_1 \in [0,1]$, $x_i \in [-1,1]$	convex under linear constraints.
CF2	[2,4,6]	1000	2	30	$x_1 \in [0,1]$, $x_i \in [-1,1]$	non-convex with non-linear constraints
CF3	[2,4,6]	1000	2	30	$x_i \in [0,1]$	discontinuous
CF4	[2,4,6]	1000	2	30	$x_1 \in [0,1]$, $x_i \in [-2,2]$	discontinuities, variable convexity
CF5	[2,4,6]	1000	2	30	$x_1 \in [0,1]$, $x_i \in [-1,1]$	discontinuities, variable convexity
CF6	[2,4,6]	1000	2	30	$x_1 \in [0,1]$, $x_i \in [-1,1]$	discontinuities, variable convexity
CF7	[2,4,6]	1000	2	30	$x_1 \in [0,1]$, $x_i \in [-1,1]$	discontinuities, variable convexity
CF8	[2,4,6]	1000	3	30	$x_1, x_2 \in [0,1]$, $x_i \in [-2,2]$	discontinuities, variable convexity
CF9	[2,4,6]	1000	3	30	$x_1, x_2 \in [0,1]$, $x_i \in [-2,2]$	discontinuities, variable convexity
CF10	[2,4,6]	1000	3	30	$x_1, x_2 \in [0,1]$, $x_i \in [-2,2]$	discontinuities, variable convexity
ZDT1	[2,4,6]	1000	2	30	$x_i \in [0,1]$	Convex
ZDT2	[2,4,6]	1000	2	30	$x_i \in [0,1]$	Concave
ZDT3	[2,4,6]	1000	2	30	$x_i \in [0,1]$	Discontinuous PF
ZDT4	[2,4,6]	1000	2	30	$x_i \in [0,1]$	Convex, multimodal
ZDT6	[2,4,6]	1000	2	30	$x_1 \in [0,1]$, $x_i \in [-1,1]$	Concave, multimodal, Biased
DTLZ1	[40]	1000	2	30	$x_i \in [0,1]$	linear, dispersed solutions, uncomplicated constraints
DTLZ2	[40]	1000	2	30	$x_i \in [0,1]$	Spherical PF
DTLZ3	[40]	1000	2	30	$x_i \in [0,1]$	Convex
DTLZ4	[40]	1000	2	30	$x_i \in [0,1]$	Uneven PF
DTLZ5	[40]	1000	3	30	$x_1 \in [0,1]$, $x_i \in [-1,1]$	Curve
DTLZ6	[40]	1000	3	30	$x_1 \in [0,1]$, $x_i \in [-1,1]$	The cutting-edge curve on PF
DTLZ7	[40]	1000	3	30	$x_1 \in [0,1]$, $x_i \in [-1,1]$	The cutting-edge curve on PF

3 Main Results

3.1 The Beluga Whale Multi-Objective Optimization Algorithm

The proposed MOBWO algorithm utilizes an elitist non-dominated ranking of solutions and a crowding distance mechanism to maintain diversity. This ranking includes the following steps:

- First, calculating the non-dominated solution;
- Second, applying non-dominated sorting (NDS);
- Third, calculating the non-dominated rank (NDR) for all non-dominated solutions;

The crowding distance (CD) is defined as follows:

$$CD_j^i = \frac{f_j^{i+1} - f_j^{i-1}}{f_j^{max} - f_j^{min}} \tag{8}$$

where f_j^{min} and f_j^{max} are the minimum and maximum values of objective function j, f_j^{i+1} and f_j^{i-1} are respectively the values of the objective function f_j for the solutions adjacent to the i-th solution in a set sorted according to this objective.

The algorithm operates as follows:

Step 1: Define control parameters such as population size, loop stopping criteria, and the maximum number of iterations;

Step 2: Randomly generate an initial population of belugas, noted as P_0, within the feasible search space, and calculate the objective function values for each individual in this population;

Step 3: Apply the elitist-based non-dominated sorting method, as well as crowding distance, to the population P_0;

Step 4: Create a new population, noted as P_j, by merging it with the population P_0 to obtain population P_i;

Step 5: Sort the population P_i using the elitist-based non-dominated criterion, along with the resulting crowding distance data;

Step 6: Create a new parent population by selecting the best solutions from population P_i.

Step 7: Repeat this process until the termination condition is met.

In summary, the algorithm aims to optimize solutions through an iterative process that maintains solution diversity and favors non-dominated solutions.

Algorithm 2. Proposed MOBWO Pseudo-Code

Require: Initially generate a population (P_0) randomly in the solution space (S).
1: Evaluate the objective space (F) for the generated population (P_0).
2: Sort the population using the elitist non-dominated sorting method and determine the non-dominated rank (NDR) and non-dominated fronts.
3: Calculate the crowding distance (CD) for each front.
4: Update the solutions (P_j) using **Algorithm 1**.
5: Merge (P_0) and (P_j) to create (P_i) = (P_0) $\cup$ (P_j).
6: Perform initialization for (P_i).
7: Sort (P_i) according to NDR and CD.
8: Replace (P_0) with the first $Npop$ members of (P_i).
Ensure: The best solution

3.2 Control Parameters of All Algorithms

In this section, MOSMA [31], MOWCA [35], and NSGA2 [3] are compared with MOBWO, and the best figure from a set of optimal Pareto solutions is presented. Table 2 summarizes all initial parameters of the listed algorithms. It should be noted that 100 populations and a maximum of 1000 iterations were used for each experiment. This section tests the effectiveness of the proposed algorithm on 32 test problems.

The effectiveness of the proposed MOBWO is evaluated using various benchmark problems, including CF, ZDT, and DTLZ. Table 1 lists the 10 CF problems, of which 7 are bi-objective and 3 are tri-objective. Next, the benchmark evaluation problems of ZDT are presented, showing that each of the five ZDT problems has two objectives. Finally, the DTLZ problems consist of two test problems, each with three objectives and 30 variables.

Table 2. Control parameters of all algorithms..

Methods	MOBWO	MOSMA	MOWCA	NSGA2
Number of Runs	10	10	10	10
Population Size//Search agent	100	100	100	100
Maximum Number of Iterations (Max_t)	1000	1000	1000	1000
Number of Function	22	22	22	32

3.3 Graphical Representation

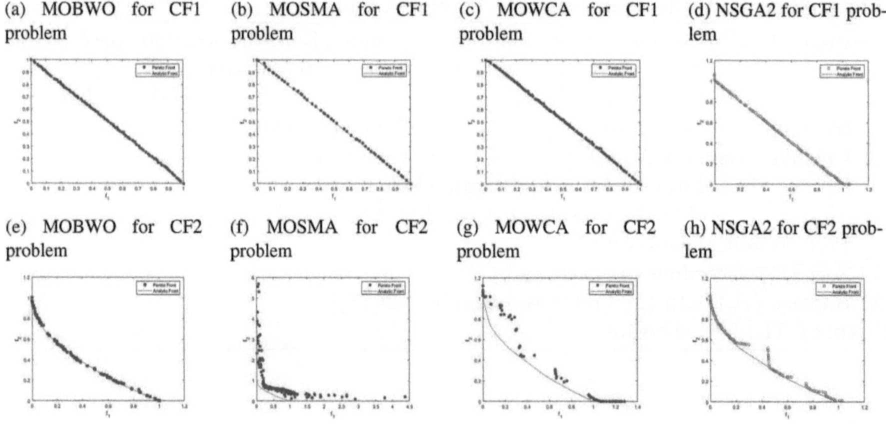

(a) MOBWO for CF1 problem
(b) MOSMA for CF1 problem
(c) MOWCA for CF1 problem
(d) NSGA2 for CF1 problem
(e) MOBWO for CF2 problem
(f) MOSMA for CF2 problem
(g) MOWCA for CF2 problem
(h) NSGA2 for CF2 problem

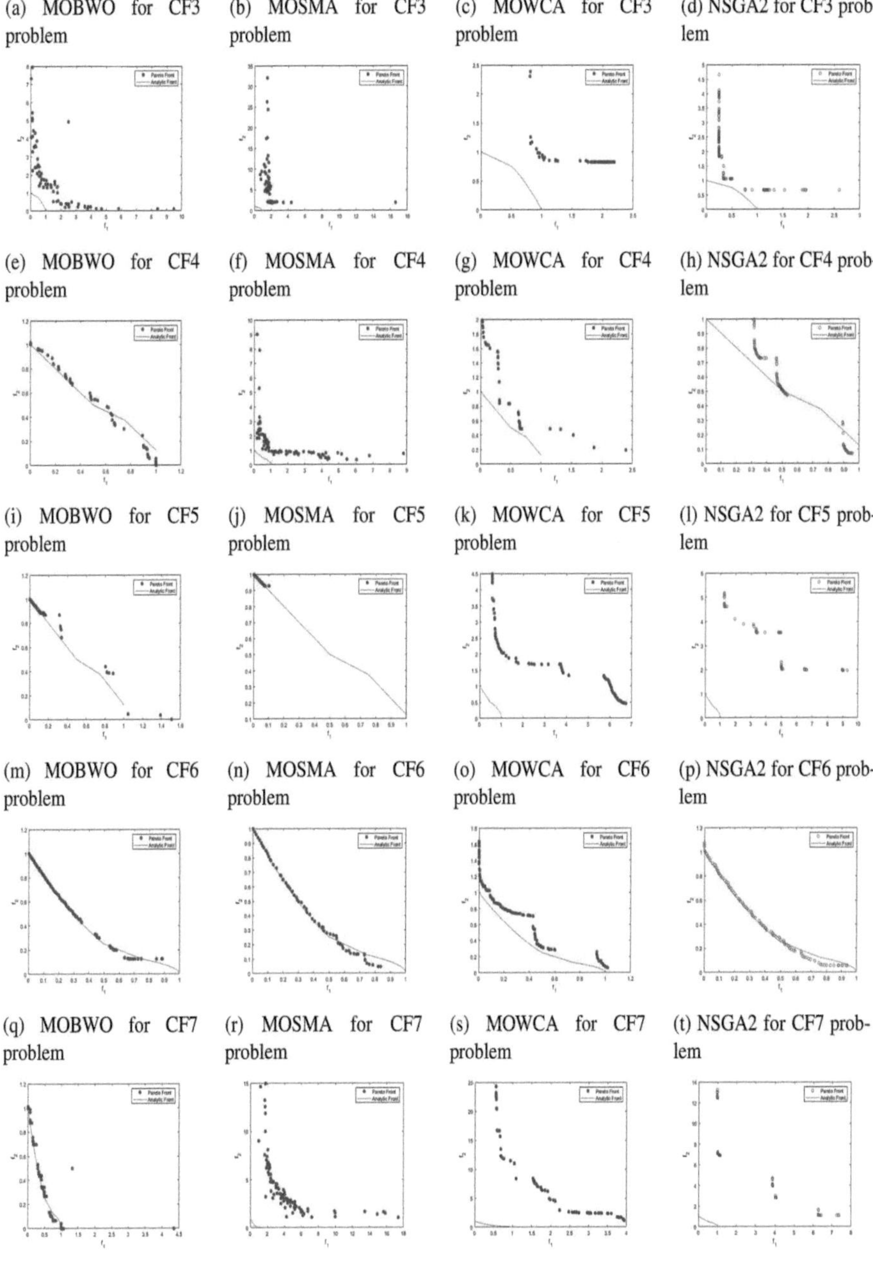

(a) MOBWO for CF3 problem (b) MOSMA for CF3 problem (c) MOWCA for CF3 problem (d) NSGA2 for CF3 problem

(e) MOBWO for CF4 problem (f) MOSMA for CF4 problem (g) MOWCA for CF4 problem (h) NSGA2 for CF4 problem

(i) MOBWO for CF5 problem (j) MOSMA for CF5 problem (k) MOWCA for CF5 problem (l) NSGA2 for CF5 problem

(m) MOBWO for CF6 problem (n) MOSMA for CF6 problem (o) MOWCA for CF6 problem (p) NSGA2 for CF6 problem

(q) MOBWO for CF7 problem (r) MOSMA for CF7 problem (s) MOWCA for CF7 problem (t) NSGA2 for CF7 problem

(a) MOBWO for CF8 problem

(b) MOSMA for CF8 problem

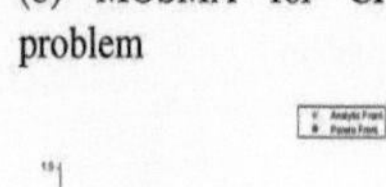

(c) MOWCA for CF8 problem

(d) NSGA2 for CF8 problem

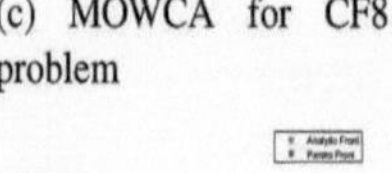

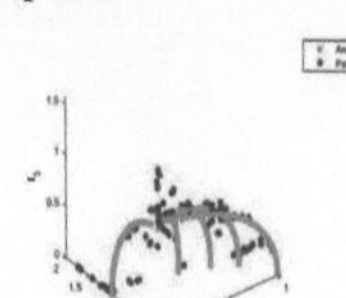

(e) MOBWO for CF9 problem

(f) MOSMA for CF9 problem

(g) MOWCA for CF9 problem

(h) NSGA2 for CF9 problem

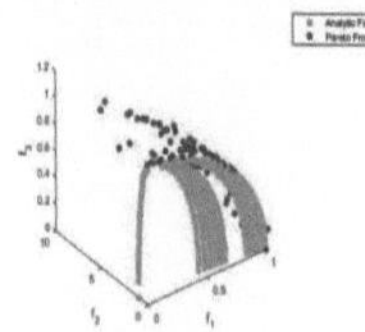

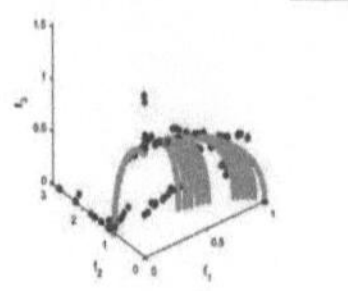

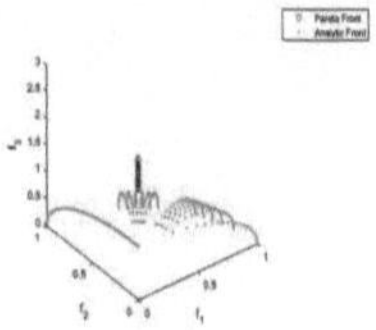

(i) MOBWO for CF10 problem

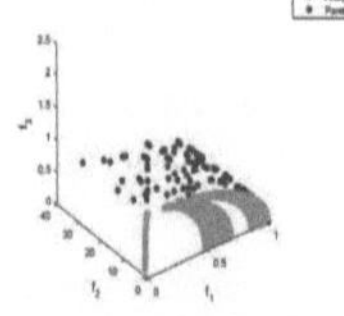

(j) MOSMA for CF10 problem

(k) MOWCA for CF10 problem

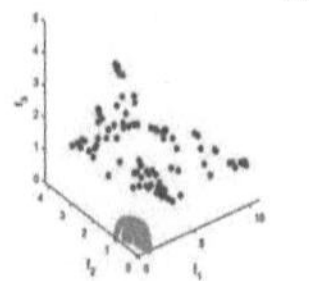

(l) NSGA2 for CF10 problem

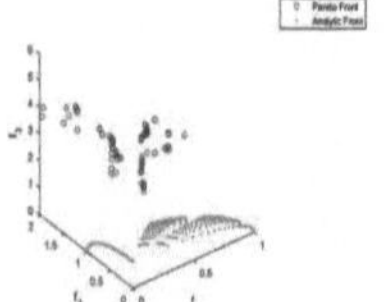

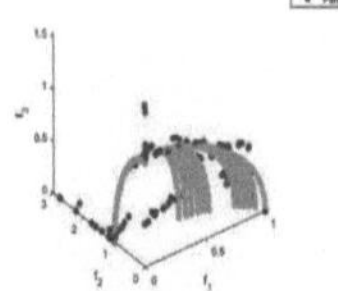

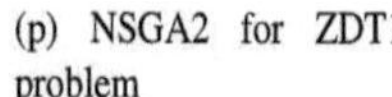

(m) MOBWO for ZDT1 problem

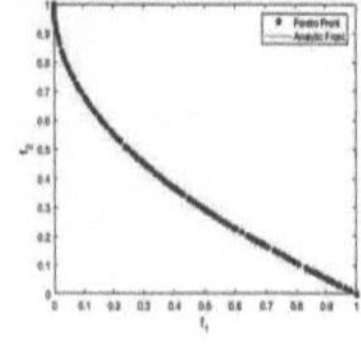

(n) MOSMA for ZDT1 problem

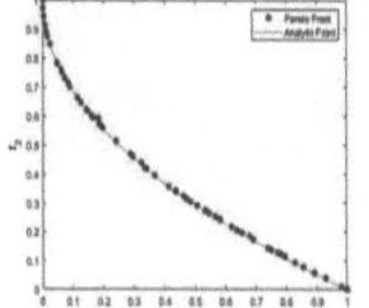

(o) MOWCA for ZDT1 problem

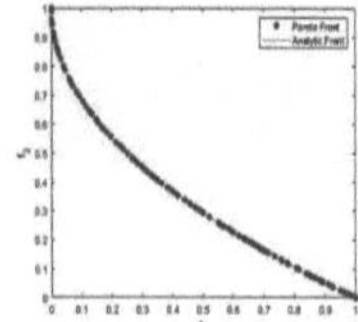

(p) NSGA2 for ZDT1 problem

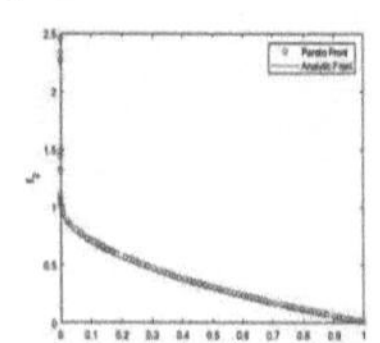

(q) MOBWO for ZDT2 problem

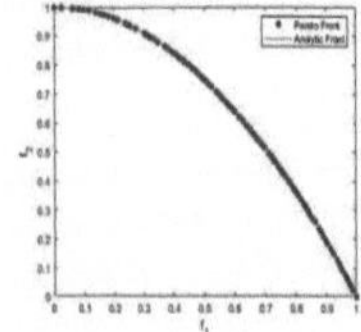

(r) MOSMA for ZDT2 problem

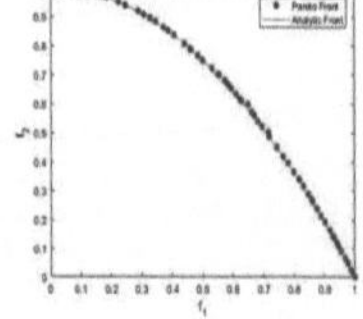

(s) MOWCA for ZDT2 problem

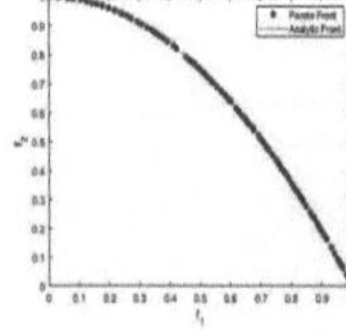

(t) NSGA2 for ZDT2 problem

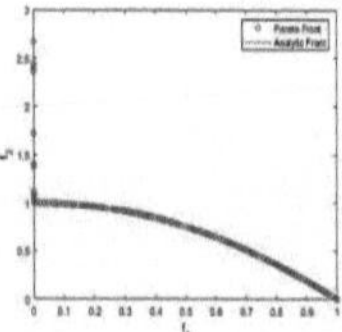

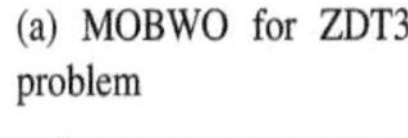

(a) MOBWO for ZDT3 problem

(b) MOSMA for ZDT3 problem

(c) MOWCA for ZDT3 problem

(d) NSGA2 for ZDT3 problem

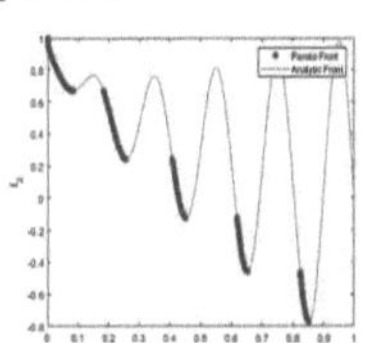 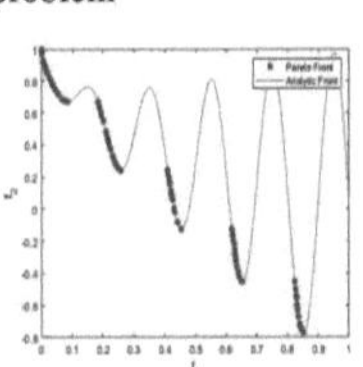 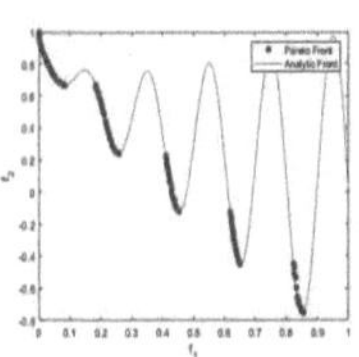 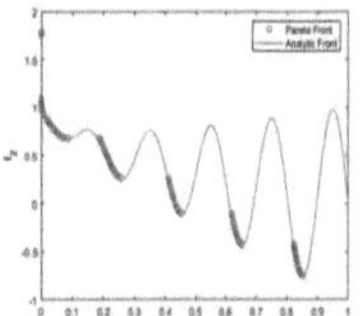

(e) MOBWO for ZDT4 problem

(f) MOSMA for ZDT4 problem

(g) MOWCA for ZDT4 problem

(h) NSGA2 for ZDT4 problem

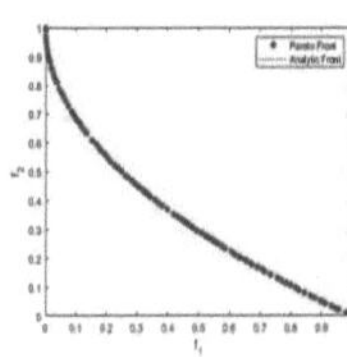 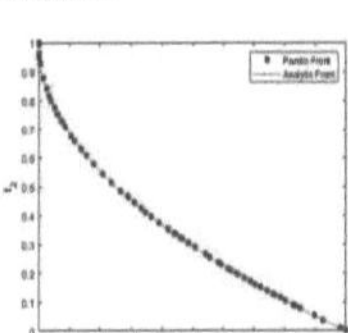 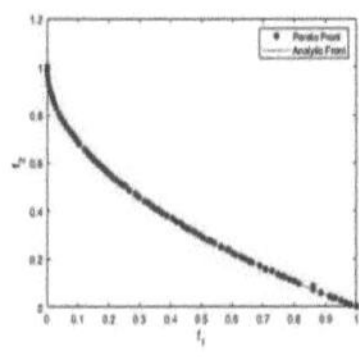 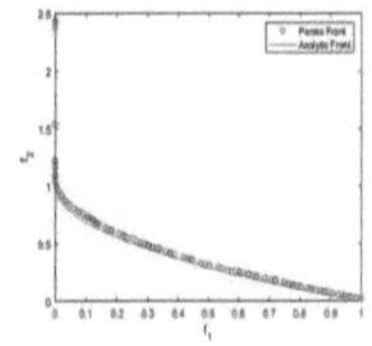

(i) MOBWO for ZDT6 problem

(j) MOSMA for ZDT6 problem

(k) MOWCA for ZDT6 problem

(l) NSGA2 for ZDT6 problem

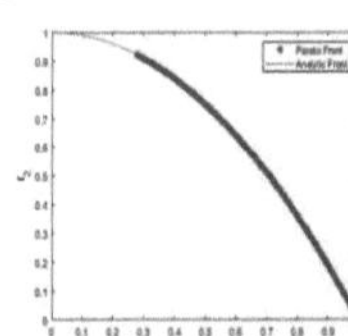 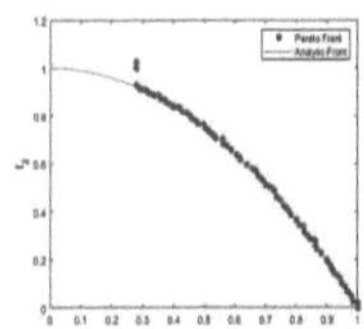 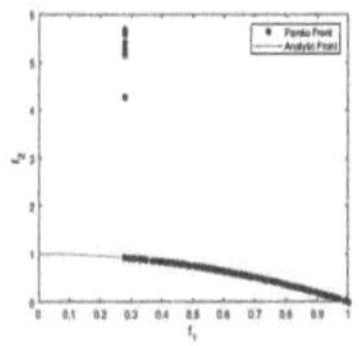 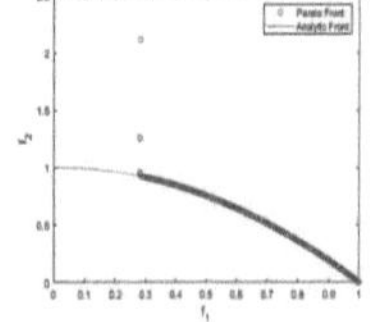

(m) MOBWO for DTLZ1 problem

(n) MOSMA for DTLZ1 problem

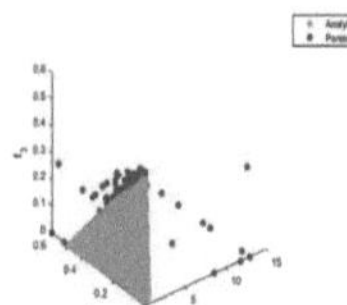

(o) MOWCA for DTLZ1 problem

(p) NSGA2 for DTLZ1 problem

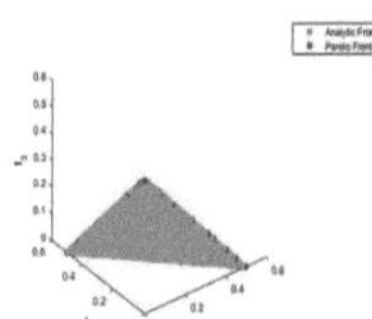  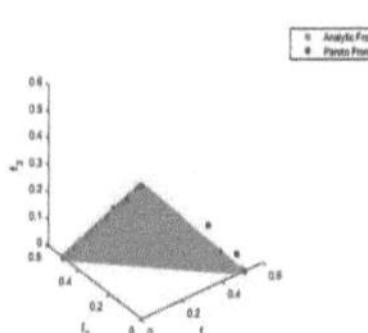 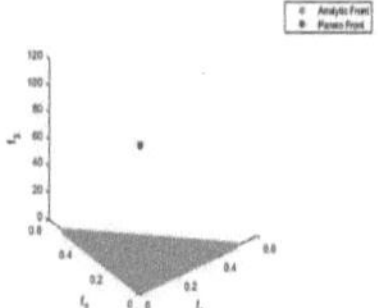

(q) MOBWO for DTLZ2 problem

(r) MOSMA for DTLZ2 problem

(s) MOWCA for DTLZ2 problem

(t) NSGA2 for DTLZ2 problem

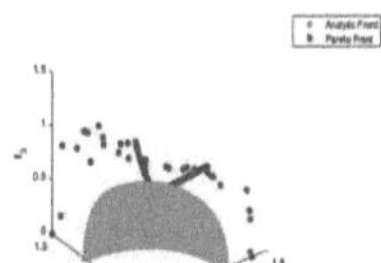 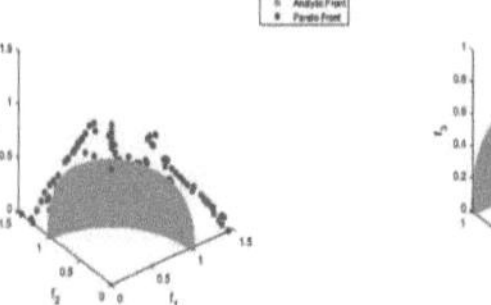 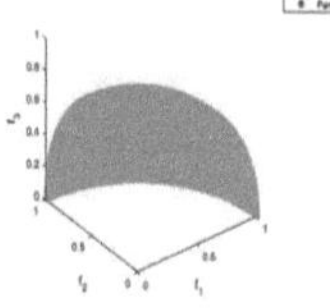

(a) MOBWO for DTLZ3 problem

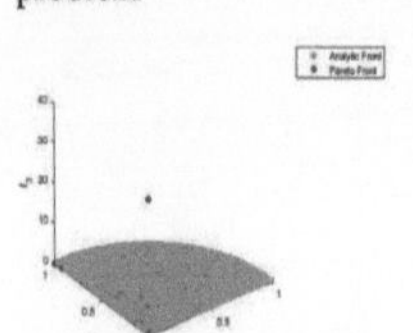

(b) MOSMA for DTLZ3 problem

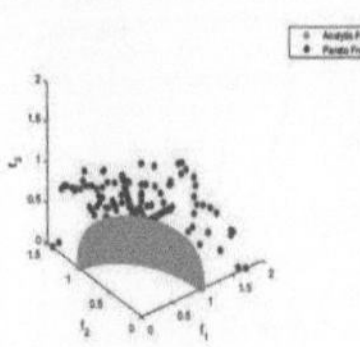

(c) MOWCA for DTLZ3 problem

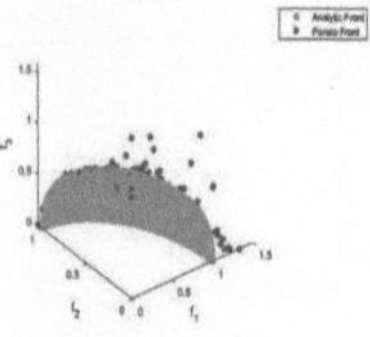

(d) NSGA2 for DTLZ3 problem

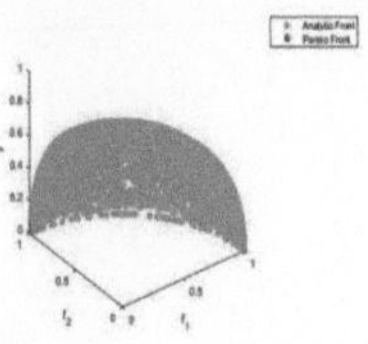

(e) MOBWO for DTLZ4 problem

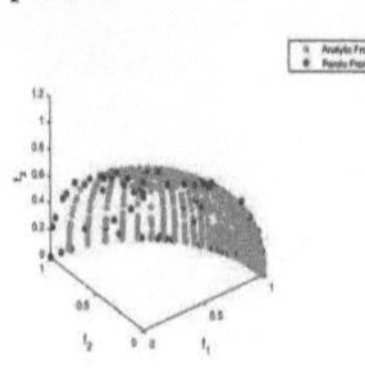

(f) MOSMA for DTLZ4 problem

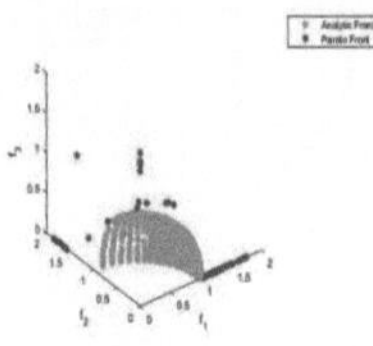

(g) MOWCA for DTLZ4 problem

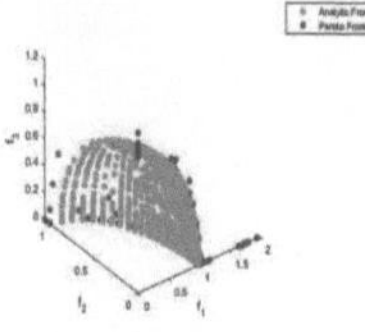

(h) NSGA2 for DTLZ4 problem

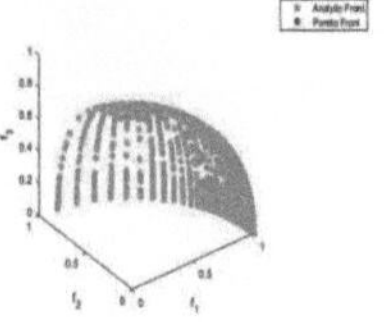

(i) MOBWO for DTLZ5 problem

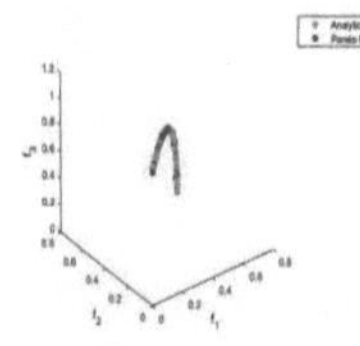

(j) MOSMA for DTLZ5 problem

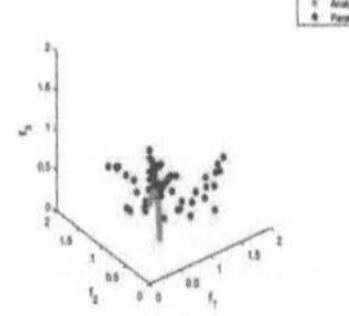

(k) MOWCA for DTLZ5 problem

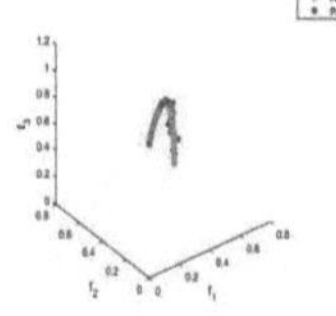

(l) NSGA2 for DTLZ5 problem

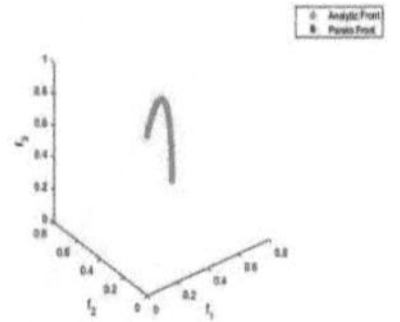

(m) MOBWO for DTLZ6 problèm

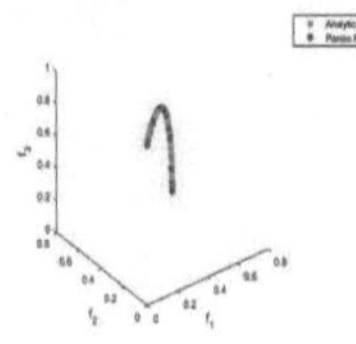

(n) MOSMA for DTLZ6 problèm

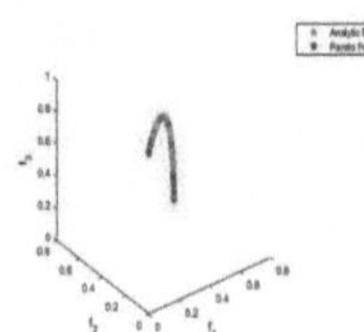

(o) MOWCA for DTLZ6 problèm

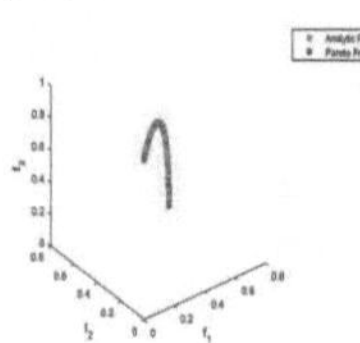

(p) MOBWO for DTLZ6 problèm

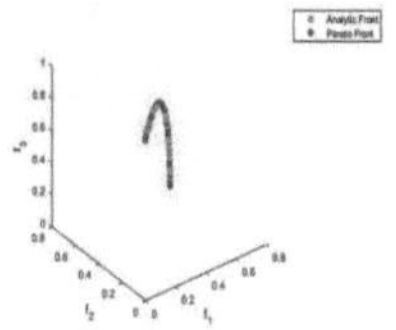

(q) MOBWO for DTLZ7 problem

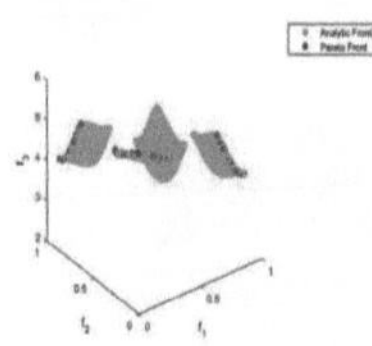

(r) MOSMA for DTLZ7 problem

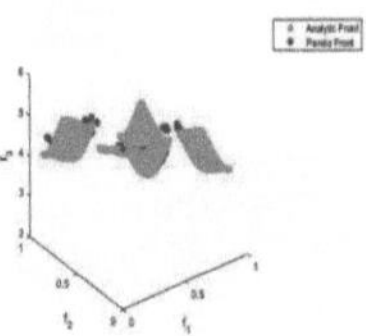

(s) MOWCA for DTLZ7 problem

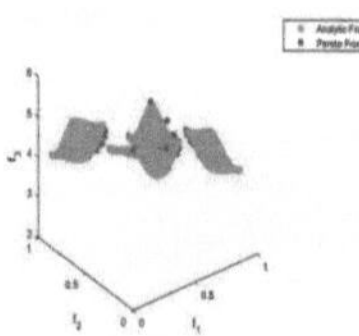

(t) NSGA2 for DTLZ7 problem

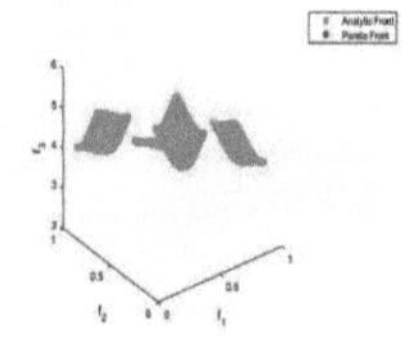

Table 3. GD-Metric Values Obtained on CF problems.

Methods	MOBWO			MOSMA			MOWCA			NSGA2		
Contente	Best	Ave	std	Best	Ave	std	Best	Ave	std	Best	Ave	std
CF1	2.0362e-03	**2.0812e-03**	**3.1155e-05**	2.0359e-03	2.0956e-03	5.4834e-05	2.1443e-03	2.9913e-03	1.0041e-03	**2.0256e-03**	2.9561e-03	1.2388e-03
CF2	**6.3610e-03**	**6.8355e-03**	**4.0411e-04**	5.1847e-02	8.5707e-02	4.1013e-02	2.0952e-02	7.7451e-02	3.1299e-02	1.2653e-02	2.4619e-01	2.0268e-01
CF3	**4.3383e-02**	**5.8931e-02**	**1.3404e-02**	4.5752e-01	8.4985e-01	4.0551e-01	3.1406e-02	4.9015e-01	4.9987e-01	3.4265e-02	1.8708e+14	2.4711e+14
CF4	5.2058e-03	**7.5790e-03**	**2.0331e-03**	2.3130e-01	5.2004e-01	2.1587e-01	4.2279e-02	2.5791e-01	1.9526e-01	**4.0496e-03**	1.1090e-02	4.9493e-03
CF5	**4.2041e-04**	**1.1875e-03**	**1.4889e-03**	5.4565e-04	1.0667e-01	1.1273e-01	1.2378e-01	4.4493e-01	2.3975e-01	3.8882e-01	5.8791e-01	1.4596e-01
CF6	**8.8697e-04**	**1.6746e-03**	**4.8180e-04**	1.5323e-03	1.4670e-02	3.9937e-02	1.7680e-02	1.1264e-01	6.5339e-02	1.0197e-02	3.5317e-02	1.0266e-02
CF7	**2.5212e-02**	**1.1313e-01**	**5.6534e-02**	5.9857e-01	7.5330e-01	1.4377e-01	4.3491e-01	1.0458e+00	4.2753e-01	1.4318e-01	4.7707e-01	1.5780e-01
CF8	5.3476e-01	1.3506e+00	3.0987e-01	**5.0941e-02**	**1.3974e-01**	**3.0087e-01**	8.9303e-01	2.1387e+00	6.3072e-01	1.8244e-01	9.6037e-01	6.6427e-01
CF9	5.8651e-02	2.3161e-01	**1.1324e-01**	**3.0539e-02**	**1.5436e-01**	1.5213e-01	4.6790e-01	7.5022e-01	2.0682e-01	5.7109e-02	5.1281e-01	4.0834e-01
CF10	**0**	8.7285e-01	7.5297e-01	1.0260e-01	**4.0746e-01**	**4.5677e-01**	1.0741e+00	1.9436e+00	5.3171e-01	3.4755e-01	1.5905e+00	6.9049e-01

3.4 Metric Values

Table 4. IGD-Metric Values Obtained on CF problems.

Methods	MOBWO			MOSMA			MOWCA			NSGA2		
Contente	Best	Ave	std	Best	Ave	std	Best	Ave	std	Best	Ave	std
CF1	**4.6702e-03**	**5.9170e-03**	**6.5728e-04**	8.3315e-03	1.0113e-02	1.2456e-03	8.3648e-03	1.7719e-02	9.4135e-03	5.3502e-03	7.9253e-03	1.1182e-03
CF2	**7.5180e-03**	**9.1431e-03**	**7.9010e-04**	7.5405e-02	1.7381e-01	9.0391e-02	7.8872e-02	1.8830e-01	6.9296e-02	1.9040e-01	2.0728e+00	1.6190e+00
CF3	**1.9132e-01**	**2.1564e-01**	2.2757e-02	1.9055e+00	1.9078e+00	**2.3021e-03**	5.1182e-01	1.2020e+00	3.0484e-01	6.6158e-01	1.8680e+15	2.4733e+15
CF4	**3.7842e-02**	**7.1729e-02**	**2.3955e-02**	3.5232e-01	6.0282e-01	9.7684e-02	9.0220e-02	2.0264e-01	7.5071e-02	1.0368e-01	2.1545e-01	1.2807e-01
CF5	**4.7881e-01**	6.1061e-01	**5.0186e-02**	2.8305e-01	**4.2002e-01**	1.1191e-01	7.4338e-01	1.2891e+00	4.1695e-01	2.4923e+00	3.8462e+00	8.2171e-01
CF6	2.6546e-02	4.1494e-02	1.8396e-02	**1.7897e-02**	**2.6125e-02**	**5.4721e-03**	8.1774e-02	1.4974e-01	4.3902e-02	9.2707e-02	1.4001e-01	8.6376e-02
CF7	**1.0354e-01**	**2.0409e-01**	**8.1572e-02**	2.7904e+00	3.3923e+00	5.2916e-01	2.6991e+00	3.2102e+00	4.9749e-01	1.4108e+00	3.0822e+00	1.0102e+00
CF8	**1.6174e-01**	3.7534e-01	9.5020e-02	1.6497e-01	**2.0399e-01**	**2.6700e-02**	5.4349e-01	3.3136e+00	1.8160e+00	1.7225e+00	7.8772e+00	5.8149e+00
CF9	**1.3349e-01**	2.4495e-01	8.3665e-02	1.6036e-01	**2.0353e-01**	**3.9908e-02**	4.6519e-01	9.0664e-01	2.9814e-01	1.0324e+00	4.4516e+00	3.8030e+00
CF10	3.7572e-01	6.9136e-01	3.0966e-01	**2.9391e-01**	**4.2535e-01**	**1.0737e-01**	1.1389e+00	3.4585e+00	1.3224e+00	2.3534e+00	9.9639e+00	6.4798e+00

Table 5. delta-Metric Values Obtained on CF problems.

Methods	MOBWO			MOSMA			MOWCA			NSGA2		
Contente	Best	Ave	std	Best	Ave	std	Best	Ave	std	Best	Ave	std
CF1	1.7886e-02	**1.8255e-02**	**3.4070e-04**	1.7887e-02	1.8538e-02	6.3077e-04	1.9091e-02	2.7140e-02	8.6651e-03	**1.7801e-02**	2.2023e-02	4.6017e-03
CF2	**3.9342e-02**	**4.3348e-02**	**3.2196e-03**	2.7214e-01	5.7976e-01	3.2755e-01	1.7667e-01	5.9682e-01	2.5372e-01	1.9040e-01	2.5526e+00	1.8597e+00
CF3	**3.2133e-01**	**4.4157e-01**	**8.0748e-02**	3.7954e+00	5.7840e+00	2.4649e+00	5.1182e-01	3.4188e+00	2.8463e+00	6.6158e-01	1.8708e+15	2.4711e+15
CF4	**4.1227e-02**	**7.4228e-02**	**2.1797e-02**	1.6797e+00	3.4149e+00	1.1926e+00	3.5705e-01	1.6001e+00	1.2834e+00	1.0368e-01	2.1545e-01	1.2807e-01
CF5	4.7881e-01	**6.1061e-01**	**5.0186e-02**	**3.1574e-01**	8.7142e-01	7.5359e-01	1.2213e+00	3.7685e+00	1.6823e+00	3.9015e+00	5.6532e+00	1.3377e+00
CF6	2.6546e-02	**4.1494e-02**	**1.8396e-02**	1.7897e-02	7.5217e-02	1.5534e-01	1.5171e-01	6.8667e-01	4.0509e-01	**9.4725e-02**	2.7042e-01	7.5882e-02
CF7	**1.6596e-01**	**4.8070e-01**	**2.5122e-01**	5.4987e+00	6.6633e+00	1.0166e+00	4.0565e+00	8.5786e+00	2.9372e+00	1.4270e+00	4.4683e+00	1.4246e+00
CF8	2.7330e+00	1.0092e+01	2.8445e+00	**2.4854e-01**	**8.3905e-01**	**6.3913e-01**	7.2449e+00	1.8889e+01	5.7161e+00	1.7734e+00	9.5219e+00	6.5929e+00
CF9	3.2838e-01	1.6238e+00	9.6848e-01	**2.3847e-01**	**8.1655e-01**	**7.4485e-01**	4.2195e+00	6.1571e+00	1.7191e+00	1.0324e+00	5.0293e+00	3.7652e+00
CF10	1.0473e+00	7.0703e+00	5.2165e+00	**7.5347e-01**	**3.1446e+00**	**3.5051e+00**	9.5344e+00	1.6731e+01	4.2618e+00	3.4242e+00	1.5355e+01	6.9914e+00

Table 6. spacing-Metric Values Obtained on CF problems.

Methods	MOBWO			MOSMA			MOWCA			NSGA2		
Contente	Best	Ave	std	Best	Ave	std	Best	Ave	std	Best	Ave	std
CF1	**5.7896e-03**	**6.3302e-03**	**2.9725e-04**	7.8733e-03	9.4321e-03	1.2370e-03	6.0191e-03	6.6051e-03	3.7226e-04	6.6140e-03	7.9548e-03	1.4008e-03
CF2	6.1624e-03	7.3962e-03	**9.5010e-04**	7.9139e-02	1.3616e-01	4.4477e-02	1.0161e-02	2.3247e-02	9.7698e-03	**7.2091e-04**	**2.7359e-03**	1.7384e-03
CF3	**2.8811e-02**	**6.6308e-02**	**3.4897e-02**	4.5001e-01	1.2087e+00	6.4830e-01	1.5288e-02	1.0757e-01	1.3991e-01	0	7.8501e+10	1.6655e+11
CF4	1.6919e-03	1.7499e-02	1.9603e-02	1.9964e-01	4.9298e-01	2.3835e-01	1.4454e-02	9.8706e-02	1.2131e-01	**1.4489e-03**	**4.1828e-03**	**1.8208e-03**
CF5	**1.2032e-04**	**4.6789e-04**	**4.8664e-04**	8.5744e-04	4.3976e-03	6.7263e-03	2.7986e-02	9.6719e-02	7.2644e-02	1.1127e-02	4.7810e-02	3.2958e-02
CF6	**3.6694e-03**	**8.4863e-03**	4.8536e-03	8.6195e-03	1.0353e-02	**2.5774e-03**	6.7565e-03	4.3627e-02	4.7995e-02	5.1481e-03	1.2056e-02	6.2375e-03
CF7	2.4144e-02	3.1078e-01	2.9221e-01	2.4076e-01	6.6282e-01	4.1063e-01	4.9715e-02	1.3332e-01	9.6679e-02	**2.1062e-03**	**3.2296e-02**	**2.5624e-02**
CF8	2.3804e-01	3.3412e-01	4.2208e-02	2.7563e-02	4.7250e-02	**1.8988e-02**	1.6431e-01	1.4892e+00	6.3077e-01	**1.1620e-02**	**3.4887e-02**	2.4841e-02
CF9	8.0947e-02	1.5932e-01	4.5584e-02	2.7736e-02	5.6940e-02	2.4534e-02	3.5459e-01	4.6440e-01	9.7825e-02	**2.7981e-03**	**1.1095e-02**	**8.6510e-03**
CF10	**0**	2.0370e-01	1.7689e-01	3.2734e-02	**9.8260e-02**	**5.6513e-02**	5.5949e-01	1.0814e+00	2.9238e-01	7.9966e-02	1.8176e-01	1.0279e-01

Table 7. spread-Metric Values Obtained on CF problems.

Methods	MOBWO			MOSMA			MOWCA			NSGA2		
Contente	Best	Ave	std	Best	Ave	std	Best	Ave	std	Best	Ave	std
CF1	**2.7313e-01**	**2.9456e-01**	**1.9754e-02**	1.6002e+00	1.7065e+00	7.4163e-02	2.8132e-01	3.2478e-01	3.4034e-02	3.4297e-01	4.2766e-01	6.7801e-02
CF2	5.9096e-01	8.0555e-01	1.2782e-01	7.6618e-01	9.6800e-01	1.4538e-01	**4.2083e-01**	**7.1829e-01**	2.1883e-01	7.9405e-01	9.5929e-01	**6.0192e-02**
CF3	1.2501e+00	1.4532e+00	9.2139e-02	1.1483e+00	1.2674e+00	7.1610e-02	1.0660e+00	1.1935e+00	1.1454e-01	**1.0000e+00**	**1.0055e+00**	**1.1270e-02**
CF4	1.1125e+00	1.3969e+00	1.9294e-01	8.5956e-01	1.0865e+00	1.3367e-01	**5.7963e-01**	1.2351e+00	3.0017e-01	7.0817e-01	**8.2936e-01**	**7.6020e-02**
CF5	9.8378e-01	**9.8975e-01**	**3.0363e-03**	1.0007e+00	1.0468e+00	8.0740e-02	**7.5301e-01**	1.0494e+00	2.5999e-01	9.6644e-01	1.0444e+00	5.5784e-02
CF6	**4.4431e-01**	**5.6358e-01**	7.1388e-02	1.1809e+00	1.2399e+00	**4.6920e-02**	4.7194e-01	7.8391e-01	2.3479e-01	5.4356e-01	6.4969e-01	6.7623e-02
CF7	1.4773e+00	1.7565e+00	1.2620e-01	**6.7287e-01**	**8.7849e-01**	1.3310e-01	8.2360e-01	9.9200e-01	8.2161e-02	1.0007e+00	1.0551e+00	**3.4631e-02**
CF8	**4.5203e-01**	**5.8193e-01**	9.2935e-02	1.0591e+00	1.1837e+00	7.6423e-02	5.1052e-01	6.7214e-01	9.8227e-02	9.9859e-01	1.0156e+00	**1.4490e-02**
CF9	**4.7348e-01**	6.3613e-01	1.3081e-01	1.1015e+00	1.1940e+00	8.0344e-02	4.9133e-01	**6.1353e-01**	7.3452e-02	1.0006e+00	1.0116e+00	**1.3682e-02**
CF10	**5.2579e-01**	7.3331e-01	2.3083e-01	1.0310e+00	1.1804e+00	9.1106e-02	5.5665e-01	**6.6266e-01**	9.4769e-02	9.5534e-01	1.0227e+00	**3.4719e-02**

Table 8. HV-Metric Values Obtained on CF problems.

Methods	MOBWO			MOSMA			MOWCA			NSGA2		
Contente	Best	Ave	std	Best	Ave	std	Best	Ave	std	Best	Ave	std
CF1	**5.7791e-01**	**5.7705e-01**	5.2301e-04	5.7231e-01	5.7150e-01	6.4691e-04	5.7278e-01	5.6081e-01	**1.2494e-02**	5.7580e-01	5.7469e-01	7.8699e-04
CF2	**7.0972e-01**	**7.0791e-01**	1.0905e-03	5.6583e-01	4.5594e-01	1.1610e-01	6.0452e-01	4.5933e-01	7.9757e-02	4.3473e-01	1.3835e-01	**1.8637e-01**
CF3	**1.2480e-01**	**9.1853e-02**	2.7582e-02	0	0	0	1.1403e-01	1.1403e-02	**3.6058e-02**	2.0964e-02	2.0964e-03	6.6294e-03
CF4	**5.3564e-01**	4.9222e-01	3.1952e-02	1.1268e-01	3.7408e-02	2.6566e-02	4.1513e-01	2.9924e-01	7.6322e-02	4.3982e-01	3.3336e-01	**1.0221e-01**
CF5	1.1404e-01	1.0942e-01	2.0479e-03	**2.3378e-01**	**1.7179e-01**	**3.4557e-02**	0	0	0	0	0	0
CF6	6.9303e-01	6.7939e-01	1.0396e-02	**7.0001e-01**	**6.9253e-01**	6.7531e-03	5.7356e-01	4.9273e-01	5.5303e-02	5.8914e-01	5.3503e-01	6.9258e-02
CF7	**5.4447e-01**	**3.7258e-01**	**1.2657e-01**	0	0	0	0	0	0	0	0	0
CF8	**3.9100e-01**	2.2575e-01	**7.7433e-02**	3.8706e-01	**3.5057e-01**	3.3964e-02	8.1995e-02	8.1995e-03	2.5929e-02	0	0	0
CF9	**4.5273e-01**	3.2879e-01	**1.0728e-01**	4.0070e-01	**3.7778e-01**	2.3768e-02	9.0097e-02	1.2668e-02	2.8472e-02	0	0	0
CF10	1.9485e-01	1.1320e-01	3.3882e-02	**2.5508e-01**	**1.6109e-01**	**5.0790e-02**	0	0	0	0	0	0

Table 9. GD-Metric Values Obtained on ZDT problems.

Methods	MOBWO			MOSMA			MOWCA			NSGA2		
Contente	Best	Ave	std	Best	Ave	std	Best	Ave	std	Best	Ave	std
ZDT1	**2.4717e-03**	**2.5816e-03**	5.9375e-05	2.5103e-03	2.6101e-03	7.5009e-05	2.5216e-03	2.5830e-03	**5.6091e-05**	2.0271e-02	5.1510e-02	2.2673e-02
ZDT2	3.0937e-05	**7.3324e-05**	**3.2443e-05**	2.1148e-04	2.7671e-04	3.6464e-05	**4.3371e-06**	3.8664e-03	7.7562e-03	5.4967e-02	1.3444e-01	4.5639e-02
ZDT3	1.6007e-02	**2.2165e-02**	3.4588e-03	3.3321e-02	3.5097e-02	**1.3871e-03**	**9.4847e-03**	2.7354e-02	9.8598e-03	3.0635e-02	5.0234e-02	1.3165e-02
ZDT4	**2.1111e-05**	**4.8103e-05**	**1.6693e-05**	9.1244e-05	1.5859e-04	4.0318e-05	1.0005e-04	1.5527e+00	1.6402e+00	2.3979e+00	NaN	NaN
ZDT6	**4.4733e-06**	**4.7671e-06**	**1.9819e-07**	1.2737e-03	1.4588e-02	1.5597e-02	1.1434e-01	2.0381e-01	7.4279e-02	2.9486e-03	6.0345e-03	4.5408e-03

Table 10. IGD-Metric Values Obtained on ZDT problems.

Methods	MOBWO			MOSMA			MOWCA			NSGA2		
Contente	Best	Ave	std	Best	Ave	std	Best	Ave	std	Best	Ave	std
ZDT1	2.6412e-01	2.6417e-01	**3.2753e-05**	2.6374e-01	**2.6413e-01**	2.3182e-04	2.6418e-01	2.6434e-01	2.9033e-04	**2.6123e-01**	2.6844e-01	1.1029e-02
ZDT2	**4.4320e-03**	**4.6635e-03**	**2.5777e-04**	7.4103e-03	8.4126e-03	8.1724e-04	4.6649e-03	1.2953e-01	1.9968e-01	3.7081e-01	1.1908e+00	3.4556e-01
ZDT3	1.6812e-01	1.7558e-01	5.6887e-03	1.6551e-01	1.6589e-01	**2.4746e-04**	1.4978e-01	1.6512e-01	5.4726e-03	**1.2681e-01**	**1.5698e-01**	1.1052e-02
ZDT4	**4.3036e-03**	**4.4314e-03**	**9.0113e-05**	7.3779e-03	7.8663e-03	3.6345e-04	4.5810e-03	2.2728e-01	2.6341e-01	2.3032e+00	NaN	NaN
ZDT6	4.5552e-02	4.6029e-02	**2.7339e-04**	4.4319e-02	4.5181e-02	6.1954e-04	4.4824e-02	6.2129e-02	2.1123e-02	**4.2788e-02**	**4.3175e-02**	3.1352e-04

Table 11. delta-Metric Values Obtained on ZDT problems.

Methods	MOBWO			MOSMA			MOWCA			NSGA2		
Contente	Best	Ave	std	Best	Ave	std	Best	Ave	std	Best	Ave	std
ZDT1	2.6412e-01	2.6417e-01	**3.2753e-05**	2.6374e-01	**2.6413e-01**	2.3182e-04	2.6418e-01	2.6434e-01	2.9033e-04	**2.6123e-01**	2.8208e-01	3.9703e-02
ZDT2	**4.4320e-03**	**4.6635e-03**	**2.5777e-04**	7.4103e-03	8.4126e-03	8.1724e-04	4.6649e-03	1.2953e-01	1.9968e-01	4.5165e-01	1.2871e+00	4.1242e-01
ZDT3	1.6812e-01	**1.7678e-01**	**5.9034e-03**	2.3824e-01	2.5541e-01	1.0718e-02	**1.4978e-01**	2.1449e-01	4.1550e-02	1.9333e-01	2.7869e-01	4.5997e-02
ZDT4	**4.3036e-03**	**4.4314e-03**	**9.0113e-05**	7.3779e-03	7.8663e-03	3.6345e-04	4.5810e-03	1.2387e+01	1.4423e+01	1.1302e+01	NaN	NaN
ZDT6	4.5552e-02	4.6029e-02	**2.7339e-04**	4.4319e-02	5.1380e-02	1.2219e-02	3.0188e-01	1.1016e+00	7.3472e-01	**4.2788e-02**	**4.3175e-02**	3.1352e-04

Table 12. spacing-Metric Values Obtained on ZDT problems.

Methods	MOBWO			MOSMA			MOWCA			NSGA2		
Contente	Best	Ave	std	Best	Ave	std	Best	Ave	std	Best	Ave	std
ZDT1	**6.1440e-03**	**6.6483e-03**	**3.2062e-04**	8.0898e-03	1.0160e-02	9.3624e-04	8.1561e-03	8.6679e-03	4.5103e-04	8.6611e-03	1.3941e-02	5.0269e-03
ZDT2	**5.8760e-03**	6.7326e-03	**5.7772e-04**	9.5312e-03	1.0324e-02	6.1504e-04	0	7.4766e-03	**6.7240e-03**	2.0832e-03	1.6675e-02	2.7274e-02
ZDT3	8.6018e-03	2.0263e-02	1.1919e-02	1.0791e-02	1.2101e-02	**1.0988e-03**	**5.9302e-03**	**1.1795e-02**	6.4824e-03	8.3664e-03	3.8509e-02	6.1075e-02
ZDT4	**6.2637e-03**	**7.1615e-03**	**6.8717e-04**	8.9093e-03	1.0820e-02	1.1664e-03	7.0280e-03	2.8787e-01	3.6939e-01	5.4518e-01	NaN	NaN
ZDT6	**4.5780e-03**	**7.1326e-03**	**1.1073e-03**	8.3141e-03	1.3013e-02	1.2244e-02	2.2770e-02	9.2213e-02	5.7336e-02	6.5156e-03	2.9540e-02	4.5065e-02

Table 13. spread-Metric Values Obtained on ZDT problems.

Methods	MOBWO			MOSMA			MOWCA			NSGA2		
Contente	Best	Ave	std	Best	Ave	std	Best	Ave	std	Best	Ave	std
ZDT1	**2.9815e-01**	**3.4426e-01**	**2.7321e-02**	1.3570e+00	1.4966e+00	8.5385e-02	4.6980e-01	5.3337e-01	4.0532e-02	3.9066e-01	5.6811e-01	9.7421e-02
ZDT2	**3.0089e-01**	**3.6204e-01**	**4.7572e-02**	1.2951e+00	1.4519e+00	1.0448e-01	4.2429e-01	7.5443e-01	2.7327e-01	7.4250e-01	9.7864e-01	1.0747e-01
ZDT3	5.7477e-01	**6.7617e-01**	1.0243e-01	1.0587e+00	1.1372e+00	**4.9104e-02**	**4.7276e-01**	7.0219e-01	2.3060e-01	5.6989e-01	7.2363e-01	1.8086e-01
ZDT4	**3.2599e-01**	**3.8060e-01**	**4.6101e-02**	1.3621e+00	1.4536e+00	8.4213e-02	3.5480e-01	8.9626e-01	5.0597e-01	1.0667e+00	NaN	NaN
ZDT6	1.0157e+00	1.2096e+00	**8.1079e-02**	9.0874e-01	**1.0537e+00**	1.0426e-01	8.2864e-01	1.2800e+00	2.9329e-01	**5.5827e-01**	7.0115e-01	2.2424e-01

Table 14. HV-Metric Values Obtained on ZDT problems.

Methods	MOBWO			MOSMA			MOWCA			NSGA2		
Contente	Best	Ave	std	Best	Ave	std	Best	Ave	std	Best	Ave	std
ZDT1	**7.2007e-01**	**7.1997e-01**	8.0383e-05	7.1501e-01	7.1389e-01	8.1952e-04	7.1988e-01	7.1949e-01	5.5934e-04	7.0852e-01	6.5140e-01	**5.9758e-02**
ZDT2	4.4440e-01	**4.4397e-01**	3.6504e-04	4.3959e-01	4.3838e-01	8.7144e-04	**4.4442e-01**	3.4160e-01	**1.6037e-01**	8.8094e-02	8.8094e-03	2.7858e-02
ZDT3	7.2164e-01	6.6959e-01	2.1108e-02	6.5889e-01	6.5817e-01	4.8425e-04	7.3400e-01	6.7601e-01	**2.3271e-02**	**7.3533e-01**	**7.0145e-01**	4.2353e-02
ZDT4	**7.2003e-01**	**7.1977e-01**	1.4729e-04	7.1629e-01	7.1543e-01	5.2668e-04	7.1963e-01	4.8107e-01	**2.3517e-01**	0	NaN	NaN
ZDT6	4.1546e-01	**4.1488e-01**	3.4285e-04	4.1288e-01	4.1181e-01	7.2956e-04	**4.1634e-01**	3.9735e-01	**2.3323e-02**	4.1469e-01	4.1389e-01	4.7302e-04

Table 15. GD-Metric Values Obtained on DTLZ problems.

Methods	MOBWO			MOSMA			MOWCA			NSGA2		
Contente	Best	Ave	std	Best	Ave	std	Best	Ave	std	Best	Ave	std
DTLZ1	**3.6076e-04**	**4.1569e-04**	**6.3803e-05**	1.1872e-01	3.7676e-01	3.9228e-01	6.6105e-04	1.0262e-01	2.6093e-01	1.4577e+01	1.5203e+01	3.6929e-01
DTLZ2	**3.1784e-03**	**6.4502e-03**	**5.2461e-03**	3.7004e-02	5.0710e-02	1.0596e-02	1.0324e-02	2.3859e-02	1.6162e-02	3.6397e-01	NaN	NaN
DTLZ3	**1.0861e-03**	**1.0033e+00**	**1.2151e+00**	1.3167e+01	1.6854e+01	2.2562e+00	1.7458e+01	2.3299e+01	4.0680e+00	2.0738e+02	NaN	NaN
DTLZ4	**5.2166e-03**	**6.4044e-03**	**5.5405e-04**	3.6906e-02	6.4737e-02	2.0277e-02	6.5804e-03	1.0140e-02	4.4489e-03	NaN	NaN	NaN
DTLZ5	**2.2236e-04**	**3.6247e-04**	**1.0313e-04**	3.3030e-02	4.9071e-02	8.4455e-03	7.9450e-04	9.9373e-03	1.5556e-02	NaN	NaN	NaN
DTLZ6	**3.6837e-04**	**4.5749e-04**	**6.0530e-05**	5.2186e-04	4.7557e-03	4.3065e-03	4.6259e-04	1.8047e-01	2.3231e-01	NaN	NaN	NaN
DTLZ7	**6.4648e-04**	**8.3203e-04**	**2.1275e-04**	4.1807e-03	5.3174e-03	7.8753e-04	2.5460e-03	6.5552e-03	4.7433e-03	NaN	NaN	NaN

Table 16. IGD-Metric Values Obtained on DTLZ problems.

Methods	MOBWO			MOSMA			MOWCA			NSGA2		
Contente	Best	Ave	std	Best	Ave	std	Best	Ave	std	Best	Ave	std
DTLZ1	**2.3004e-02**	2.3733e-02	5.7798e-04	1.0197e-01	1.2723e-01	2.2924e-02	2.6078e-02	4.5226e-02	2.7900e-02	1.2601e+02	1.3090e+02	2.9303e+00
DTLZ2	**6.7117e-02**	**7.2180e-02**	**3.7845e-03**	2.7993e-01	3.3025e-01	3.2397e-02	1.0753e-01	1.6669e-01	4.3247e-02	3.8594e+00	NaN	NaN
DTLZ3	**6.8712e-02**	2.9139e+00	3.0721e+00	4.9150e-01	**5.1822e-01**	**6.1804e-02**	4.9150e-01	5.7335e+00	5.6061e+00	2.0588e+03	NaN	NaN
DTLZ4	**3.6147e-02**	**4.5262e-02**	**5.8325e-03**	3.1608e-01	3.6605e-01	3.4278e-02	5.3836e-02	8.7163e-02	4.9987e-02	NaN	NaN	NaN
DTLZ5	**6.0747e-03**	**6.3464e-03**	**2.4526e-04**	1.5982e-01	2.0933e-01	3.0508e-02	7.7266e-03	2.7558e-02	2.6550e-02	NaN	NaN	NaN
DTLZ6	**5.4011e-03**	**6.0132e-03**	**3.4666e-04**	4.0574e-02	1.1751e-01	1.2115e-01	4.7265e-03	3.8170e-01	5.7226e-01	NaN	NaN	NaN
DTLZ7	3.3064e-01	3.4958e-01	1.4537e-02	**1.4144e-01**	**1.5577e-01**	**1.1848e-02**	8.0684e-02	2.4576e-01	3.1570e-01	NaN	NaN	NaN

Table 17. delta-Metric Values Obtained on DTLZ problems.

Methods	MOBWO			MOSMA			MOWCA			NSGA2		
Contente	Best	Ave	std	Best	Ave	std	Best	Ave	std	Best	Ave	std
DTLZ1	**2.3004e-02**	**2.3733e-02**	**5.7798e-04**	6.1295e-01	2.6025e+00	3.1791e+00	2.8421e-02	6.8483e-01	1.9522e+00	1.4485e+02	1.5107e+02	3.6622e+00
DTLZ2	**6.7117e-02**	**7.2180e-02**	**3.7845e-03**	3.1214e-01	4.2879e-01	9.4347e-02	1.0753e-01	2.0322e-01	1.1737e-01	3.8594e+00	NaN	NaN
DTLZ3	**6.8712e-02**	**4.4272e+00**	**4.2480e+00**	1.2391e+02	1.6556e+02	2.4421e+01	1.7112e+02	2.2700e+02	3.9496e+01	2.0738e+03	NaN	NaN
DTLZ4	**3.6147e-02**	**4.7305e-02**	**5.5161e-03**	3.2046e-01	5.0823e-01	1.4704e-01	5.3836e-02	9.4042e-02	4.9479e-02	NaN	NaN	NaN
DTLZ5	**6.0747e-03**	**6.3464e-03**	**2.4526e-04**	2.1377e-01	3.6614e-01	7.5357e-02	7.7266e-03	6.3684e-02	9.6863e-02	NaN	NaN	NaN
DTLZ6	**5.4011e-03**	**6.0132e-03**	**3.4666e-04**	4.0574e-02	1.1751e-01	1.2115e-01	4.7265e-03	1.4938e+00	2.0460e+00	NaN	NaN	NaN
DTLZ7	3.3064e-01	3.4958e-01	1.4537e-02	**1.4144e-01**	**1.5577e-01**	**1.1848e-02**	8.0684e-02	2.4576e-01	3.1570e-01	NaN	NaN	NaN

Table 18. spacing-Metric Values Obtained on DTLZ problems.

Methods	MOBWO			MOSMA			MOWCA			NSGA2		
Contente	Best	Ave	std	Best	Ave	std	Best	Ave	std	Best	Ave	std
DTLZ1	**1.7074e-02**	**2.0651e-02**	**1.7132e-03**	2.2908e-01	1.1362e+00	1.5912e+00	2.2480e-02	6.1949e-02	7.6646e-02	1.1285e+00	1.3491e+00	1.1635e-01
DTLZ2	5.2036e-02	**5.9549e-02**	**5.2045e-03**	1.1932e-01	1.4433e-01	2.2916e-02	6.1370e-02	8.0083e-02	2.2528e-02	**3.0071e-02**	NaN	NaN
DTLZ3	**6.4539e-02**	**4.2088e+00**	8.9878e+00	1.2443e+01	1.8396e+01	**3.5381e+00**	3.4259e+00	2.1915e+01	8.2728e+00	1.7021e+01	NaN	NaN
DTLZ4	5.5560e-02	**6.7292e-02**	**6.2763e-03**	9.9149e-02	1.8663e-01	6.2783e-02	**2.2096e-02**	7.5173e-02	4.8441e-02	NaN	NaN	NaN
DTLZ5	1.0461e-02	**1.1555e-02**	**8.0896e-04**	7.1383e-02	9.3882e-02	1.4648e-02	**7.6609e-03**	1.6338e-02	1.1178e-02	NaN	NaN	NaN
DTLZ6	**1.0543e-02**	**1.2412e-02**	8.6250e-04	**0**	2.9519e-02	5.4804e-02	7.9865e-03	8.6101e-02	7.8626e-02	NaN	NaN	NaN
DTLZ7	**1.7215e-02**	**2.4640e-02**	7.9623e-03	3.0746e-02	3.9930e-02	**5.6132e-03**	7.1187e-02	8.9573e-02	2.2843e-02	NaN	NaN	NaN

Table 19. spread-Metric Values Obtained on DTLZ problems.

Methods	MOBWO			MOSMA			MOWCA			NSGA2		
Contente	Best	Ave	std	Best	Ave	std	Best	Ave	std	Best	Ave	std
DTLZ1	**3.6848e-01**	**4.1971e-01**	3.5372e-02	6.8858e-01	1.1632e+00	3.1537e-01	4.5690e-01	7.2279e-01	2.8865e-01	7.5925e-01	8.0711e-01	**2.2593e-02**
DTLZ2	**3.8996e-01**	**4.3625e-01**	**3.6473e-02**	5.9513e-01	8.7282e-01	1.5519e-01	6.0002e-01	6.9974e-01	7.5018e-02	8.4726e-01	NaN	NaN
DTLZ3	**7.5102e-01**	**1.1647e+00**	4.4090e-01	9.7803e-01	1.4812e+00	2.8367e-01	1.2588e+00	1.6560e+00	1.9038e-01	8.0083e-01	NaN	NaN
DTLZ4	6.3181e-01	7.2252e-01	**6.6413e-02**	1.1715e+00	1.3306e+00	1.4499e-01	**5.0269e-01**	**6.7289e-01**	2.6504e-01	NaN	NaN	NaN
DTLZ5	6.0007e-01	6.9231e-01	**6.4352e-02**	8.6586e-01	1.0295e+00	1.2503e-01	**2.9304e-01**	**4.7875e-01**	1.4236e-01	NaN	NaN	NaN
DTLZ6	6.5923e-01	1.1222e+00	**2.2641e-01**	1.0000e+00	1.5554e+00	4.6248e-01	**3.6664e-01**	**1.0502e+00**	5.0985e-01	NaN	NaN	NaN
DTLZ7	**4.0150e-01**	**4.5659e-01**	**3.3268e-02**	1.1774e+00	1.2671e+00	4.3468e-02	4.3507e-01	7.3470e-01	3.7346e-01	NaN	NaN	NaN

Table 20. HV-Metric Values Obtained on CF problems.

Methods	MOBWO			MOSMA			MOWCA			NSGA2		
Contente	Best	Ave	std	Best	Ave	std	Best	Ave	std	Best	Ave	std
DTLZ1	**8.2999e-01**	**8.2631e-01**	2.3138e-03	5.9919e-01	4.8290e-01	**6.6394e-02**	8.1687e-01	7.6461e-01	5.0211e-02	5.8155e-01	5.6002e-01	2.6494e-02
DTLZ2	5.2787e-01	**5.2306e-01**	5.9920e-03	1.8611e-01	1.5374e-01	1.5009e-02	4.5578e-01	3.4084e-01	**8.3232e-02**	**8.8939e-01**	NaN	NaN
DTLZ3	**5.4809e-01**	**2.7284e-01**	**2.8760e-01**	1.0623e-01	8.9629e-02	2.6186e-02	1.0623e-01	2.1714e-02	4.0264e-02	2.2235e-01	NaN	NaN
DTLZ4	**5.3920e-01**	**5.3598e-01**	2.0548e-03	9.0909e-02	9.0909e-02	7.7953e-07	5.3111e-01	4.6452e-01	**6.2406e-02**	NaN	NaN	NaN
DTLZ5	**1.9905e-01**	**1.9874e-01**	2.7235e-04	7.4842e-02	6.5833e-02	3.2361e-03	1.9672e-01	1.7960e-01	**2.2288e-02**	NaN	NaN	NaN
DTLZ6	1.9948e-01	**1.9904e-01**	2.6963e-04	1.7649e-01	1.5161e-01	2.8804e-02	**2.0000e-01**	1.2450e-01	**8.9554e-02**	NaN	NaN	NaN
DTLZ7	**2.4535e-01**	**2.3746e-01**	5.7318e-03	2.3476e-01	2.2925e-01	4.6176e-03	2.6737e-01	2.3203e-01	**4.6912e-02**	NaN	NaN	NaN

3.5 Discussion of Test Functions

Table 3 presents the statistical results of mathematical functions (i.e., CF) in terms of the Generational Distance (GD) performance metric. The proposed MOBWO algorithm achieves better results compared to other methods (MOSMA, MOWCA, and NSGA2). The proposed MOBWO obtained the best results in 7 out of 10 test cases (i.e., CF1 to CF7), closely followed by MOSMA, which achieved the best results in 3 out of 10 test cases (i.e., CF8 to CF10). Thus, the results demonstrate the ability of the proposed MOBWO to solve complex multi-objective optimization problems. It performed excellently in most tested problems, measured by statistical parameters such as the best solution (Best), average solution (Ave), and standard deviation (sdt).

Table 4 presents the statistical results of mathematical functions (i.e., CF) in terms of the Inverted Generational Distance (IGD) performance metric. It was found that the proposed MOBWO achieves better results compared to other methods (MOSMA, MOWCA, and NSGA2). The proposed MOBWO obtained the best results in 6 out of 10 test cases (i.e., CF1 to CF5 and CF7), closely followed by MOSMA, which achieved the best results in 4 out of 10 test cases (i.e., CF6, CF8, CF9, and CF10). Thus, the results illustrate the capability of the proposed MOBWO to solve complex multi-objective optimization problems.

It performed excellently in most tested problems, with statistical parameters such as the best solution (Best), average solution (Ave), and standard deviation (sdt).

Table 5 presents the statistical results of mathematical functions (i.e., CF) in terms of the Spread (Δ) performance metric. It shows that the proposed MOBWO achieves better results compared to other methods (MOSMA, MOWCA, and NSGA2). The proposed MOBWO obtained the best results in 7 out of 10 test functions (i.e., CF1 to CF7), closely followed by MOSMA, which achieved the best results in 4 out of 10 tested functions (i.e., CF7 to CF10). Thus, the results demonstrate the ability of the proposed MOBWO to solve complex mathematical multi-objective optimization problems. It performed excellently in most tested problems, with statistical parameters such as the best solution (Best), average solution (Ave), and standard deviation (sdt).

Table 6 presents the statistical results of the tested functions (i.e., CF) in terms of the Spacing (S) performance metric. The proposed MOBWO and NSGA2 achieve equally good results compared to the other two methods (MOSMA and MOWCA). The proposed MOBWO obtained the best results in 4 out of 10 test cases (i.e., CF1, CF3, CF5, and CF6), closely followed by MOSMA, which achieved the best results in 4 out of the 10 tested functions (i.e., CF2, CF4, CF7, and CF9). Thus, the results demonstrate the ability of the proposed MOBWO and NSGA2 to solve complex multi-objective optimization problems. They performed excellently in most tested problems, with statistical parameters such as the best solution (Best), average solution (Ave), and standard deviation (sdt).

Table 7 presents the statistical results of mathematical functions (i.e., CF) in terms of the Maximum Spread (MS) performance metric. The proposed MOBWO achieves equally good results compared to the other comparative methods (MOSMA, MOWCA, and NSGA2). The proposed MOBWO obtained the best results in 4 out of 10 test cases (i.e., CF2, CF5, CF6, and CF8). The remaining cases were distributed among the other methods. Thus, the results demonstrate the ability of the proposed MOBWO to solve complex mathematical multi-objective optimization problems. It performed excellently in most tested problems, with low values for the best solution (Best), average solution (Ave), and standard deviation (sdt).

Table 8 presents the statistical results of mathematical functions (i.e., CF) in terms of the Hypervolume (HV) performance metric. It is clear that the proposed MOBWO achieves better results compared to the other comparative methods (MOSMA, MOWCA, and NSGA2). The proposed MOBWO obtained the best results in 7 out of 10 test cases (i.e., CF1, CF2, CF3, CF7, CF8, and CF9), closely followed by MOSMA, which achieved the best results in 4 out of 10 test cases (i.e., CF4, CF6 to CF10). Thus, the results demonstrate the ability of the proposed MOBWO to solve complex mathematical multi-objective optimization problems. It performed excellently in most tested problems, with statistical parameters such as the best solution (Best), average solution (Ave), and standard deviation (sdt).

Table 9 presents the statistical results of the ZDT problems for the Generational Distance (GD) performance metric. The results are satisfactory for the proposed MOBWO algorithm. In terms of the best value, mean, and standard deviation, the respective proportions are 40%, 10%, 10%, and 40%; 100%, 0%, 0%, and 0%; 60%, 20%, 20%, and 0% for the multi-objective algorithms MOBWO, MOSMA, MOWCA, and NSGA2, respectively. This demonstrates that the proposed method achieves better results compared to other algorithms.

Table 10 presents the statistical results of the ZDT problems for the Inverted Generational Distance (IGD) performance metric. The results are satisfactory for the proposed MOBWO algorithm. In terms of the best value, mean, and standard deviation, the respective proportions are 40%, 0%, 0%, and 60%; 40%, 20%, 20%, and 40%; 80%, 20%, 0%, and 0% for the multi-objective algorithms MOBWO, MOSMA, MOWCA, and NSGA2, respectively. This demonstrates that the proposed method achieves better results compared to other algorithms.

Table 11 presents the statistical results of the ZDT problems for the Spread (Δ) performance metric. The results are satisfactory for the proposed MOBWO algorithm. In terms of the best value, mean, and standard deviation, the respective proportions are 40%, 0%, 20%, and 40%; 60%, 0%, 40%, and 0%; 80%, 20%, 0%, and 0% for the multi-objective algorithms MOBWO, MOSMA, MOWCA, and NSGA2, respectively. This demonstrates that the proposed method achieves better results compared to other algorithms.

Table 12 presents the statistical results of the ZDT problems for the Spacing (S) performance metric. The results are very satisfactory for the proposed MOBWO algorithm. In terms of the best value, mean, and standard deviation, the respective proportions are 80%, 0%, 20%, and 0%; 60%, 0%, 20%, and 0%; 80%, 20%, 0%, and 0% for the multi-objective algorithms MOBWO, MOSMA, MOWCA, and NSGA2, respectively. This demonstrates that the proposed method achieves better results compared to other algorithms. Table 13 presents the statistical results of the ZDT problems for the Maximum Spread (MS) performance metric. The results obtained are entirely satisfactory for the proposed MOBWO algorithm. Regarding the best value, mean, and standard deviation, the respective proportions are 60%, 0%, 20%, and 20%; 80%, 20%, 0%, and 0%; 80%, 20%, 0%, and 0% for the multi-objective algorithms MOBWO, MOSMA, MOWCA, and NSGA2, respectively. This demonstrates that the proposed method achieves better results compared to other algorithms.

Table 14 presents the statistical results of the ZDT problems for the Hypervolume (HV) performance metric. The results obtained are satisfactory for the proposed MOBWO algorithm. In terms of the best value, mean, and standard deviation, the respective proportions are 40%, 0%, 40%, and 20%; 80%, 0%, 0%, and 20%; 0%, 0%, 80%, and 20% for the multi-objective algorithms MOBWO, MOSMA, MOWCA, and NSGA2, respectively. This demonstrates that the proposed method achieves better results compared to other algorithms.

Table 15 presents the statistical results of the DTLZ problems for the Generational Distance (GD) performance metric. The results obtained are entirely satisfactory for the proposed MOBWO algorithm. In terms of the best value, mean, and standard deviation, the respective proportions are 100%, 0%, 0%, and 0%; 100%, 0%, 0%, and 0%; 100%, 0%, 0%, and 0% for the multi-objective algorithms MOBWO, MOSMA, MOWCA, and NSGA2, respectively. This demonstrates that the proposed method achieves better results compared to other algorithms.

Table 16 presents the statistical results of the DTLZ problems for the Inverted Generational Distance (IGD) performance metric. The results obtained are satisfactory for the proposed MOBWO algorithm. In terms of the best value, mean, and standard deviation, the respective proportions are 86%, 14%, 0%, and 0%; 57%, 43%, 0%, and 0%; 57%, 43%, 0%, and 0% for the multi-objective algorithms MOBWO, MOSMA, MOWCA, and NSGA2, respectively. This demonstrates that the proposed method achieves better results compared to other algorithms.

Table 17 presents the statistical results of the DTLZ problems for the Spread (Δ) performance metric. The results obtained are satisfactory for the proposed MOBWO algorithm. In terms of the best value, mean, and standard deviation, the respective proportions are 86%, 14%, 0%, and 0%; 86%, 14%, 0%, and 0%; 86%, 14%, 0%, and 0% for the multi-objective algorithms MOBWO, MOSMA, MOWCA, and NSGA2, respectively. This demonstrates that the proposed method achieves better results compared to other algorithms. Table 18 presents the statistical results of the DTLZ problems for the Spacing (S) performance metric. The results obtained are very satisfactory for the proposed MOBWO algorithm. Regarding the best value, mean, and standard deviation, the respective proportions are 42%, 14%, 28%, and 14%; 100%, 0%, 0%, and 0%; 57%, 28%, 0%, and 14% for the multi-objective algorithms MOBWO, MOSMA, MOWCA, and NSGA2, respectively. This demonstrates that the proposed method achieves better results compared to other algorithms.

Table 19 presents the statistical results of the DTLZ problems for the Maximum Spread (MS) performance metric. The results obtained are entirely satisfactory for the proposed MOBWO algorithm. Regarding the best value, mean, and standard deviation, the respective proportions are 57%, 0%, 43%, and 0%; 57%, 0%, 43%, and 0%; 71%, 0%, 0%, and 29% for the multi-objective algorithms MOBWO, MOSMA, MOWCA, and NSGA2, respectively. This demonstrates that the proposed method achieves better results compared to other algorithms.

Table 20 presents the statistical results of the DTLZ problems for the Hypervolume (HV) performance metric. The results obtained are satisfactory for the proposed MOBWO algorithm. Regarding the best value, mean, and standard deviation, the respective proportions are 71%, 0%, 15%, and 14%; 100%, 0%, 0%, and 0%; 14%, 14%, 71%, and 0% for the multi-objective algorithms MOBWO, MOSMA, MOWCA, and NSGA2, respectively. This demonstrates that the proposed method achieves better results compared to other algorithms.

4 Conclusion

In this paper, a new MOBWO algorithm for solving multi-objective problems is proposed. This algorithm is based on the recently reported BWO algorithm, initially developed as a single-objective approach. A mechanism for non-dominated sorting and crowding distance was integrated into the BWO algorithm.

To verify the effectiveness of this new algorithm, we validated it on 22 contextual case studies. The results demonstrated that MOBWO efficiently ranks the true Pareto optimal fronts for all optimization problems.

Performance indicators, such as the GD, IGD, S, MS, Δ, and HV metrics, showed the superiority of MOBWO. Based on these findings, we conclude that the MOBWO algorithm offers advantages over several existing multi-objective algorithms. Therefore, it can be used to solve practical engineering problems with multiple local fronts.

References

1. Zoungrana, A., Somé, K., Poda, J.: Obtaining optimal pareto solutions using a hybrid approach combining ϵ-constraint and MOMA-Plus method. Int. J. Numer. Methods Appl. **23**, 90C29 (2023). https://doi.org/10.17654/0975045223006
2. Abdollahzadeh, B., Gharehchopogh, F., Khodadadi, N., Mirjalili, S.: Mountain gazelle optimizer: a new nature-inspired metaheuristic algorithm for global optimization problems. Adv. Eng. Softw. **174**, 103282 (2022). https://doi.org/10.1016/j.advengsoft.2022.103282
3. Deb, K., Pratap, A., Agarwal, S., Meyarivan, T.: A fast and elitist multiobjective genetic algorithm: NSGA-II. IEEE Trans. Evolut. Comput. **6**, 182–197 (2002). https://doi.org/10.1109/4235.996017
4. Tripathi, P., Bandyopadhyay, S., Pal, S.: Multi-objective particle swarm optimization with time variant inertia and acceleration coefficients. Inf. Sci. **177**, 5033–5049 (2007). https://doi.org/10.1016/j.ins.2007.06.018
5. Kennedy, J., Eberhart, R.: Particle swarm optimization. In: Proceedings Of ICNN'95-international Conference On Neural Networks, vol. 4, pp. 1942–1948 (1995). https://doi.org/10.1109/ICNN.1995.488968
6. Mirjalili, S., Saremi, S., Mirjalili, S., Coelho, L.: Multi-objective grey wolf optimizer: a novel algorithm for multi-criterion optimization. Expert Syst. Appl. **47** pp. 106–119 (2016). https://doi.org/10.1016/j.eswa.2015.10.039
7. Fu, X., Fortino, G., Li, W., Pace, P., Yang, Y.: WSNs-assisted opportunistic network for low-latency message forwarding in sparse settings. Futur. Gener. Comput. Syst. **91**, 223–237 (2019)
8. Wen, D., Zhang, X., Liu, X., Lei, J.: Evaluating the consistency of current mainstream wearable devices in health monitoring: a comparison under free-living conditions. J. Med. Internet Res. **19**, e68 (2017)
9. Xie, J., Wen, D., Liang, L., Jia, Y., Gao, L., Lei, J., et al.: Evaluating the validity of current mainstream wearable devices in fitness tracking under various physical activities: comparative study. JMIR MHealth UHealth. **6**, e9754 (2018)
10. Singh, V., Gu, N., Wang, X.: A theoretical framework of a BIM-based multi-disciplinary collaboration platform. Autom. Constr. **20**, 134–144 (2011)
11. Lv, Z., Xiu, W.: Interaction of edge-cloud computing based on SDN and NFV for next generation IoT. IEEE Internet Things J. **7**, 5706–5712 (2020)
12. Sun, G., Xu, G., Jiang, N.: A simple differential evolution with time-varying strategy for continuous optimization. Soft Comput. **24**, 2727–2747 (2020)

13. Yildiz, A.: A novel hybrid whale Nelder Mead algorithm for optimization of design and manufacturing problems. Int. J. Adv. Manuf. Technol. **105**, 5091–5104 (2019). https://doi.org/10.1007/s00170-019-04532-1
14. Tougma, A., Somé, K., Compaoré, A.: Extension of the projected gradient and Armijo's rule concepts for solving convex nonlinear multiobjective optimization problems. Appl. Anal. Optim. **7**, 263–278 (2023). https://doi.org/10.21203/rs.3.rs-2491296/v1
15. Yildiz,, B., Yildiz,, A., Pholdee, N., Bureerat, S., Sait, S., Patel, V.: The Henry gas solubility optimization algorithm for optimum structural design of automobile brake components. Mater. Test. **62**, 261–264 (2020). https://doi.org/10.3139/120.111479
16. Panagant, N., Pholdee, N., Bureerat, S., Kaen, K., Yildiz,, A., Sait, S.: Seagull optimization algorithm for solving real-world design optimization problems. Mater. Test. **62**, 640–644 (2020). https://doi.org/10.3139/120.111529
17. Yildiz, B., Yildiz, A., Pholdee, N., Bureerat, S., Sait, S., Patel, V.: The Henry gas solubility optimization algorithm for optimum structural design of automobile brake components. Mater. Test. **62**, 261–264 (2020)
18. Yildiz, B.: The mine blast algorithm for the structural optimization of electrical vehicle components. Mater. Test. **62**, 497–502 (2020)
19. Yildiz, B., Yildiz, A., Albak, E., Abderazek, H., Sait, S., Bureerat, S.: Butterfly optimization algorithm for optimum shape design of automobile suspension components. Mater. Test. **62**, 365–370 (2020)
20. Mirjalili, S., Jangir, P., Mirjalili, S., Saremi, S., Trivedi, I.: Optimization of problems with multiple objectives using the multi-verse optimization algorithm. Knowl.-Based Syst. **134**, 50–71 (2017)
21. Jangir, P., Jangir, N.: A new non-dominated sorting grey wolf optimizer (NS-GWO) algorithm: development and application to solve engineering designs and economic constrained emission dispatch problem with integration of wind power. Eng. Appl. Artif. Intell. **72**, 449–467 (2018)
22. Mirjalili, S., Jangir, P., Saremi, S.: Multi-objective ant lion optimizer: a multi-objective optimization algorithm for solving engineering problems. Appl. Intell. **46**, 79–95 (2017). https://doi.org/10.1007/s10489-016-0825-8
23. Wolpert, D., Macready, W.: No free lunch theorems for optimization. IEEE Trans. Evol. Comput. **1**, 67–82 (1997)
24. Deb, K., Pratap, A., Agarwal, S., Meyarivan, T.: A fast and elitist multiobjective genetic algorithm: NSGA-II. IEEE Trans. Evol. Comput. **6**, 182–197 (2002)
25. Zhang, Y., Gong, D., Ding, Z.: A bare-bones multi-objective particle swarm optimization algorithm for environmental/economic dispatch. Inf. Sci. **192**, 213–227 (2012)
26. Helmreich, S.: Recombination, rationality, reductionism and romantic reactions: culture, computers, and the genetic algorithm. Soc. Stud. Sci. **28**, 39–71 (1998)
27. Zhang, Y., Gong, D., Cheng, J.: Multi-objective particle swarm optimization approach for cost-based feature selection in classification. IEEE/ACM Trans. Comput. Biol. Bioinform. **14**, 64–75 (2015)
28. Zhang, Y., Gong, D., Ding, Z.: Handling multi-objective optimization problems with a multi-swarm cooperative particle swarm optimizer. Expert Syst. Appl. **38**, 13933–13941 (2011)
29. Li, H., Zhang, Q.: Multiobjective optimization problems with complicated Pareto sets, MOEA/D and NSGA-II. IEEE Trans. Evol. Comput. **13**, 284–302 (2008)

30. Premkumar, M., Jangir, P., Sowmya, R., Alhelou, H., Mirjalili, S., Kumar, B.: Multi-objective equilibrium optimizer: framework and development for solving multi-objective optimization problems. J. Comput. Des. Eng. **9**, 24–50 (2022)
31. Premkumar, M., Jangir, P., Sowmya, R., Alhelou, H., Heidari, A., Chen, H.: MOSMA: multi-objective slime mould algorithm based on elitist non-dominated sorting. IEEE Access **9**, 3229–3248 (2020)
32. Pandya, S., Jangir, P., Trivedi, N.I.: Multi-objective moth flame optimizer: a fundamental visions for wind power integrated optimal power flow with FACTS devices. Smart Sci. **10**, 118–141 (2022)
33. Buch, H., Trivedi, I.: A new non-dominated sorting ions motion algorithm: development and applications. Decis. Sci. Lett. **9**, 59–76 (2020)
34. Mirjalili, S., Mirjalili, S., Saremi, S., Faris, H., Aljarah, I.: Grasshopper optimization algorithm for multi-objective optimization problems. Appl. Intell. **48**, 805–820 (2018). https://doi.org/10.1007/s10489-017-1019-8
35. Kumawat, I., Nanda, S., Maddila, R.: Multi-objective whale optimization. In: Tencon 2017-2017 IEEE Region 10 Conference, pp. 2747-2752 (2017)
36. Premkumar, M., Jangir, P., Kumar, B., Alqudah, M., Nisar, K.: Multi-objective grey wolf optimization algorithm for solving real-world BLDC motor design problem. Comput. Mater. Contin. **70** (2022)
37. Kumar, S., Jangir, P., Tejani, G., Premkumar, M., Alhelou, H.: MOPGO: a new physics-based multi-objective plasma generation optimizer for solving structural optimization problems. IEEE Access **9**, 84982–85016 (2021). https://doi.org/10.1109/ACCESS.2021.3087739
38. Abdollahzadeh, B., Gharehchopogh, F., Mirjalili, S.: African vultures optimization algorithm: a new nature-inspired metaheuristic algorithm for global optimization problems. Comput. Ind. Eng. **158**, 107408 (2021). https://doi.org/10.1016/j.cie.2021.107408
39. Li, S., Chen, H., Wang, M., Heidari, A., Mirjalili, S.: Slime mould algorithm: a new method for stochastic optimization. Futur. Gener. Comput. Syst. **111**, 300–323 (2020)
40. Khodadadi, N., Abualigah, L., El-Kenawy, E., Snasel, V., Mirjalili, S.: An archive-based multi-objective arithmetic optimization algorithm for solving industrial engineering problems. IEEE Access **10**, 106673–106698 (2022). https://doi.org/10.1109/ACCESS.2022.3212081
41. Michael Gertz, E.: A quasi-Newton trust-region method. Math. Program. **100**, 447–470 (2004)
42. Liu, L., Liu, S.: Integrated production and distribution problem of perishable products with a minimum total order weighted delivery time. Mathematics **8**, 146 (2020)
43. Liu, S., Chan, F., Ran, W.: Decision making for the selection of cloud vendor: an improved approach under group decision-making with integrated weights and objective/subjective attributes. Expert Syst. Appl. **55**, 37–47 (2016)
44. Chen, H., Qiao, H., Xu, L., Feng, Q., Cai, K.: A fuzzy optimization strategy for the implementation of RBF LSSVR model in Vis-NIR analysis of pomelo maturity. IEEE Trans. Ind. Inf. **15**, 5971–5979 (2019)
45. Mantegna, R.: Fast, accurate algorithm for numerical simulation of Levy stable stochastic processes. Phys. Rev. E **49**, 4677 (1994)
46. Li, X., Zhu, Y., Wang, J.: Highly efficient privacy preserving location-based services with enhanced one-round blind filter. IEEE Trans. Emerg. Top. Comput. **9**, 1803–1814 (2021)

47. Liu, Y., Yang, C., Sun, Q.: Thresholds based image extraction schemes in big data environment in intelligent traffic management. IEEE Trans. Intell. Transp. Syst. **22**, 3952–3960 (2021)
48. Ni, T., et al.: Non-intrusive online distributed pulse shrinking-based interconnect testing in 2.5D IC. IEEE Trans. Circuits Syst. II: Express Briefs **67**, 2657–2661 (2020)
49. Fu, X., Pace, P., Aloi, G., Yang, L., Fortino, G.: Topology optimization against cascading failures on wireless sensor networks using a memetic algorithm. Comput. Netw. **177**, 107327 (2020)
50. Khodadadi, N., Azizi, M., Talatahari, S., Sareh, P.: Multi-objective crystal structure algorithm (MOCryStAl): introduction and performance evaluation. IEEE Access **9**, 117795–117812 (2021). https://doi.org/10.1109/ACCESS.2021.3106487
51. Zhong, C., Li, G., Meng, Z.: Beluga whale optimization: a novel nature-inspired metaheuristic algorithm. Knowl.-Based Syst. **251**, 109215 (2022)
52. Mirjalili, S.: Dragonfly algorithm: a new meta-heuristic optimization technique for solving single-objective, discrete, and multi-objective problems. Neural Comput. Appl. **27**, 1053–1073 (2016). https://doi.org/10.1007/s00521-015-1920-1
53. Mirjalili, S., Gandomi, A., Mirjalili, S., Saremi, S., Faris, H., Mirjalili, S.: Salp swarm algorithm: a bio-inspired optimizer for engineering design problems. Adv. Eng. Softw. **114**, 163–191 (2017). https://doi.org/10.1016/j.advengsoft.2017.07.002
54. Mirjalili, S., Mirjalili, S., Saremi, S., Faris, H., Aljarah, I.: Grasshopper optimization algorithm for multi-objective optimization problems. Appl. Intell. **48**, 805–820 (2018)
55. Tripathi, P., Bandyopadhyay, S., Pal, S.: Multi-objective particle swarm optimization with time variant inertia and acceleration coefficients. Inf. Sci. **177**, 5033–5049 (2007)
56. Yang, X.: Multiobjective firefly algorithm for continuous optimization. Eng. Comput. **29**, 175–184 (2013)
57. Som, A., Some, K., Compaore, A.: Hybrid method based on exponential penalty function and moma-plus method for multiobjective optimization. J. Comput. Sci. Appl. Math. **5**, 35–51 (2023)
58. Poda, J., Somé, K., Compaoré, A., Somé, B.: Adaptation of the MOMA-Plus method to the resolution of transportation and assignment problems. JP J. Math. Sci. **22**, 25–44 (2018)
59. Compaoré, A., Somé, K., Poda, J., Somé, B.: Efficiency of MOMA-Plus method to solve some fully fuzzy LR triangular multiobjective linear programs. J. Math. Res. **10**, 77–87 (2018)
60. Costa, M., Rocha, A., Fernandes, E.: An artificial fish swarm algorithm based hyperbolic augmented Lagrangian method. J. Comput. Appl. Math. **259**, 868–876 (2014)
61. Greenwood, G., Zhu, Q.: Convergence in evolutionary programs with self-adaptation. Evol. Comput. **9**, 147–157 (2001)
62. Tougma, A., Kaboré, A., Somé, K. Hyperbolic augmented Lagrangian algorithm for multiobjective optimization problems. Gulf J. Math. **16**, 151–170 (2024). https://doi.org/10.56947/gjom.v16i2.1876

Author Index

A. Sere et al. (Eds.): AFRI2 2025, CCIS 2536, p. 181, 2026.
https://doi.org/10.1007/978-3-031-98327-6

MIX
Papier aus verantwortungsvollen Quellen
Paper from responsible sources
FSC® C105338

If you have any concerns about our products,
you can contact us on
ProductSafety@springernature.com

In case Publisher is established outside the EU,
the EU authorized representative is:
Springer Nature Customer Service Center GmbH
Europaplatz 3, 69115 Heidelberg, Germany

Printed by Libri Plureos GmbH
in Hamburg, Germany